FIXING MEDICAL PRICES

FIXING MEDICAL PRICES

HOW PHYSICIANS ARE PAID

MIRIAM J. LAUGESEN

 Harvard University Press

Cambridge, Massachusetts
London, England
2016

First printing

Library of Congress Cataloging-in-Publication Data

Names: Laugesen, Miriam, author.

Title: Fixing medical prices : how physicians are paid / Miriam J. Laugesen.

Description: Cambridge, Massachusetts : Harvard University Press, 2016. |
   Includes bibliographical references and index.

Identifiers: LCCN 2016015003 | ISBN 9780674545168 (alk. paper)

Subjects: LCSH: American Medical Association. | Medical economics—United States. |
   Medical care—United States—Evaluation. | Medicare. | Health services
   administration—United States.

Classification: LCC RA410.53 .L385 2016 | DDC 338.4/73621—dc23
   LC record available at https://lccn.loc.gov/2016015003

Contents

Preface

In 2007, my neighbor, who happened to be a physician, told me (with a resigned shrug) why internists were poorly paid. According to her, Medicare's fee schedule was tilted toward the needs of specialists. Our discussion was a spark that reignited my longstanding interest in this issue. I had published a paper that touched on the topic during my postdoctoral training, but put it aside.

Ever since my first health policy class a decade earlier, I had considered the way Medicare sets prices an enigma. I remembered Professor Joseph Newhouse explaining how Congress believed primary care physicians should be paid more, so that their fees reflected the true cost of providing their services. Congress changed the way Medicare paid physicians in 1989, in an effort to achieve that goal. If my neighbor was correct, Congress's efforts to ensure that primary care doctors' fees better reflected the value of their services had failed. That was unfortunate, because the rationale underlying the 1989 legislation was that rewarding the effort associated with primary care would potentially improve health outcomes.

An article I coauthored with my colleague Sherry Glied gave credence to the misdirection of these goals. While orthopedic surgeons' incomes and fees were the highest among the countries we studied, primary care incomes and fees in the United States were more similar to those in other countries. The larger gap between specialty and primary care incomes in the United States was suggestive of a problem, and a paper by physicians Christine Sinksy and David Dugdale showed that Medicare fees for screening colonoscopies and cataract extractions were 368 percent and 486 percent, respectively, of the amount earned by physicians for the same time spent on office visits; these procedures can generate more revenue in one to two hours than a primary care physician receives for an entire day's work (Sinsky and Dugdale 2013).

Without the right economic incentives, it is difficult to persuade more physicians to become primary care physicians. Although many non-monetary factors influence medical students' residency choices, higher-income specialties are naturally more attractive. The relative allocation of resources among physicians has profound consequences, and ultimately it can even influence the kinds of services people receive. Over decades, many well-designed research studies have shown that when fees are increased or decreased, physicians pivot to the kinds of services that are more rewarding. Yet for most Americans, these kinds of financial incentives are imperceptible and operate invisibly.

In starting this book, I wanted to know whether my neighbor was right: had the congressional effort to pay for the true cost of primary care failed, and if so, why? I suspected the representation of specialists in the policy process might be a factor. From my earlier preliminary work, I knew that the American Medical Association (AMA) plays a key role in advising Medicare on how much physician "work" was associated with providing specific services. That struck me as unusual. I also wondered how such a potentially important policy process was hiding in plain sight.

Starting around 2006, other researchers were critiquing this process and considering its impact on physician fees. I soon became a policy detective, trying to unravel the mystery of Medicare fees. One of my first papers on the topic, published in 2012, showed that the AMA committee advising federal officials was highly successful: Medicare was adopting 90 percent of its recommendations. But why? This book attempts to understand how and why the AMA makes its recommendations, and why Medicare often agrees with them.

As is often the case, the reality is complicated and nuanced. The way we price services reflects decades of effective advocacy by physicians' organizations. The message of this book is that medicine has successfully advanced the idea that when it comes to payment policy, "doctor knows best." The philosophy built on itself: In a policy vacuum such ideas were reinforced, and physician organizations filled up the space. Physician-directed payment policy was aided by a complementary billing infrastructure that dovetailed elegantly. A physician-designed billing code system developed for private insurers was later mandated for Medicare and became the industry standard across the entire health care system. Indeed, Medicare's policy choices, which have typically been physician-friendly, compounded medicine's influence. A fluid symbiosis developed, whereby the private sector adopted Medicare standards and rules. In the private sector, prices were confirmed by the light touch of state governments regulating the health insurance industry.

Since 1989, these factors almost guaranteed that the intentions of Congress would come undone. *Fixing Medical Prices* makes the case that understanding how and why we value different medical services is a necessary step toward fixing our health care system.

Abbreviations

AAFP	American Academy of Family Physicians
ABMS	American Board of Medical Specialties
ACA	Affordable Care Act
ACR	American College of Radiology
ACS	American College of Surgeons
AMA	American Medical Association
ASTRO	American Society for Radiation Oncology
CBO	Congressional Budget Office
CMA	California Medical Association
CMS	Centers for Medicare & Medicaid Services
CPR	Customary, prevailing, and reasonable charge
CPT	Current Procedural Terminology
CRVS	California Relative Value Scale
DOJ	Department of Justice
DRG	Diagnosis-related group
E&M	Evaluation and management
FTC	Federal Trade Commission
GAO	Government Accountability Office
GDP	Gross domestic product
HCFA	Health Care Finance Administration
HCPAC	Health Care Professionals Advisory Committee
HCPCS	Healthcare Common Procedure Coding System

HMO	Health maintenance organization
ICD	International Classification of Diseases
IPAB	Independent Payment Advisory Board
MEI	Medicare Economic Index
MIPPA	Medicare Improvement for Patients and Providers Act of 2008
OBRA	Omnibus Budget Reconciliation Act
ORDS	Office of Research, Demonstrations, and Statistics
OTA	Office of Technology Assessment
PPRC	Physician Payment Review Commission
RBRVS	Resource-Based Relative Value Scale
RUC	Specialty Society Relative Value Scale Update Committee
RVS	Relative value scale
RVU	Relative value unit
SCAI	Society for Cardiovascular Angiography and Interventions
SGR	Sustainable growth rate
SNM	Society of Nuclear Medicine
SPECT	Single-photon emission computed tomography
TCG	Technical Consulting Group
UCR	Usual, customary, and reasonable charge

FIXING MEDICAL PRICES

To conceal ingenuity is ingenuity indeed.

—François, duc de La Rochefoucauld

ONE

Introduction: The House of Medicine and Medical Prices

HIGHER PRICES FOR health care contribute to higher health expenditure in the United States (Anderson et al. 2003; Laugesen and Glied 2011). Over time, increases in prices (as well as other factors) lead to higher health insurance premiums and out-of-pocket expenditures.

Rising health expenditure is having a negative impact on Americans' standard of living, particularly among middle-income Americans. For many Americans, higher health care expenses have cancelled out income gains. After accounting for increases in health care expenditure, workers' wages increased only $95 between 1999 and 2009. Had the increase in health care costs been less than or the same as the rate of inflation, on average a family would have been $545 wealthier each month (Auerbach and Kellermann 2011).

Many factors influence the growth of health expenditure, including the fact that people might increase their use of health care. People may benefit from increases in their quality of life from treatments that are more effective, but cost more than old treatments. Even so, understanding why prices are high, and why prices increase, is important. That knowledge base is increasing, because outside of public programs like Medicare and Medicaid, we mainly relied on "sticker" prices, which made it difficult to know the prices that insurers and patients actually pay, which were lower. We did know that in the hospital sector, prices display idiosyncratic variations (Ginsburg 2010), are "chaotic," and lack rationality (Reinhardt 2006). Today, increasing access to better data has not contradicted what we already knew, but has given us greater precision. The data show that on average, prices vary by a factor of three for identical services in the same geographic area (Cooper et al. 2015). There is no question that higher prices lead to higher expenditures. There is a direct relationship between hospital prices paid by private health insurers in different parts of the United States, which can vary by a factor of eight, and differences in health care expenditure, with higher prices leading to higher health expenditure (Cooper et al. 2015).

This suggests something is awry, and the level of concern is apparent in discussions about health care, which increasingly touch on the issue of prices. Pharmaceutical prices received extensive attention in 2015 after one manufacturer, Turing Pharmaceuticals, increased the prices of a drug by 5,000 percent. In a series in the *New York Times* called "Paying Till It Hurts," Elisabeth Rosenthal highlighted international differences in prices and the high cost of care in the United States (Rosenthal 2013–2014). Likewise, an article in a best-selling issue of *Time* by Steven Brill challenging hospital pricing (2013) prompted Congress to ask Brill to testify before the Senate Committee on Finance. Brill railed against the ways that the health care market does not function as a marketplace and said that health care "is a casino where the house holds all the cards" (US Senate Committee on Finance 2013).

At the same time, much of the public debate is necessarily broad, and fails to touch on important subtleties of health care prices. For example, not all physician fees are uniformly higher than in other countries. Fees for office visits are not significantly higher in Medicare than they are in other public programs around the world (Laugesen and Glied 2011). If some prices are too high, while others are too low, the issue of prices moves from being a financial or economic problem to one that more directly influences health, because relative prices influence the kinds of medical services people receive. Services with greater returns to a provider, such as laboratory tests and surgical services, are more likely to be provided, and when prices change there are measurable effects on the number and mix of services provided to patients (Cromwell and Mitchell 1986; Gruber, Kim, and Mayzlin 1999; Hadley et al. 2003; Rice 1983). One study showed how, when prices for chemotherapy drugs for patients with metastatic breast, colorectal, and lung cancer changed, physicians switched to more expensive drugs. In doing so, they earned more, because drugs with higher prices are more profitable (Jacobson et al. 2006). Such responses to price changes are rational responses to the economic incentive structure currently in place.

Medicare Prices for Medical Services

While hospital and pharmaceutical prices have generated increasing attention, there has been less attention paid to the fees charged by physicians. About 20 percent of health expenditure is spent on physician services, which is twice the amount we spend on pharmaceuticals. As mentioned, new analyses of claims data today means we have a better understanding of the prices physicians and medical groups charge private insurers. Yet, such data do not take us closer to more important questions, such as why we pay more for some services and not others, and where prices come from. This book shows that differences in fees for physician services are largely a reflection of the preferences of physician organizations advising Medicare on how much their services are worth in relation to other services. As organized currently, physician organizations' role in Medicare payment policy leads to decisions that are based on a lack of sound evidence and made in a process that is needlessly opaque.

This book focuses on Medicare payment policies, but the analysis has broader implications. What happens in Medicare does not necessarily stay in Medicare. Most Americans are unaware that, regardless of where they get their insurance, Medicare has an outsized influence over what they pay for physician service. Medicare publishes a fee schedule every year, and although the dollar amounts for each service are not identical, private payers peg their fees against Medicare's common fee schedule. When Medicare increases the price of a service by $1, private insurers typically increase their fees for that service by $1.30 (Clemens and Gottlieb 2013). One estimate found that three-quarters of the services physicians billed to private insurers are benchmarked to Medicare's relative prices (Clemens, Gottlieb, and Molnár 2015). Likewise, Tri-Care, the program for active military health care personnel, uses Medicare fee schedules. State Medicaid programs and state workers' compensation programs use Medicare rates as a benchmark.[1] Therefore, Medicare price changes ripple across the US health care system.

In this book, I will focus on the numeric value of the units published each year in the Medicare fee schedule and how they are decided. Medicare's fee schedule includes over 7,400 services (Centers for Medicare & Medicaid Services 2013). Every service, such as a hip replacement or colonoscopy, has a billing code number and an associated unit value that payers from across the public and private sectors can plug into their own billing systems. Therefore, the fee schedule provides an exchange rate of sorts for paying physicians that can be readily adapted because relative value units are simply multiplied by a dollar "conversion" factor, which can be set by the payer.

The number of units associated with any given service is supposed to reflect its true cost. In theory, a service with a unit value equal to another means that the total resources needed to provide the service are identical—that is, the physician work, which is time and effort expended by the physician; the cost of materials and practice costs; and the cost of malpractice insurance premiums.

When the method for estimating these costs, called the Resource-Based Relative Value Scale (RBRVS), was approved by Congress in 1989, the idea was that Medicare would be able to capture the true cost of providing primary care services. At that time, like today, policy makers and physician groups were concerned that primary care physicians were being underpaid, while fees for surgical and procedure-oriented services were too high. Congress believed that increases in relative value units under the RBRVS would be budget neutral, and that increases in Medicare expenditure would also be restrained by an overall expenditure target.

The RBRVS is one of the most curious anomalies in US public policy. It was created in the 1980s under a Republican administration during the heyday of Reaganite market deregulation. Regulatory policies for other sectors for the economy, such as "transportation, telecommunications, and banking," moved "the opposite way" (Brown 1992, 19). Some critics found it jarring that Medicare could determine how much work a physician was expending, reminiscent of Karl Marx's labor theory of value (Moffit 1992), while others claimed that it was akin to socialism under a centrally planned system (Baumgardner 1992). Critics described the RBRVS as "alien to a free market system, where supply and demand have always been the best instruments by which to determine prices, including the price of labor" (Wasley 1993, 15). The system would "skew the demand for various types of physicians, with the government encouraging more students to become family practitioners and fewer to become surgeons" (Wasley 1993, 16). As it turned out, predictions of excessive government control or a socialist takeover missed the mark by a wide margin. Although it was designed to be a scientific measurement of physician work and other inputs, physician groups rather than bureaucrats were centrally involved. In theory, the American Medical Association (AMA) committee only advises the Centers for Medicare & Medicaid Services (CMS) on fee schedule updates. As said, while physician organizations do not determine Medicare physician fees directly—CMS is responsible for Medicare and publishes the RBRVS—physician organizations are influential in the policy process. The AMA has a quasi-official role in advising the government on relative value units through a committee it coordinates, called the Specialty Society Relative Value Scale Update Committee—commonly known as RUC but referred to throughout the book as the "Update Committee" or "committee"—except when quoting other sources. The Update Committee advises CMS on how much services should be "worth" (in relative value units) compared to other services. The Update Committee is quasi-institutionalized as the leading advisor for CMS. The relative value units published by CMS mostly mirror the Update Committee's recommendations. Between 1994 and 2010, the Update Committee's recommendations were accepted unaltered 87.5 percent of the time (Laugesen, Wada, and Chen 2012).

The Update Committee is composed of 30 individuals plus a chairperson; other than a representative of osteopathic physicians and one of non-MD professionals, almost all voting members of the Update Committee represent national medical societies. The Update Committee holds meetings three times a year. Also attending the meeting are representatives of more than 100 specialty societies who are members of the update Advisory Committee. The Advisory Committee members do not vote on proposals (although members participate in ad hoc committees). Advisory Committee members present proposals to the Update Committee for changes (or to keep a value the same). After questioning the society and discussing their recommendation, Update Committee members vote and the organization sends a recommendation to CMS (more detail about the process is provided in Chapter 4).

Committee members perceive their role as ensuring that relative value units accurately reflect the physician work involved and are fairly distributed. As will be shown in subsequent chapters, the reality is more complicated. The Update Committee's treatment of specialty society recommendations can seem remarkably pro forma, and committee recommendations invariably either preserve current favorable values or increase relative value units.

The Premature Decline Narrative and the Rise of Regulation

This book asserts that organizations representing physicians continue to be powerful rather than weak, and that physician organizations are at the center of policy decisions relating to payment. In the domain of physician payment, greater federal regulation has afforded the profession more influence, not less. This extends from earlier work that showed physician groups influence payment policy (Laugesen 2009; Laugesen and Rice 2003).

In this book, the term *House of Medicine* is used to refer to organizations representing US physicians. The term reflects the lexicon of the physicians interviewed, who themselves talk about the House of Medicine. Above all, interviewees who are part of the Update Committee process used the term when they wanted to emphasize physicians' organizations as standing together and/or cohesively responding to societal or policy changes. Here, *the House of Medicine* refers to the collective representation of physicians. Scholars have traditionally used the term *organized medicine;* frequently, this term was shorthand only for the AMA. Over time, that term has become somewhat pejorative in its connotation (although not universally), but more important, it fails to reflect the ever-increasing specialization within medicine and the relationships among and across organizations. Above all, the term *organized medicine* does not capture the AMA's role in relation to other groups. The AMA was the architect, draftsperson, and builder of the House. Without it, the House of Medicine would have no foundation, no roof, and no walls.

Historically, the AMA was the most visibly involved in policy making. Payment policies and the advent of a national fee schedule have served to foster a House of Medicine, in which the AMA has taken a lead role—but critically, the AMA is not the only member of the House. The threats to the fee-for-service model in the 1980s and the creation of the RBRVS brought physician organizations together. This would appear to be a challenge; after all, American medicine is famously specialty and subspecialty oriented: currently, physicians can take residency programs in 130 different specialty and subspecialty programs (Accreditation Council for Graduate Medical Education 2016). Board certification is awarded in more than 145 specialties and subspecialties (American Board of Medical Specialties 2010). This may explain why physicians are inclined to see their specialty organizations as their "home" (Stevens 2001).

There is a tendency to assume that the growth of specialty medicine has diminished the power of the AMA. In fact, the organization has skillfully adapted to a countervailing need for coherence and coordination and has recast itself as an organization that can bring medicine together. The process of greater incorporation of specialty organizations developed starting in 1978, when the AMA allowed societies to hold seats in the House of Delegates, a parliament of sorts for US physician organizations and the official policymaking body of the AMA. The House of Delegates has more than 600 members representing 50 state medical societies and around 185 specialty organizations.

Later, the Board of Trustees of the AMA funded a $2 million project called the "Report of the Study of the Federation," which reported on "how to restructure organized medicine into a true federation of the many county and state medical societies, national specialty societies, and other physician groups—in sum, how to put the 'organized' back into 'organized medicine'" (Gesensway 1995). In 1996, the AMA put specialty societies on the same footing as state medical societies by equalizing the formula for allocating seats in the House of Delegates. Thus, over the past two decades, the AMA has established itself as a place "where physician organizations come together," and the House of Delegates is "medicine's most important crossroad" (American Medical Association 2011a, 5). The AMA calls the House of Delegates the "federation" of medicine.[2]

At the same time, using the term does not imply that the organizations are necessarily united. Nor should the primacy of the AMA be diminished in referring to the House—it is still an important organization. The AMA maintains a powerful position in the House of Medicine, and its leadership, the AMA's Board of Trustees, has been described as "arguably the most powerful physician leaders in the nation" (Gesensway 1995). If the House of Medicine today is powerful, the AMA has been a major contributor to that powerbase. After all, it has been said that Congress never approves health policy legislation without a clear understanding of "where does the AMA stand on this?" (Boyle 1989). Likewise, when the AMA put its support behind the Affordable Care Act in 2009, Senator John Dingell described this support as "a true milestone" and said that the "historical significance of the AMA's support should not be underestimated." Indeed, that the AMA has substantially influenced US health policy has been demonstrated in many books and studies of the subject and is widely accepted. At key points in the development of the US health care system, the AMA and local affiliates shaped the organization and financing of health care in the United States. Historically, the AMA was at the vanguard of the politics of health care, not necessarily specialty organizations. It discouraged affordable and lower-cost insurance products such as integrated and prepaid practice from developing (Starr 1982), thus reinforcing the dominance of fee-for-service medicine.

A combination of strong associations and privately delivered and financed health care renders interest groups enormously important for understanding the US health care system and its ongoing challenges. In other countries, scholars showed that physicians were also powerful, but usually groups found themselves subdued as government control over health care grew. Paul Starr asserted that organized medicine shaped its own economic destiny in the United States through the skillful use of the political process and an unrivalled legitimacy in the health care policymaking arena. In his book, *The Social Transformation of American Medicine*, Starr traced the rise of the medical profession, its ability to leverage its professional authority for political ends, and its formidable opposition to national health insurance. Starr proposed that based on developments in the 1970s, it was likely that the political and economic power of organized medicine had reached its apex. The trajectory of organized medicine's power would slope downward. Thus Starr's book launched a persuasive scholarly narrative documenting and reinforcing the "rise and decline" of organized medicine (Stevens 2001). In the wake of Starr's book, that narrative was largely unquestioned and unchallenged (Stevens 2001).

The narrative proposed that the physician's power was decelerating at a faster rate compared to other professions: "No profession in our sample has flown quite as high in guild power and control as American medicine, and few have fallen as fast" (Krause 1999, 36). Physician political power was eroding due to the increasing role of organizational payers of health care, such as employers and government. "Medicine had overdrawn its credit and it had also aroused a variety of new social movements to much bolder opposition" (Starr 1982, 383). Ultimately, Starr contended, physicians would be enlisted by a corporate transformation of medicine.[3] Likewise, even though the House of Medicine was remarkably resilient, buyers dictated the terms, and for the House, it "has ceased to be their game" (Light 1993, 79). Some authors even suggested that physicians had fallen so far that medicine had become "proletarian" (McKinlay and Arches 1985).

At the core of this decline narrative was the idea that physicians had lost both professional autonomy and professional authority due to state and corporate control. Professional authority is often discussed in terms of clinical authority, but it includes the ability to shape public policies (Schlesinger 2002). Like other professions, medicine was no longer outside of state control, and was subject to state action by organizations such as the Federal Trade Commission (FTC) (Krause 1999, 34). These changes were seen as symptoms of decline. Indeed, creating a Medicare fee schedule based on relative value units was thought to have "effectively removed control of Medicare fees or prices from the hands of the medical profession" (Culbertson and Lee 1996, 126–127). As this book shows, that prediction did not come true.

To be sure, some scholars challenged the narrative and argued that it was too early (Haug 1988) to conclude that the House was now less significant. Others said they were skeptical that power had significantly eroded (Mechanic 1991) and that "organized medicine was weakened but not vanquished" (Quadagno 2004, 831). To put the power of the House in a zero-sum game between the state and the House was also wrong, because "under certain circumstances a more rationalized and bureaucratic health care system may actually promote an expansion of medical hegemony" (Hafferty 1988, 206).

The influence of the House of Medicine on payment policy through the Update Committee suggests that the narrative of decline should be recalibrated. However, rather than see professional power or state power on an upward or downward trajectory, we should focus on the dynamic and changeable nature of policy influence, and the fact that the private sector also introduces new venues of influence (Oliver, Lee, and Lipton 2004). To date, we have tried to chart a course using a linear line. Yet policy tends to change in bursts or punctuations that are unpredictable, and we can overlook the flexibility and resilience of policy participants such as the House of Medicine (Baumgartner and Jones 1993). The House of Medicine's political power and influence have not diminished. The role of the House in policymaking has been underestimated. Rather than occupying the lower decks, the House of Medicine sits in Medicare's wheelhouse. The power of the House, especially in the regulatory arena, can be easily overlooked. Influence is exerted in different arenas, such that analysts of professional decline may miss the fact that policy occurs in many "venues," as Baumgartner and Jones (1993) call them. Indeed, we have tended to focus on the dynamic between the AMA and legislators, but after the Medicare fee schedule was adopted, the venue changed and the politics changed. With some exceptions, such as the public campaigns mounted by the AMA that advocated ending expenditure targets in Medicare, much of the House of Medicine's public stance and interaction with government today contrasts starkly with the AMA's highly visible campaigns against national health insurance in earlier decades. In the Truman era, large billboards announced to the American public the political agenda of the House of Medicine (the AMA juxtaposed the slogan "keep politics out of this picture" on a famous painting by Sir Luke Fildes of a doctor sitting with a sick child through the night). The AMA, in particular, had a highly public role in debates over national health insurance and Medicare. As James A. Morone described it, the AMA's tactics in the 1940s were "political theater as much as genuine power brokering" (Morone 1990, 259), but that political theater influenced policy elites and the public. The AMA's lower profile in recent decades is not indicative of a diminished role.

Today, the House of Medicine excels at what some characterize as "quiet politics" (Culpepper 2010). The complexity of the RBRVS makes public sloganeering less realistic—and likewise serves to understate the influence of the House of Medicine. Therefore, this book stresses the role of agency officials and interest groups as key actors in the process. Implementation is equally important as the politics of policy adoption, and this book contributes to our understanding of the power of the House of Medicine by closely examining the advisory and regulatory mechanisms over time. The implementation of policy, which commonly involves delegation to the bureaucracy or control to the states, allows agency staff and interest groups to reshape programs (Pressman and Wildavsky 1984). This book concurs, but suggests that when they are complex regulatory policies, the policies are continuously renegotiated in the regulatory process. When agencies write rules, they do not simply "execute" the law; rather, they are forced to replay many of the same policy questions debated by Congress—albeit on a miniature scale—and those small changes can lead to substantial deviations from core principles.

As a study of the content of policy and the politics of Medicare, this book adds to earlier work on Medicare, the implementation of the RBRVS, and the 1989 payment reform legislation (Mayes and Berenson 2006; Oberlander 2003; Oliver 1993; Smith 1992). A quarter century has passed since the RBRVS was implemented, and it is a key component of Medicare. Yet we lack an understanding of the RBRVS and its update process as well as the effectiveness of the Update Committee as a policy advisory organization.

This book reviews how the RBRVS conceives of physician work. The law defines work and therefore sets the parameters for CMS and the Update Committee. Researchers who developed the RBRVS made a concerted effort to be transparent in their approach to measuring work. After they completed their study, researchers published their research methods in peer-reviewed journals. However, their work mostly reported on the technicalities of developing and validating the RBRVS rather than its political history. That has left a gap in our understanding of its prehistory and how the concept was actually operationalized later, especially by the Update Committee. Without that information, our understanding of what the committee does and how it works is necessarily incomplete.

For the most part, until recently we have been reliant on the AMA's description of the committee, which asserts that the committee is a panel of independent experts that uses a rigorous and evidence-based method. However, in 2006 a former member and internist threw down the gauntlet on the Update Committee's perceived lack of attention to primary care reimbursement (Goodson 2007). Fee increases via Medicare's updates were shown to account for a substantial proportion of increases in Medicare expenditure, even controlling for other factors (Maxwell, Zuckerman, and Berenson 2007). Reports and journal articles over the years (Bodenheimer, Berenson, and Rudolf 2007; Braun and McCall 2011a; Cromwell et al. 2006; Ginsburg and Berenson 2007; Goodson 2007; Maxwell, Zuckerman, and Berenson 2007; McCall, Cromwell, and Braun 2006) suggested there were fundamental problems that were not being addressed.

The book adds to the findings of these prior studies. Members of the committee are not necessarily independent experts. They represent their specialty societies and engage in political advocacy related to physician payment. There are weaknesses in the process that the committee uses to measure and estimate physician work. We should therefore be concerned about the accuracy of payments that Medicare makes for more than 7,400 services, both in terms of paying too little for some services and overestimating the work associated with others.

The Origins, Development, and Maintenance of Medical Prices

The Update Committee reflects a series of historical choices and larger systemic factors. Chapter 2 considers the historical evolution of physician payment in the United States. Medicine flourished under the assumption that professionals and private institutions were the best judge of how to run their own affairs: the medical profession's interests prevailed (Starr 1982). After successfully heading off national health insurance for more than half a century, Medicare locked in a payment system that served physicians' economic self-interest—and fueled subsequent medical inflation (Peterson 2001). Adamant that physicians should continue to determine their own fees and work under a fee-for-service payment system, the AMA demanded that their payments be left alone. Therefore, government policies served to re-inforce professional power, such that the issues of professional autonomy and guild power cannot be understood in isolation of government (Beyer and Mohideen 2008, 191). The House of Medicine secured favorable payment policies (Marmor 2000) that were supposedly designed to preserve the prac-tices of private insurers that paid on the basis of prevailing charges. However, it is also true that at that time, insurers did not use one method to calculate fees; typically, if they used a prevailing charge system, they also had to rely on relative value–based fee schedules in use at the time. A combination of fee schedules and prevailing charges was the norm.

Fee schedules based on relative values had developed earlier for several reasons. Starting in 1956, the California Medical Association and some spe-cialty societies created relative value–based fee schedules for their members. After the growth of private health insurance in the 1950s, many physicians (mostly specialists) wanted to know how much they should charge insurers; they needed administrative systems to facilitate billing.[4] Likewise, insurers liked fee schedules because they did not always have enough charge data to rely on prevailing charges alone. Organizations such as the California Med-ical Association typically updated their fee schedules in a process not too dissimilar from the processes used by the Update Committee today.

The emphasis on surgical and procedural services in the design of the RBRVS may reflect larger attitudes reinforced by the structure and history of our health insurance system that we see replicated in the development of the fee schedule. As Chapter 2 suggests, physicians in the United States may have monetized or compounded underlying differences more readily, however. The US reverence for subspecialty and procedural medicine was fostered by generous private insurance payments that mushroomed without the visible hand of government. The decline of general practice began in the early 1950s—until then, general practitioners formed the majority of the phy-sician workforce. In other countries, the growth of procedural specialties may have been moderated by public payers or limited by the fact that specialists were paid salaries and employed in hospitals. Payment from private insurers in the United States may have increased income expectations among sur-gical and procedural specialties.

As Chapter 3 shows, our current payment policy structure was forged in the transition after the FTC outlawed specialty society fee schedules in the mid-1980s. The FTC prevented almost all medical societies from updating their fee schedules in the 1970s. Meanwhile, Congress was concerned about the rising cost of Medicare. Congress introduced cost containment policies in the 1970s and also cut some fees in the 1980s.

During this period, the AMA was alert to the possibility that more radical policy changes might be afoot. Societies representing internal medicine physicians advocated reform, and there were also concerns about the supply of physicians. When Congress took an interest in reforming physician payment in the 1980s, leaders of physician groups decided they needed a strategy to preserve fee-for-service payment. The AMA encouraged Congress to develop a relative value fee schedule approach in the early 1980s to head off capitation—a payment method that was perceived by physicians as potentially disastrous for the entire profession (Todd 1988). The House of Medicine became the major proponent of relative value–based payment.

Organizations representing physicians persuaded Congress to request and fund a report on relative value payment models (Hsiao 1995). These developments created an ironic juxtaposition: a few years after the FTC had eliminated relative value–based fee schedules, Congress was sponsoring a study that would encourage the development of them. Of course, the new approach was considered different because it was resource based rather than based on existing charges.

After the project began, the AMA had "extensive involvement" in what became known as the Hsiao study after the lead author, William Hsiao (Rubin, Segal, and Sherman 1989). Some organizations also contributed funding to have their specialty included. When the fee schedule was implemented, the AMA and specialty societies were already familiar with the RBRVS, having participated to some extent in its creation.

Chapter 3 explores concerns that emerged early in the payment reform discussion regarding what could happen if the House of Medicine determined changes to the RBRVS. Even before Congress enacted legislation, this issue was already on the radar of policy makers. At that time, a logical choice for this task might have been the Physician Payment Review Commission (PPRC). In 1989, the commission reported to Congress that updates to the RBRVS would need to be determined objectively and independently (Physician Payment Review Commission 1989, 176). After the law was passed, the commission began convening physician groups to help the agency revise parts of the RBRVS while the executive branch began writing rules and designing the model fee schedule.

The AMA created an Update Committee and offered the committee's expertise to the Health Care Financing Administration,[5] which accepted the

Update Committee's offer to advise the agency on updates to the RBRVS. The committee soon became institutionalized as the "go-to" source for advice on RBRVS updates. Chapter 3 shows how what some former agency heads have described as an almost "accidental" policy change underestimated the committee—despite widespread awareness among other agencies that close involvement of the House of Medicine constituted a significant conflict of interest.

Chapter 4, "How Doctors Get Paid," describes the contemporary structure of Medicare payment policy and the role of the Update Committee and CMS in updating the RBRVS. The organization of and interaction between specialty societies and the Update Committee are also examined, including why and how specialty societies participate and how the committee has evolved over time.

Chapter 5 shows that the process used by the Update Committee to evaluate physician work has significant weaknesses. Had the RBRVS successfully addressed two problems it was designed to solve—reducing primary-specialty care differentials and lowering Medicare expenditure growth—there might be no reason to investigate the Update Committee's role in updating the RBRVS. Unfortunately, after 25 years, payment reforms appear to have fallen short of their original goals. Given failures in cost containment and disparities in primary-specialty fees, the effectiveness and integrity of the process have come under more scrutiny. The mean relative value unit of physician work has increased substantially since 2000, suggesting that the update process may lead to higher fees (but not necessarily for all kinds of services). Although changes to the RBRVS are perceived as being made in a budget-neutral fashion, it is unclear whether budget neutrality operates as a real constraint.

Physician work units are a composite of time, mental effort, judgment, technical skill, physical effort, and psychological stress (psychological stress on the physician is thought to be higher where there is a larger likelihood of complications or mortality). Metrics of work directed toward technical skill, physical effort, and psychological stress on the physician may better lend themselves to the kind of work that procedural and surgical specialists do. In addition, some procedures may be especially stressful for physicians to perform when they are new but gradually become routinized and established. Some services therefore become overvalued over time. Yet, it is also important to consider the contribution of the RBRVS itself. Committee members work within the constraints of the law enacted by Congress and its definition of work. Might the RBRVS itself have an inherent bias toward procedurally based medicine?

As said, the historical roots of fee schedules in general reflect the fact that insurance coverage of specialty services occurred earlier and was therefore structured largely for the needs of specialty physicians. At that time, the generalist medicine was both more widespread but also taken for granted rather than lauded as a concept; today primary care stands for a philosophy that believes primary care is an essential tool in the prevention of diseases and chronic disease management. Structural features of the payment system, even the categorization of services developed for specialty billing purposes and a discrete set of tasks that can be broken down into steps, may have unintended effects on how the committee defines and conceives of physician work. The Current Procedural Terminology (CPT) system, copyrighted and trademarked by the AMA, has thousands of highly granular surgical and procedural service codes.[6] Such services are often differentiated by characteristics such as incision size or the weight of tissue removed. There are fewer codes for office visits, and these codes are less differentiated (Kumetz and Goodson 2013). Office visit codes include more generic descriptions with less specificity regarding the work performed. Procedural specialists may have more opportunities to distinguish services and create more lucrative service codes. Generalists have traditionally treated a wide range of diseases within the all-encompassing office visit, which by its nature—perhaps unless diagnosis-based—defies such levels of granularity.

The balance of surgical, procedural, and nonprocedural codes in the CPT shows how the definition of work breaks down in practice, because it is influenced by other factors, in this case the billing system (and vice versa). With more codes for surgical and procedural services, the committee may be more accustomed to evaluating such work, which in turn influences its standard operating procedures. When physicians fill out surveys on work, for example, they are asked to estimate their work in a specific sequence that starts with scrubbing up, draping, positioning the patient, and performing an incision—what the committee calls "skin to skin." A linear, temporally defined flow of physician work in the committee's evaluation process is organized around an operating room scenario where the patient might be anesthetized. For genuinely complex and time-intensive services, generally speaking, the longer and more complicated the procedure, the greater the accuracy of the Update Committee's valuation, as discussed in Chapter 5. As said, the surgical or procedurally oriented approach to work is task-driven, and that may be harder to adapt to services with a broader range of clinical issues, less defined temporal sequences, and a more nonlinear workflow, as found in the management of chronic conditions.

Of course, if the Update Committee or the RBRVS elevates certain kinds of medical work, some might argue that such a tendency is reinforced by larger cultural attitudes and societal norms, as well as attitudes within the profession regarding specialty medicine. In short, we tend to hold highly technical and more specialized physician work in high regard. For once, this is not a US phenomenon alone: throughout all health care systems, physicians and the public give higher status rankings to surgeons or physicians who perform complex procedures (Norredam and Album 2007; Rosoff and Leone 1991; Schwartzbaum, McGrath, and Rothman 1973; Shortell 1974).

A related issue is how precisely work can be measured. Granted, quantifying "work" is not easy, but the updates of the RBRVS rely on a shaky evidence base and may be influenced by not wholly disinterested participants. Chapter 5 describes how voting members are integrated into their specialty society's governance structure. In private, participants admit that there are known techniques used to increase the value of codes. There are significant weaknesses in the evidence used and the quality of decision making. The data used to evaluate work are typically based on small surveys of physicians (often drawn from society membership lists). In the past, the committee has allowed samples as small as six—even though its own rules require a minimum of 30 to 50 survey respondents. Small and nonrandom samples likely explain why estimates of how long surgical procedures take are usually inaccurate and much longer than those recorded in surgical operating theater logs, which found discrepancies as large as 300 percent (McCall, Cromwell, and Braun 2006). Longer time estimates usually translate into higher work units (and higher payment).

Due to nonrandom sample selection processes, survey samples may not be wholly independent or unbiased. Physicians are sometimes solicited from standing panels of physicians who repeatedly fill out surveys and/or serve on society payment committees, or they may be selected from lists provided by device manufacturers (American Academy of Orthopedic Surgeons 2014). Time estimates based on self-reports of how people spend their time at work or how many hours they worked are an unreliable method of measuring time (Robinson and Bostrom 1994; Robinson, Chenu, and Alvarez 2002). There are inherent limitations to expert decision making in small group processes of the type used by the Update Committee. Likewise, participants indicated that randomness and chance often determine committee decisions.

While Chapter 5 mainly reviews the terrain of the processes inside the Update Committee, Chapter 6 explores the internal politics of the committee in relation to the external policy process, particularly why the venue where policy is made and the technical characteristics of the fee schedule serve to influence that relationship. As said, if people believe the influence of the House of Medicine has declined, it may be because sometimes we can confuse lower visibility with diminished influence. In the two decades since the RBRVS was created, the House of Medicine has operated the committee quietly, largely behind the scenes.

Today, the House of Medicine lobbies on the technicalities of the Medicare fee schedule, the elements of various Medicare payment formulas, and the details of rules around payments for specific services. Small technical changes to policies might appear insignificant, yet a single change might disproportionately benefit one specialty or a small subset of physicians. On occasion, when more substantial changes are proposed in the regulatory process, Congress has made legislative amendments that freeze or temporarily suspend payment reductions, add sunset clauses to reductions or restrictions, or exempt services or specialties from budgetary impact requirements. While Congress continues to play a role, the real action, however, is in the sometimes plodding and dry minutiae of regulation. Like other interest groups, the House of Medicine actively participates in the rulemaking process: one survey of interest groups reported that 82 percent of respondents said they participated in rulemaking, and most groups said it was an important part of their lobbying strategy (Furlong and Kerwin 2005).

Even so, the participation of the House of Medicine and the Update Committee is not simply a way for groups to comment on proposed rules, and it exhibits differences due to its private but elevated position in the rulemaking process. The committee and the rulemaking process constitute a repeated policy game providing participants multiple chances to renegotiate terms. Over time, interest groups may achieve small victories that cumulatively mitigate intended policy effects, a process called policy drift, where changes in the operation or impact of policies occur without significant changes in program structure (Hacker 2004; Thelen 2004). Policy drift is partly facilitated by the fact that payment policy is obscured by detail and complexity. Chapter 6 measures the complexity of the RBRVS and draws on theories of regulatory capture from political science, finance, and legal scholarship, explaining how the complexity of policy enables greater influence by the House of Medicine.

Policy complexity allows interest groups to achieve their objectives under the cover of exhaustive layers of detail. As said, the RBRVS has more than 7,400 services, each with a work unit and a malpractice unit, as well as two different practice expense units (facility and nonfacility units). Not unexpectedly, annual updates to the fee schedule published in the *Federal Register* run to hundreds of pages.

Chapter 7 reviews the lessons learned from the analysis in preceding chapters and changes under the Affordable Care Act (ACA). In light of the findings of the book, the ACA, and recent developments, various policy options are discussed.

Information Sources and Data Used

The AMA and the staff and leadership of the Update Committee kindly accommodated the author at the September to October 2010 meeting, the February and April 2011 meetings, and an April 2012 meeting. The author also attended the CPT committee meeting in February 2015. No access restrictions were placed on the author to individuals inside or outside the committee meetings. The author signed the same nondisclosure agreement that all other participants sign.

In preference to using information that is not publicly accessible, the author sought publicly available versions of the information available to maximize accessibility to original sources and the transparency of sources. For example, specialty societies sometimes republish material from the Update Committee meetings, and publicly accessible documents are available on specialty society websites, including letters, meeting minutes, and internal memos. Articles cited included those from newsletters and peer-reviewed journals by former or current participants, all of which were publicly accessible. Congressional bills addressing physician fee schedules and fee schedule cuts, press releases, archival documents, congressional testimony and committee reports, Medicare Payment Advisory Commission reports, Physician Payment Review Commission reports, and legislation were all reviewed. Multiple editions of the AMA's official publication on the RBRVS, *RBRVS: A Physician's Guide,* starting with the 1993 edition, as well as other publications from the AMA, including annual reports and Internal Revenue Service 990 forms, were reviewed.

Since the author began the study, the Update Committee has increased the availability of information on its website, and it now makes more material accessible, such as meeting minutes, that was previously not publicly available at www.ama-assn.org. For example, a data set of voting counts, published by the AMA, was used (American Medical Association 2014).

For the purposes of measuring changes in relative value units, the author compiled a database of relative value units and recommendations from CMS sources, including the *Federal Register* and data files from CMS.gov. An original database was compiled from the *Federal Register* of all RUC recommendations and CMS decisions for the period 1994–2010, and readability statistics were also calculated for federal rulemaking documents. The author reviewed the *Federal Register* for the period beginning in 1991 and read recent and specialty society comments on rules that are available at Regulation.gov.

Before each meeting, the AMA provided documents to the author on CD-ROMs. These include internal policy statements, reports and analyses of issues related to the update process, reports of subcommittees and their meetings such as conference calls on specific issues, and detailed documentation supporting each society's request for review. The total page count for each of these disks is around 5,000 pages.

Committee meetings may not be recorded or photographed. The author took extensive notes documenting exchanges between presenting societies, Update Committee members, AMA staff, CMS staff, and the content of specialty society presentations during meetings. The author took notes at pre- and postfacilitation meetings, where smaller groups of participants deliberated on work values. Meeting notes are noted in the text as "Author's meeting notes."

General observations about the committee were made based on unsolicited information provided to the author by individuals. The information was delivered on the condition that identities of the individuals remained anonymous. These materials were not obtained in connection with the author's participation in the committee processes. These are noted as "anonymous source." All reasonable efforts have been made to verify the information using publicly available sources.

The book includes information from confidential interviews. The Columbia University Medical Center Institutional Review Board approved the interview protocol and recruitment method. Forty individuals who were Update Committee members or Advisory Committee members were contacted by mail. Contact information for the members was based on publicly available information. The AMA never saw the interviewee list or vetted the names of the people the author approached. However, some of the interviewees told the author that they had checked with the AMA before agreeing to be interviewed, so they voluntarily disclosed their choice to be interviewed to the AMA, but the author does not have information regarding who did and did not contact the AMA regarding voluntary disclosures made to the author.

The initial sample of interviewees included 40 current Update Committee and Advisory Committee members who were recruited via letters, with follow-up by telephone to those who did not respond. Some other individuals volunteered to be interviewed. Thirteen people who participated in the committee process agreed to be interviewed, and one joined an in-person interview uninvited, bringing the total number of people interviewed to 14; these people had served as voting members or were on the Advisory Committee at the time of the interview, with a small handful having recent service. Two interviews failed to be completed due to scheduling issues. Among those interviewed, all 14 were MDs who were currently or had served on the Update Committee or the Advisory Committee.

To the extent that the information obtained from interviews reflects any kind of selection bias based on the interviewees who responded or volunteered to be interviewed, the information should be assessed based on the understanding that the responses are both consistent with and confirmed by other publicly available information. In addition, all information from individuals interviewed should be construed in connection with the context of both the chapter in which it appears as well as the overall content of the book.

The author also interviewed current and former specialty society staff or consultants, and she approached payment policy experts and researchers for interviews, including two who had served in the government at different times, all of whom agreed to be interviewed.

Including the participants and others, the author interviewed 24 individuals between 2010 and 2013 by telephone and in person. The interviews were conducted using a semi-structured interview protocol. Of these, 22 of the interviews were audio-recorded and transcribed. Only one member declined to be taped, and one interview with a payment policy researcher was not taped; however, the author took detailed notes of both conversations. Professor Rick Mayes, University of Richmond, kindly provided transcripts from two interviews he had previously conducted. Another publicly available set of 43 interviews with former secretaries, administrators, members of Congress, and others from CMS and the Health Care Finance Administration (HCFA) (Smith and Moore n.d.) was also used, although only some of the material was relevant to the study. The author used a qualitative software analysis program, MaxQDA, to code the transcript quotes by topic.

Verbatim quotes from the interviews are used throughout the book. For some quotes, it was necessary to protect the anonymity of the interviewee by redacting identifying words or names and removing any individual information about gender or dates, length of service on the committee, or time periods served that would make it possible to link the information to a particular individual, consistent with human subjects research best practice. Certain speech "fillers" (e.g., "um," "yeah," "you know," and "like") were removed from the quotes for clarity and conciseness, and minor grammatical errors were corrected.

Conclusion

For many years it seemed as if the thorny issue of physician reimbursement had been settled, due to the significant reforms enacted in 1989 that reshaped physician payment in Medicare. Researchers saw this as a problem that had been solved and believed these reforms had brought discipline to the process of setting physician fees. A powerful decline narrative asserted that the House of Medicine had lost power and influence.

This book argues that while the House of Medicine may now compete for influence on many health policy issues with other groups, the House dominates policies relating to pricing of medical care. The Update Committee has mostly flown under the radar, at least partly because of the complexity of the fee schedule nested within an increasingly multi-layered Medicare program that dilutes sustained attention. As one scholar put it, it is impossible to generalize about the political economy and policy actors involved in Medicare, given that this is not a single program but four. There is no single politics of Medicare: the politics of Medicare varies across Medicare's four programs (hospital, physician and suppliers, prescription drugs, and managed care), which have increasingly diverged (Oberlander 2003).

What this book shows is that it is easy to miss the importance and influence of the House of Medicine and the centrality of this committee, yet it is vitally important to understand both. To date, we have lacked an in-depth understanding of the implementation of one of the most important changes in health care since Medicare was created—the creation of the RBRVS—and we have underestimated the role of the House of Medicine in shaping physician payment. The complexity of the update process and the RBRVS, along with confidentiality requirements, may have discouraged efforts to research this topic. Through the use of multiple sources of data and theoretical models of how policy is made, *Fixing Medical Prices* overcomes both barriers and explores the organization at the center of US physician payment policy.[7]

Skeptics might argue that we can learn little from one committee that, at first glance, appears to have a small footprint. Yet, the Update Committee's impact is large: understanding the politics of physician payment and the updating of the RBRVS by the Update Committee is crucial for understanding the US health care system.

What we pay for medical services as well as how we pay for them speaks to what we value: what kind of medical care we want, how we want to allocate resources, and how to fairly compensate physicians doing very different kinds of work. How the Update Committee operates and how the policy process around the RBRVS functions are fundamental issues for scholars and policy makers—and the public. Because upward revision of RBRVS codes is one cause of higher Medicare expenditures, developing accurate prices for physician services is necessary to contain the cost of health care in the United States. The next six chapters explore the development of physician payment and the role of the House of Medicine in formulating physician payment policy, how we got here, and the gap between the hopes of reformers and reality when they designed the RBRVS.

TWO

The Enduring Influence of the House of Medicine over Prices

THE HOUSE OF Medicine stifled alternatives to fee-for-service and fought early efforts to create organizations that resembled health maintenance organizations (HMOs). In a period of prosperity and growth in private health insurance after World War II, the House of Medicine further institutionalized a fee-for-service payment system by creating a more convenient method for insurers to pay physicians, based on relative value units. The ability of the House to do so was facilitated by US political institutions and limited regulation of health insurers.

The RBRVS reflects the longstanding power of the House to shape the prices of medical care in the US health care system and the House of Medicine's success in developing and controlling the core architecture of the health care system—fee schedules, medical nomenclature, and billing. Medicare's introduction acted to encourage greater private-sector standardization that drew from physician-created systems. After the California Medical Association created a fee schedule in the 1950s called the California Relative Value Scale (CRVS), the norms of its design influenced the administration of Medicare. With some exceptions, the CRVS became a shadow fee schedule for the Medicare program itself. Private claims processors for Medicare needed a way to process fees for thousands of providers and millions of claims, and gradually many payers adopted a coding system developed by the AMA. That coding system became the industry standard after Medicare and Medicaid were legislatively required to adopt the system in the 1980s. Thus, the RBRVS was a culmination of an incremental adaptation of prior payment practices and physician-driven fee schedules that adapted and complemented public programs such as Medicare.

To understand the policy approach to physician prices and fees requires tracing the origins of the health care system that were shaped by the role of the government and a privately driven standardization of the health care system. Only by understanding why and how the House of Medicine was positioned decades earlier can we understand current policy arrangements.

American Political Development and the US Health Care System

A mélange of public and private actors is involved in funding and providing physician services, which speaks to the contradictions and challenges of US health care policy as betwixt and between, neither fish nor fowl. Private insurers finance the largest share of expenditure on physician services (46 percent of total physician expenditures). On the other hand, the US health care system has evolved to become more "public" over the past 50 years than ever, with government financing just over one-third (35 percent) of the expenditure on physician services provided, of which Medicare accounts for two-thirds. Patients pay for 10 percent of the cost of physician services, and the remaining 10 percent is financed by a variety of other sources, including employer-based clinics, workers' compensation, and grants to states. If physician services are increasingly financed from public sources, greater public control over private providers and insurers, however, has not matched the shift of dollars. The following discussion traces the historical dominance of the private sector in both financing and providing health care.

As said, the public-private dynamic of the US health sector reflects longstanding contradictions around whether health care is indeed a public or private activity. Often, the tendency toward private sector mechanisms in public policy is attributed to core US values. We tend to believe that, on balance, people will prefer the private sector and that liberty is embedded in the US national DNA. It reflects the fact that "Americans want government programs but dislike government. In the abstract, many Americans profess a desire for small government and low taxes, and are skeptical about government" (Morgan and Campbell 2011, 6–7). Yet, digging deeper, shrewd analysts of public opinion and public policy observe that Americans are more enthusiastic about government programs that protect them against life's vagaries (Morgan and Campbell 2011, 6–7). Additionally, there is good evidence that the public does not see the many ways they personally benefit from programs offered in a "submerged state," or public programs veiled by private sector provision (Mettler 2011). In health care, the public is prone to misinterpret the role of government. For example, not-for-profit hospitals benefit from tax-exempt status, while Medicare subsidizes the cost of graduate medical education. The use of the private sector to administer and deliver social policy constitutes the "delegated state," which reflects and perpetuates such misperceptions (Morgan and Campbell 2011).

Medicare's supporters and the internal design of the program "buttressed and reinforced the idea that health care belonged first and foremost to the private sector, that health insurance was to be purchased in the market place." To win support for the program, the elderly were painted as an anomaly that the market could not serve—"the elderly were carved out as an 'exception' for government policy" (Rothman 1997, 69). At times, the private sector has profited from the ambiguity of whether health care is public or private. While sometimes asserting complete market freedom, at other times health care providers and payers have sought special tax protection or exceptions to the strictures and restraints placed on other market actors.

In other countries, these ambiguities (which, to be sure, exist in pockets of all health care systems) were less difficult to resolve and could not flourish to the same extent as they did in the United States. The ability of the House of Medicine to shape prices reflects the fact that the countervailing powers in US health care were weaker than in other countries (Light 1993; Mechanic 1991). For example, in countries like New Zealand, hospitals came under state control after government offered substantial subsidies for patient care (Laugesen and Gauld 2012). Social insurers and governments acted to brake cost growth, and if not subject to actual public control, hospitals retained a stronger charity-based focus. Hospitals in the United States were, as Rosemary Stevens notes, able to embrace the practice of charging fees rather than being purely charity-driven institutions as in Europe (Stevens 1999). Hospitals that were fee-driven maintained the veneer of a voluntarism, however, which allowed the House of Medicine and hospital associations to benefit from public funding of hospital construction (Stevens 1999). The 1946 Hospital Construction Act (known as the Hill-Burton Act) provided public largesse while maintaining the House of Medicine's authority. The profession used the funds to "build up a sophisticated institutional infrastructure for the private practice of medicine" (Morone 1993, 727). Health care has long been a public-private partnership where public funding is followed by delegation of control that ultimately strengthens private actors.

The ambiguity of the private-public role in health care is reinforced by a private health insurance system that is weakly regulated. The House of Medicine's power to monopolize the payment methods available in both the market and the public sector reflects a pattern of American political development that weakened state capacity for careful stewardship of the health care system. The role of the House of Medicine in setting fees must therefore be understood as being intertwined with larger societal and historical forces influencing US health care more generally.

If current financing and delivery arrangements and nuanced relationships between the private sector and the state are longstanding, that is not unusual: in all countries, current policies and possibilities for change reflect the "accidental logics" of every health system, each unfolding and shaped by unique histories and critical junctures (Tuohy 1999, 445).[1] For example, in Europe, World War II left many countries devastated; the private-sector health care system was therefore less dominant than in the United States,[2] and citizens became more accustomed to government intervention in health care. The UK government took the opportunity to reorganize and centralize control over hospitals following each of the two world wars.

In the United States, political institutional structures designed by the country's founders were intended to constrain state power, and the administrative capacity that flows from expansion of government never developed to the same extent as it did elsewhere (Skowronek 1982). Thus, the power of the House of Medicine emerged and solidified within a US constitutional structure that encourages power distribution and divides influence over policy decisions through a separation of powers and other unique institutional structures (Weaver and Rockman 1993). More favorable institutional structures in other countries gave governments greater leverage over organizations that tried to block national health insurance; in many countries, elected officials had unilateral control, allowing them to override objections from medical societies that fought the creation of public health insurance programs (Immergut 1992). As persuasively demonstrated by other scholars, federalism and political and constitutional structures shape the opportunities for the state to assume greater or lesser control in health care (Gray 1991; Immergut 1992; Obinger, Leibfried, and Castles 2005; Steinmo and Watts 1995).

Even programs beginning with limited coverage of workers only, such as Bismarck's Germany, shape the expectations and bureaucratic capacities that subsequently enable expansion. Furthermore, the institutionalization of publicly funded health care structures allows public permanence to be established and feedback effects reinforce expectations of public coverage. They also endow more power to government by creating bureaucratic institutions to manage and govern these programs, as well as encourage new interest groups to form and mobilize when programs are threatened by cuts (see Pierson 1993). Thus, once introduced, physician organizations found that national health insurance is almost impossible to remove. Therefore, the structure of political institutions is a powerful determinant of whether and when national health insurance and welfare states develop and grow.

Where public programs are weak, as in the United States, the operation of private markets critically determines the extent of government influence over fees. If the private health insurance market is strong, it strengthens professional power relative to government. Encouraged by the House of Medicine, private health insurance developed to such a great extent that government would be unable to replace what people had come to expect. This is the flipside of the idea of policy feedback, which is a theory that when governments get involved in providing services or creating new policies, public expectations change or new expectations are created (Campbell 2003; Mettler 2002; Patashnik 2014; Pierson 1993). The private health insurance industry's growth and the ability of Americans to purchase health insurance reinforced the idea that government should be limited in this area: "Blue Cross helped to secure the definition of healthcare coverage as a personal and private responsibility." Blue Cross had the expressed purpose, according to David Rothman, of "reducing the possibilities of government intervention. It was not the cunning of history but the cunning of Blue Cross that helps explain the early failure to enact national health insurance" (Rothman 1997, 19).

During World War II, health insurance was exempt from wage controls and gained in popularity among employers. At that point, health insurance was taxed as compensation but could be used as a benefit in lieu of wage increases. Then, in 1943, the Internal Revenue Service issued a ruling that allowed health insurance to be excluded from employees' "income," allowing employers to deduct the cost as a business expense. A reversal 10 years later of this ruling was countered by Congress, which solidified the favorable tax treatment of health insurance in 1953 (Hyman 2007, 309).

The number of people with health insurance increased during World War II, partly because providing health insurance was exempted from wartime wage freezes. As said, after the war, these exemptions remained, and more employers offered health insurance coverage to their employees. These policies typically covered inpatient care and physician services in the hospital, leaving individuals to pay for physician visits and physician services outside the hospital (Delbanco, Meyers, and Segal 1979), which often required significant out-of-pocket expenses. Private health insurance coverage of physician services outside the hospital was modest in the immediate decade after the war: in 1948, only 12 percent of the population had it. When Medicare was passed, 46 percent of the population had coverage (Feldstein 1970, 132).

Tax subsidies introduced during the war and then extended by Congress paved the way for the development of employer-sponsored health insurance. That development "would vastly complicate the challenge facing future advocates of national health insurance," even though costs increased, because once employer-sponsored insurance spread, reformers had to consider approaches that would "work around the burgeoning system of private insurance rather than supplant it" (Hacker 2002, 222). Indeed, Hacker argues that scholars focusing too much on the bluster of the AMA understate the role of private insurance as raising the bar for developing and successfully passing new public insurance programs (Hacker 2002, 226).

By the late 1950s, expectations had become locked in, and Hacker is correct that it was not only the AMA that was responsible for the defeat of national health insurance. In fact, the public was not so much against the state but in favor of private health insurance—and as said, had highly variable views about what the private/public roles should be. Policy makers knew this, however, and reformers were acutely aware of public opinion. Lawrence Jacobs's study of policy maker use of polling shows us that those driving reform were well informed by public opinion. One key architect of Medicare, Wilbur Cohen, said that reformers closely analyzed polling data and concluded that the AMA's communications campaign had not necessarily convinced the American public that public insurance was akin to "socialized medicine." Officials honed their proposals for public solutions in some areas but not in others (L. Jacobs 1993, 89–90).

Even as the private sector grew larger, it was not matched by corresponding increases in government oversight. In other countries, a similar tension exists between the public and private role in health care, but as mentioned, the ability to treat medicine as a market good and constrain costs is naturally limited by greater control from countervailing powers. Those countervailing powers can be social insurance organizations (regulated by government), single-payer national health service systems, and single-payer national health insurance programs. Until the Affordable Care Act was passed, health insurance regulation by the federal government had been relatively limited. Health insurers were also given certain privileges and exemptions from antitrust law, beginning in 1945 after the McCarran-Ferguson Act. The insurance industry faced a solvency crisis, and the McCarran-Ferguson Act was an effort to require insurers of all kinds to maintain larger reserves. While health insurance was given a more lenient antitrust structure, it was treated exactly as other insurers that were state-regulated. As such, there was "relatively limited direct regulation of health insurance" (Hyman 2007, 310). Weak and inconsistent benefit and premium price regulations across all 50 states limited cost containment.

In the decades after the expansion of private insurance, the House of Medicine benefited from this weak regulatory framework. Physicians could increase their fees (not unreasonably or dramatically, of course), which could be passed on by the insurers in the form of higher premiums. The lack of state intervention in this area meant that insurers did not face a difficult task of trying to hold down fee increases from year to year. As said earlier, rather than a strong national state keeping a watchful eye over health care costs and premiums, in the United States, we have always had a weakened and decentralized state. As said above, programs establish bureaucratic capacity, and the United States has long lacked the bureaucratic capacity commonly found in other countries (Skowronek 1982).

Insurance spreads risk, but in the absence of close state supervision, commercial insurers were able to transfer risk to premium holders through medical underwriting and risk selection (Stone 1993). While also employer sponsored in Europe, health insurance there was premised on redistribution and balancing out risk: this ensured social solidarity and a smoothing of insurance premium prices. Risk equalization ensured compensation of low-versus high-cost groups (Jost 2004).

If insurers avoided putting downward pressure on fees or failed to restrain price growth, such pressure was unlikely to come from the profession, which discouraged such efforts. As early as the eighteenth century, physicians created common minimum fee schedules to ensure fees would not fall (Blumberg 1984). The House of Medicine established professional sanctions early on against price competition from lower-cost payment models: the AMA's first resolution against "contract" practice was passed in 1869. Contract practices, also known as "lodge" arrangements, were characteristic of immigrant communities from Europe and not the norm in the general population in the United States (Rosen 1977). Efforts to limit prepaid practice continued before World War II (Schwartz 1965; Williams 1939, 1940), and medicine followed a small business model where individual practitioners set their own fees and physicians were paid in cash or services were bartered (Bodenheimer and Grumbach 1994), sometimes for a loaf of bread or a chicken (Levitsky 1996, S14).

The Sherman Antitrust Act of 1890 excluded the "learned professions" because they do not engage in "trade or commerce" (Grad 1978). Granted, the use of fee schedules declined after the passage of the act anyway (Showstack et al. 1979), but that did not last. Instead, the House successfully straddled the gray area between voluntarism and the market, at once able to take monopoly-like actions but not subject to the constraints of commercial entities. Indeed, professional "ethics" were used to justify anticompetitive behavior: participating in prepaid insurance schemes and salaried payments were violations of the AMA ethics code (Rayack 1968). Medical societies boycotted insurers who wanted to create capitated or prepaid medical plans. They also penalized renegade members of the profession by ostracizing physicians and preventing them from even exploring salary-based compensation. Even the Hill-Burton Act, which Morone (1993) notes fueled the expansion of health care under the oversight of the House of Medicine (Morone 1993), was used in some cases to boycott rural hospitals, and government found itself unable to recruit physicians for these hospitals (Krause 1999, 38).

Local, state, and national medical societies such as the AMA held physicians to the party line by imposing a severe penalty on physicians: expulsion from local medical societies. Physicians wanting to practice medicine outside of the fee-for-service model were banned from joining medical societies—a ban that deprived them of malpractice insurance, patient referrals, hospital admitting privileges, and other crucial benefits (Enthoven 1988, 32–33; Kessel 1958; Olson 1965). Hospital privileges became increasingly valuable as more medical care was provided in hospitals. These privileges were essential for physicians to practice medicine: their absence would "dry up referrals, an important source of patients," compromise specialty certification, and ultimately increase the cost of medical malpractice insurance for physicians (Canby and Gellhorn 1978, 547).

The learned professions exemption offered the House of Medicine some protection from restraint-of-trade accusations, but not complete immunity.

On occasion, the enforcement of antitrust laws acted to limit egregious restraints of trade by medical societies. For example, in the 1940s, medical societies' anticompetitive practices were challenged when the Group Health Cooperative in Washington State clashed with the AMA. Department of Justice (DOJ) investigators presented evidence to a grand jury that indicted the AMA and the District of Columbia Medical Society for violation of the Sherman Antitrust Act. The decision of the court was that the medical associations involved were engaged in an effort to restrain trade and maintain fee-for-service payment (*Group Health v. King County Medical Society* 1951).

Traditionally, nonprofit organizations were also not investigated by the FTC (Costilo 1981, 1100). If the FTC chose to investigate an organization, it would focus on indicators of commercial activities on a case-by-case basis (Costilo 1981, 1100). In 1979, the FTC investigated the AMA. It asserted jurisdiction over the AMA in light of lobbying activities directed at Congress and government agencies concerning "economic interests," "AMA practice-management programs aimed at enhancing the efficiency and profits of doctors' offices; legal advice provided to doctors on such subjects as model partnership agreements, taxes, and the sale and disposition of medical practices; and AMA law-suits challenging such government programs as price controls" (Costilo 1981, 1100).

Throughout history, the House of Medicine cultivated the idea that regulating fees was akin to regulation of medical care itself and that it amounted to government intervention in the physician-patient relationship. The House of Medicine promoted the notion that physicians could be trusted to set fees responsibly and that professional norms would ensure appropriate fee setting unmotivated by a desire for profit. Medicine has therefore long been defined by some but not all as a noncommercial activity in the United States that should be based on the "the best interests of the patient and by science—and distinctly not by the pecuniary interests of the doctor." In public, the story was cultivated that "doctors practiced medicine untainted by the influence of money" (Stone 1997, 535). The AMA amended its ethical code in 1934 to make it "unprofessional for a physician to permit 'a direct profit' to be made from his work." Profitmaking, according to this code, "is beneath the dignity of professional practice, is unfair competition with the profession at large, is harmful alike to the profession of medicine and the welfare of the people, and is against sound public policy" (Starr 1982, 216). Medicine developed under laws of commerce that were unrestrained.

In many European countries, medicine was not commercialized, but developed behind a scaffolding of state control nevertheless. This reflected also the timing of the growth of democracy and government. "In the United States, professional organization has generally preceded state involvement in health care, though government intervention has often been an impetus to organizational activity of the medical profession. Bismarck introduced compulsory government health insurance in 1883, before there was any significant professional organization" (Stone 1977, 38).

Though democratic earlier than other countries, in the United States government was weaker relative to European countries, and lacked monarchical or bureaucratic institutions. The political development of the United States ensured that centralized control of the medical profession was absent. Elsewhere, under the monarchy, medicine was a royally sanctioned activity, not controlled by associations as in the United States. Physicians were subject to strong statist regulatory machinery that kept professions under the control of the government, thus ensuring that the guild-like behavior that medicine would be prone to want to engage in would be constrained. As early as the eighteenth century and prior to democratization, the statist monarchical history of these countries provided the foundation for a subsequent governance structure over medicine that was decidedly unguild-like. Medical schools were owned by the government in France, and in Germany, the minister of the interior could set examination material and oversee these (Roemer 1968, 440). That key role for the state persisted, such that by the mid-twentieth century, licensing agencies in many countries were historically the national Ministry of Health (Japan, Sweden, and Colombia); an independent national body, governmental or quasigovernmental (United Kingdom and France); or state or provincial authorities, as in the Federal Republic of Germany and Poland (Roemer 1968, 440). In the United Kingdom, the General Medical Council was "an independent governmental corporation with members nominated by the Crown, chosen by the universities and Royal Colleges, and a proportion (but not a majority) nominated by the medical profession" (Roemer 1968, 442). Given the power of this body historically to define standards and medicines used in the practice of medicine, surgery, and midwifery (Roemer 1968), it is notable that members included nonphysicians.

While Germany had state rather than federal control, federal or national oversight was more the norm in European countries (Krause 1999, 31). For example, France sought to reorganize health under state bureaucratic control as early as 1707 in order to encourage more uniformity in medical training. The Société Royale de Médecine was founded in 1730 (in 1878, it was renamed the Société de Médecine de Paris), and the Académie royale de chirurgie (Royal Academy of Surgery) was established in 1731. The monarchy made a declaration requiring a degree from a French university to study medicine in 1743. Medicine was modeled on similar scientific and cultural institutions under royal patronage and control and "embodied a statist rather than corporate conception of medicine and provided the intense hostility of the Paris Faculty of Medicine." Another force for state control was the organization of public health systems and the need for technical expertise around these issues. Prussia and Austria were ahead of France in reorganizing public health. Reform programs espoused would affirm the powers of the state against the traditional corporate groups (Weisz 1995, 5).

In contrast, in the United States, the profession was licensed "through independent governmental agencies composed mainly of private practitioners representing the state medical associations," and in many states, medical associations had significant control over appointments to government bodies (Roemer 1968, 431).

Institutionalization and Formalization of Payments after 1945

Three processes of institutionalization have occurred in US payment policy since 1945. First, a change in the financing of health care toward greater third-party coverage by private insurers increased the need for the market to define and price services. Second was the development of standardized coding methods and increasing uniformity of medical nomenclature. Third, medical societies developed fee schedules that were later adopted by Medicare.

Across all health care systems—but especially in fee-for-service systems—patients, physicians, and payers need common and consistent definitions of medical services and prices associated with each service. In the process, physicians and payers have to agree on how they will define and name services. Typically, such formalization might follow the passage of national health insurance legislation. In the absence of national health insurance, in the United States the House of Medicine took the lead on formalizing and institutionalizing payment systems or setting standards relating to the exchange and classification of clinical and billing information.

Formalization gradually led to the institutionalization of payment methods and fees benefitting payers and providers. In addition, organizations such as the AMA recognized the need to develop fee schedules, albeit for other reasons: "if medicine does not undertake this activity, it may be done by other[s] who are much less qualified" (AMA, quoted in Somers and Somers 1961, 55). Transaction costs theory suggests that for any economic exchange, the parties seek to minimize or internalize (through integration of the supply chain) the costs associated with performing that exchange, such as monitoring and enforcing the conditions or contracts associated with it. As the number and range of services provided by physicians increased, so too did the need for greater institutionalization of physician payments to minimize transaction costs.

Private insurance coverage of physician specialty services, both in and out of hospitals, and the subsequent creation of Medicare encouraged greater formalization and institutionalization of physician payment. Even though coverage of physician services began slowly, it had a significant impact on physicians by increasing their incomes and changing their methods of billing and payment. Increased coverage led to a "major metamorphosis" because physicians' income shifted from "the modest means of the average patient to the seemingly limitless insurance funds or tax dollars" (Roe 1981, 41). When payment for medical care was primarily a direct transaction between physicians and patients, providers developed their own methods of defining services and how much each one cost.

As third-party payment grew, interacting with third-party payers over an expanding number of services encouraged physicians to formalize and standardize descriptions of services and payments. The new demands of computerized or automated billing—claims processing—also drove the effort to formalize nomenclature. Computerized billing requires standard terminology, so that physicians identify "with precision the services performed and can communicate those services to the computers which handle the billing and reimbursement functions" (US Senate Permanent Subcommittee 1979, 5).

At least since the early 1950s, the House of Medicine has been the principal arbiter of how services are described in billing codes. Having control over naming and defining services, especially holding ownership of this system under intellectual property law, has given organized medicine a key role in defining what is considered a "medical" service. Increasing granularity in these descriptions of payment structures can potentially have an inflationary effect (Baradell and Hanrahan 2000; Kessler 2008). In the 1950s, medical societies likely did not predict the implications; they were focused on how payers and providers needed a standardized way of describing and classifying services.

The AMA published its nomenclature, called the CPT, in 1966. According to the AMA, the CPT was created primarily to "expedite the reporting of therapeutic and diagnostic procedures of surgery, medicine, and obstetrics." The first edition of CPT "also included terms for supplementary and/or related services, as visits consultations, examinations, evaluations, and miscellaneous studies and/or management" (Health Care Financing Administration 1979, 10). Today, the CPT is a registered trademark of the AMA and in widespread use in the United States and around the world. New CPT codes are introduced every year, and some codes are retired or their descriptions may change.

The coding system and reimbursement are closely connected. When the CPT was first introduced, payers could easily pair CPT codes to the CRVS. The AMA was keen to encourage national use of the CPT by private insurers and public payers, and by 1969, 14 states were using the AMA-CPT system, in combination with the 1969 CRVS. Updates to the CPT were published periodically, and with each, the number of services listed exploded. The biggest increase came between 1966, when there were 2,084 services, and 1977, when there were 6,132 services. By 1985, there were 7,040 services (US Congress Office of Technology Assessment 1986, 224).

The use of CPT spread, but physicians still used a variety of coding methods. By the late 1970s, an estimated 250 different coding systems were used across the United States. In 1981, the federal Health Care Financing Administration undertook a study to determine which, if any, could be used by Medicare as a national uniform standard (Harris 1997). The agency adopted the AMA's coding system in its claims processing but created a set of additional codes, which, combined with the AMA codes, constitute the Healthcare Common Procedure Coding System (HCPCS). According to the AMA, the government chose its system because it was compatible with existing data-processing activities, it was acceptable to the medical profession, and the profession was committed to maintaining it (Harris 1997). By 1997, approximately 95 percent of services provided by physicians were reported using the CPT coding system (Harris 1997). The AMA believes that "the medical profession must maintain its code sets," and the AMA is "best suited to handle that responsibility" (Harris 1997).

After the RBRVS was adopted, the link between reimbursement and nomenclature tightened. The CPT system was now formally linked to a Medicare fee schedule, and "many specialty societies realized that the existence of codes and the manner in which procedures were segmented might have a profound influence on the eventual flow of Medicare dollars to their members" (Harris 1997). Today, participants pay close attention to the CPT and repeatedly emphasize the importance of CPT codes. This is partly because the Update Committee must often develop relative value units for these codes but also, and more important, because defining services is a strategy in itself—societies craft codes with great care to ensure payment is maximized. While the CPT has long been underappreciated by scholars (Kumetz and Goodson 2013), it is critically important because it became the standard way of coding and billing for physician services by all payers. When the RBRVS was created, the CPT system had recently become the government standard, so services were defined using CPT codes. From the start, the RBRVS was tied closely to the CPT. This facilitated the involvement of the AMA in the update process later.

The growth of standardized nomenclature developed symbiotically with fee schedules increasingly in use after the 1950s. Because insurers mainly covered surgical services, these were the first to be standardized. Initially, medical specialties and office visits "lacked such an extensive elaboration of identifiable procedures" (Health Care Financing Administration 1979, 19).

Fee schedules were seen as necessary to resolve "several varieties of chaos," including the fact that county medical societies were using different conventions to describe services and the "chaos of some private insurance company fee schedules, which express no rational relationship between fees" (Health Care Financing Administration 1979, 8). Physicians in California decided they needed guidance regarding their fees and wanted to know more about what their colleagues were charging. The California Medical Association (CMA) created a subcommittee charged with defining principles for a new fee schedule. The Alameda County Medical Association of California and the CMA commissioned a study of fees by a recent émigré from Vienna, a psychologist named Ernest Dichter. His study examined physicians' attitudes to fees and proposed that physicians should avoid price discrimination and charge the same fees to all. Some believed that less scrupulous colleagues were overcharging patients and that the reputation of the profession would therefore suffer. The CMA was concerned that wide variation in prices would prompt insurers to develop their own fee schedules, which would replace a usual-customary and reasonable charge system. Rather than have an insurer-determined schedule, the CMA proposed creating its own schedule (Sandy et al. 2009). In addition, physicians found billing difficult: patients had different coverage levels, which varied from full coverage of visits to substantial copayments by patients (Delbanco, Meyers, and Segal 1979).

The 1974 CRVS was separated into five categories for which it listed relative values: (1) medicine, (2) surgery (3) anesthesia, (4) radiology/nuclear medicine, and (5) pathology. Most codes were in the surgery and anesthesia categories (67 percent), followed by pathology (14.9 percent), medical services (9.9 percent), and radiology (7.4 percent) (US Senate Permanent Subcommittee 1979, 17).[3]

The CMA Relative Value Studies Committee of 14 voting members and five consultants updated the CRVS—and was likely a precursor to the Update Committee today. Specialty society leadership formed subcommittees to review specialty-specific codes. The basis for decisions was less than transparent. The subcommittees relied on "informal surveys" of small numbers of colleagues (e.g., cardiovascular codes involved around 15 "reputable" vascular surgeons) (US Senate Permanent Subcommittee 1979, 63), but no one could verify the findings of these surveys after the decision had been made (US Senate Permanent Subcommittee 1979, 52a). Some report that the CRVS was based on median charges reported by California Blue Shield (Monk and Burger 2001). Others contend that average dollar charges were used as a baseline and the CMA worked backward to calculate relative value units, which were then determined through consensus (US Senate Permanent Subcommittee 1979, 51). A significant constraint on this process, however, was that less than 20 percent of the services had sufficient charge data.

Critics said that charge-based data were used selectively and did not in fact reflect actual average charges. Compared with computerized charge data, they did not match: "the procedure descriptors and values in certain specialty sections are, in fact, based on the subjective judgment of a few physicians practicing in the corresponding specialties, rather than historical charge data" (Law and Ensminger 1986, 51).

The CRVS became popular: Blue Shield used it to pay physicians for privately insured patients, and it was also used by the Medi-Cal program in California (US Senate Permanent Subcommittee 1979). More than 20 states adopted some parts or all of the CRVS, and later some states used it to determine Medicaid payments. The use of the underlying relative value–based approach grew to encompass "seventeen state medical societies and six national specialty societies" (Eisenberg 1980, 442).

Medicare's Approach to Physician Payment

The House of Medicine was already involved in developing fee schedules by the time Medicare was enacted.[4] In 1959, the AMA issued a report on the matter, concluding it was in the interest of the profession to develop fee schedules (Somers and Somers 1961, 55). What the House of Medicine opposed was not the schedules but rather government determination of fees and control by private insurers. Such opposition is not limited to the United States: fee setting by physicians rather than by government is naturally favored around the world as a way to protect incomes (Immergut 1992).

Rather than making promises, the Medicare bill "opened with promises to alter almost nothing at all" (Morone 1993, 727). Medicare was a victory for three major actors in the health care system,

> who, accepting that they could not any longer block action, had persuaded Congressional leaders to substitute the designs and gimmicks of private indemnity insurance. The insurance industry—strongly aided and abetted by "organized medicine" and hospital leadership—had won on three fronts: their insurance patterns were preserved and indeed emulated; they had achieved relief from difficult and expensive insurance obligations for the aged; and they now had a statutory privilege of functioning as fiscal intermediaries for the hospital costs (Title XVIII, Part A) and as insurance carriers for the supplementary medical service costs (Title XVIII, Part B) of the public program. The hospitals had won guarantee of full cost reimbursement at whatever levels, and the medical profession had obtained guarantees for the payment of usual and customary prevailing charges, constituting for both the institutional and personal providers signed blank checks on the program's funds. (Falk 1973, 18)

Private insurance companies were a politically acceptable buffer between physicians and government when Medicare was created. Private insurance "carriers" processed claims submitted by physicians and, as before, had the discretion to determine payment levels, maintaining a firm separation of pricing decisions from direct control by the government. Policy makers borrowed the benefit design (such as the number of days in hospital covered) from Blue Cross. For Part B, the story was different: they modeled the program for physician services on the most generous federal employee benefit plan, which was Aetna's high-option plan.[5]

The conventional wisdom is that Medicare's approach, called the "customary, prevailing and reasonable charge" method, was based on how most private insurers paid physicians, called the "usual, customary, and reasonable" charge (UCR). In fact, Medicare did not mimic the norms of the private sector on payment rates. After 1965, many states and Medicare used a system of relative values to determine physician fees (US Senate Permanent

Subcommittee 1979). UCR-based insurance contracts such as Aetna's were more generous than Blue Shield contracts, which were based on fee schedules and therefore placed limits on what physicians could be paid by the insurer for a service (Delbanco, Meyers, and Segal 1979). As said, Medicare's approach was purportedly based on Aetna's UCR. Section 1842(b)(4) of the 1965 law instructed carriers to determine "reasonable charges," which referred to "customary charges for similar services generally made by the physician or other person furnishing such services, as well as the prevailing charges in the locality for similar services." This became known as the "customary, prevailing, and reasonable" charge (CPR) method. Adoption of CPR reflected heavy lobbying by the AMA and political compromises, and as a result, language was influenced by AMA lobbyists (Roe 1981). The AMA gave the impression that introducing CPR would ensure parity between the private sector and Medicare, but by 1970, Medicare rates exceeded those of Blue Shield (Delbanco, Meyers, and Segal 1979).

Indeed, the evidence strongly suggests that Medicare carriers had to change their practices and were also unprepared to do so:

> In 1966 the common methods used by organizations administering third-party payment programs for reimbursing medical claims were relative value studies with conversion factors, fixed-fee schedules for selected procedures, or in a few cases prevailing fee schedules (usually set at the 90th percentile of prevailing fees in a carrier's service area). Very few health insurance plans routinely considered a physician's customary (usual) charge in their reimbursement policies. Thus, the introduction by Medicare of a new basis for determining an allowable amount for a physician's service presented administrative difficulties for most of the carriers. (Health Insurance Benefits Advisory Council 1973, 7)

Part B carriers needed to "understand the customary-prevailing-reasonable standard (CPR), and to develop the data for screening a physician's charge accordingly" (Health Insurance Benefits Advisory Council 1973, 7).

When Medicare was introduced, the organizations processing the claims were ill prepared since they lacked the administrative systems and the data required (Health Insurance Benefits Advisory Council 1973, 7). Although regulations were written that gave detail to the simple legislative definition, in general, carriers had "almost complete discretion about implementing this methodology" (Schieber et al. 1976, 1090). Therefore, there were "fee schedules for 'customary' charges," more or less frequently updated charges, and usage of the 75th and 95th percentiles to adjust for the "prevailing" charge (Health Insurance Benefits Advisory Council 1973, 7).

The choice of CPR for determining Medicare rates had far-reaching consequences, because charge systems such as these served physicians' economic interests and fueled subsequent medical inflation (Starr 1982). Essentially, this meant that physicians were paid based on what they had previously charged and/or what their colleagues charged for the same service in the geographic area of the carrier or claims processor.

Medicare's CPR was the catalyst for UCR (the private-sector equivalent) to develop, not the other way around. Only after Medicare began using CPR did UCR become an industry standard. Medicare shifted the practices of the private insurance industry and "caused a large majority of Blue Shield and commercial plans to adopt it as well" (Ginsburg 1989, 760). Ironically, perhaps, whereas private-sector practices would normally be independent from a public insurance scheme, the decision to give carriers broad payment authority tied Medicare and the private insurance system together. Presumably, carriers preferred a standard billing approach that could be used to process claims from both private insurers and Medicare.

A misconception developed that CPR/UCR was the only basis for fees after Medicare was created. However, it was difficult administratively, so carriers had to combine it with other methods. Determining a charge for thousands of procedures requires "the processing of tens of millions of claims each year, followed by numerous adjustments," all of which is "extraordinarily burdensome administratively" (Holahan 1989, 870). William Hsiao, an economist and former actuary who later developed the RBRVS, recalled, "The number of transactions in physician services is roughly 1.4 billion. In the '60s and '70s remember there was no sophisticated computer. You have so many transactions for different services you can never monitor and control what a physician is charging." Most Blue Shield insurers lacked sufficient data for each service and each physician's charge profile to implement the prevailing charge system (Hsiao 1995, 388).

These problems surely decreased as computing power increased, but for many years, CPR/UCR was not the primary basis of insurance reimbursement. Instead, "most carriers use[d] relative value studies" (Schieber et al. 1976, 1090) of state medical societies, such as the CRVS and/or those developed by six national specialty societies (Eisenberg 1980). Insurers and carriers also fell back on physician estimates, basing their payment limits on the medical director's guesstimate of an upper limit. According to

Hsiao (1995), decisions made by medical directors in consultation with other physicians were largely arbitrary:

> He sets an arbitrary number and talks to his physician friends to see whether they agree. They might agree that for an uncomplicated appendectomy any charge that exceeds $700 was unreasonable. Then that number was put into the claim payment system, which says, "When you see an appendectomy that charges more than $700, kick it out for review." In other words, it's a review by exception system. That made it feasible to administer. (388)

During the 1970s and 1980s, some insurers decided to define the customary fee as the 80th percentile and would pay all fees up to it (Delbanco, Meyers, and Segal 1979). Because payers used these shortcuts to simplify payment, the notion that charges were based on an individual's profile eroded, and pricing was determined by fee ceilings. Recalling this two decades later, the architect of the RBRVS described how fee ceilings made it easy to find out where an individual physician stood relative to his or her colleagues: Hsiao said all they had to do was submit a high fee and see if the claim was paid. If a claim was accepted, the billing was below the customary level (Hsiao 1995).[6] People thought this method encouraged higher fees because physicians tended to compare themselves with others who were charging more (not less):

> The surgeon who has been quite satisfied with his charges is not likely to stand still when he learns that one of his less experienced and less skillful colleagues has arbitrarily established a higher "profile" and is being paid substantially more. The senior surgeon simply remodels his "profile" by charging similar or higher fees (without necessarily collecting any difference from the patient) and eventually he too gets third party payment at a higher scale. This ridiculous chain of events has no end in sight. (US Senate Permanent Subcommittee 1979, 126)

The charge-based approach came to be seen as a "boondoggle," given its "virtual invitation to abuse" (Roe 1981, 41). Essentially, there were no standard prices. Fees reflected subjective judgments of medical directors, and payers had an inconsistent and complicated system of adjusting the charges (as private insurers continue to do today). Furthermore, while some carriers paid physicians using the reasonable charge system, many carriers and states maintained versions of the California schedule approach. In short, Medicare had legislated a private-sector UCR approach, but before Medicare, fees were based on a variety of methods, and one of those methods was a relative value unit fee schedule.

The Demise of Specialty and Medical Societies' Relative Value Scales

A landmark 1975 Supreme Court decision, *Goldfarb v. Virginia State Bar*, removed the exemption for "learned professions" from the Sherman Act, leaving medicine more vulnerable to FTC enforcement of the law. Soon after, the FTC investigated physician-created fee schedules and sought voluntary agreements with professional societies to cease publishing them. Today, antitrust law remains an important constraint on prices and price setting for physician services. Some scholars believe, however, that antitrust enforcements relating to prices, as opposed to other areas of health care such as mergers, have since been underused (Hammer and Sage 2002).

The 1975 Supreme Court decision was the first nail in the coffin of the CRVS. Until *Goldfarb*, the FTC had not investigated the health care sector, but fee schedules developed by physician societies were now perceived as anticompetitive (Havighurst and Kissam 1979). After this case, relative value fee schedules published by medical societies (which appear to have been the main or only source of relative values) were investigated and challenged by two agencies enforcing antitrust laws, the FTC and the DOJ (Pfizenmayer 1982).

Subsequently, Congress also got involved, because legislators knew that Medicare based some of its payments on the CRVS. Had CPR/UCR been the only factor in determining Medicare payment, it is unlikely that in 1977,[7] Congress would have launched an investigation focused on the use of CRVS by Medicare and the relationship between a California carrier (the California Physicians' Service)[8] and the CMA.

The three principal concerns Congress had regarding the CRVS are eerily similar to some of the concerns discussed today in relation to the RBRVS. First, investigators wanted to know if the CRVS had contributed to cost growth. Carriers and payers objected to the 1974 update of the CRVS because they perceived it as inflationary—and the CRVS almost immediately lost credibility.[9]

At that time, unlike today, code growth was discussed as a cause of health care inflation. The first CRVS, published in 1956, listed 1,000 services. Subsequent updates caused disgruntlement, but this was mild compared to that triggered by changes in 1974.[10] What caught the attention of payers in the 1974 edition was that in 1969, there were 3,682 services, but five years later, there were 5,542—an increase of 1,860 services. Most of the increase occurred in surgical services, which grew from 2,517 to 3,759 or 67.8 percent of the total growth in codes. In the general medical services category, the number of services increased too but accounted for only 10 percent of the growth in codes, from 268 in 1969 to 550 services in 1974. In theory, these additions were due to changes in service descriptions in response to changes in the "state-of-the-art of medical practice," coding clarifications, procedure number code changes, or consolidation of codes. As the Office of Technology Assessment noted in its 1986 report, however, along with technological change, "substantial increases came from fragmenting procedures into a number of detailed codes in place of a single descriptor," and when Medicare carriers in California switched "from the 1964 edition to the expanded 1969 version terminology changes caused fees to rise up to 5 percent for office visits and 7 to 8 percent for hospital visits." Private insurers said the update dramatically increased fees (US Congress Office of Technology Assessment 1986, 161–162).

Investigators wanted to know if the number of codes had been increased for the economic benefit of its members. Fragmentation—"breaking down existing procedure descriptors into component procedures"—was increasing costs (US Senate Permanent Subcommittee 1979, 34d). While changes in medical practice and new technologies need to be incorporated into updates of any fee schedule, an increase in and fragmentation of billing codes is a potential strategy for increasing fees by shifting from the lower to the higher valued code. Instead of there being an "average" surgical case, there were now highly differentiated services: for example, vaginal delivery codes expanded from one to seven specific separate procedures. An "incidental" appendectomy, in which the appendix was removed while the surgeon performed another service, was now a separately reimbursed procedure. In some cases, "fragmentation creates hard to evaluate differences in descriptors on the basis of the intensity of service performed, such as in the degree of difficulty of a surgical procedure or the time and skill involved" (US Senate Permanent Subcommittee 1979, 9).

The Senate committee concluded that increased expenditure in Medicare and Medicaid was due to "shifts toward billing to higher valued patient visit services even when the options available for reporting the complexity of the service remained constant" (US Senate Permanent Subcommittee 1979, ix). A wide range of organizations—the Social Security Administration, insurers, and Medicare carriers in some states—concurred that the growth in billing codes had led to increased fees (US Senate Permanent Subcommittee 1979, 10).

Just as primary care physicians today argue that the RBRVS is biased against primary care, the investigation into the CRVS raised questions about whether it was a truly "relative" fee schedule. Examining shifts in relative values, Congress found that there was a shift to the higher-valued levels of the fee schedule (US Senate Permanent Subcommittee 1979). A professor from the University of California at San Francisco School of Medicine who submitted testimony on the CRVS argued that systems based on relative values tend to "rigidify the pattern of delivery of medical services, as well as providing incentives to perform overvalued (high charges in relation to cost) services" (US Senate Permanent Subcommittee 1979, 68). Medical directors from insurance companies argued that the CRVS of 1974 was not only devised to increase physician fees for their economic gain but also specifically designed to increase payments to "the high paid super-specialist at the expense of the primary care physician" (Schroeder and Showstack 1977, 180).

Yet another issue was the integrity of the CRVS. The Senate subcommittee found that CRVS revisions used an ad hoc and unsystematic method (US Senate Permanent Subcommittee 1979, 77). While Congress was investigating the CRVS, the DOJ and FTC continued to investigate relative value–based fee schedules. Medical societies opposed this intervention on the grounds that relative value–based fee schedules did not violate antitrust law, because agreements to set relative values were not equivalent to fee setting (US Senate Permanent Subcommittee 1979). The American Society of Anesthesiologists was one of a handful of societies that were granted exemptions under the law, but the widespread enforcement actions discouraged further development and updating of fee schedules by medical societies. The FTC and DOJ reached settlements with several medical societies (Kallstrom 1978; Pfizenmayer 1982), and others agreed under consent decrees with the FTC to cease from developing the fee schedule. The last fee schedule to be challenged was the CRVS, which the CMA, under FTC investigation, agreed to stop updating (Pfizenmayer 1982).

Not made illegal, however, was the use of a relative value scale (RVS) by payers. The CRVS lived on, "updated" not by physician societies but informally by each payer. According to one account as late as 1993, the dominant approach to processing physician reimbursement claims recombined fee screens with the CPT and CRVS (Pfizenmayer 1982).

Conclusion

The United States has had a tendency to hand over many state activities to the commercial and nonprofit sector, in what has been described as the "delegated state" (Morgan and Campbell 2011), a key example of which is the process of updating fees in Medicare. Private providers and insurers generally have had weak incentives to contain costs. At the same time, both the discipline of the market and government action were often lacking or uncoordinated. Health care has evolved as a private activity in the United States, and yet it has not been subject to extensive price regulation or cost-containment strictures because, just as the medical profession was exempt from antitrust law, health care has not been seen as part of the "market." Despite openly engaging in efforts to restrain trade in the ways described above, the House of Medicine was very rarely subject to the same enforcement that other monopolies were subjected to.

Resistance to public health insurance by the House of Medicine is not unique to the United States: in every country, medical organizations recognized that greater governmental control would likely reduce their incomes. In other countries, however, the growth of (albeit limited) social insurance schemes (starting in the late nineteenth century in Europe) limited private health insurance and put physician fees within the bailiwick of the public interest. In the United States, the House of Medicine was more successful than in other countries in protecting itself partly because the nation entered the postwar years with relatively greater prosperity and was buoyed by tax incentives that encouraged the growth of private insurance.

That private health insurance developed before government health insurance proved favorable for physicians. Private-insurer fee schedules were established by the time government introduced Medicare and Medicaid. Medical societies in California created the CRVS using a relative value–based fee schedule that was more convenient for both physicians and insurers. Insurers were receptive to such methods because it was technically difficult to develop charge-based fee schedules for every physician in practice.

A key factor that later influenced the entry of the House of Medicine into the update process was its control over a billing and coding system that government later adopted. The House of Medicine consistently helped drive more standardization toward physician-owned or updated nomenclature and payment systems. The CMA's fee schedule was adopted throughout the country, and it soon became the dominant way physician services were reimbursed (Sandy et al. 2009). As the California fee schedule developed, the AMA established and developed a complementary billing code system, which further eased the work of payers and ensured the continued feasibility of fee-for-service. Insurers seemed to have few incentives to pressure prices downward: Blue Shield, which dominated the market for insurance, was created by physicians and overseen by governing boards dominated and sometimes directly elected by medical society members. In other countries, a more assertive public sector often (but not always) subdued fees and/or worked in a corporatist manner with physician organizations to develop social insurance schemes. In the United States, by contrast, private insurance was encouraged as an alternative to government, and physician fees increased in a vacuum of close government supervision.

The political compromises needed to pass Medicare entailed acquiescence to physician demands. From the AMA's perspective, acceptable terms for physician reimbursement in Medicare included continued physician control over fees. Most readings of the historical record emphasize that Medicare legislation defined reimbursement as what a physician had charged previously or what other physicians charged for the same service; the implementation of the law did not in fact reflect charge-based fees. Claims processors continued to use fee schedules to determine prevailing charges, and those fee schedules were determined by physician organizations. These arrangements proved disastrous for program costs. Chapter 3 shows how Medicare expenditure on physician services increased and led to the development of a national fee schedule.

THREE

The Science of Work and Payment Reform

IN THE 1970S, the alarm over Medicare expenditure grew in Congress year by year, and interest in changing payment policies gathered steam. Policy makers in the executive and legislative branches made efforts to rein in Medicare physician expenditure, both through fee reductions and by commissioning research on policy options. As early as 1981, the Health Care Financing Administration was aware of a resource-based method of valuing physician services proposed by Professor William Hsiao, an economist and former actuary who taught at the Harvard School of Public Health and published an influential paper in 1979 (Hsiao and Stason 1979). Under Congress's direction, the Health Care Financing Administration called for proposals to develop a resource-based system, and Professor Hsiao was awarded the contract to develop a resource-based payment system in 1985.

This chapter surveys Congress's efforts to address Medicare expenditure and payment reform legislation, the research effort underpinning the Resource-Based Relative Value Scale (RBRVS), the development of the new resource-based payment system, and the rulemaking process that followed. The legislative lead-up and the methods of the Hsiao study have been discussed extensively (Ginsburg and Lee 1989; Lee 1990; Lee and Ginsburg 1988, 1991; Lee et al. 1989). One aspect of the process of creating the RBRVS that has received less scrutiny is the role of the House of Medicine in encouraging this system to develop, in the face of alternatives they felt would be detrimental for the profession.

After the law passed, many adjustments to the RBRVS were made. During the rulemaking process, changes were made to Hsiao's recommended values,

47

because each specialty fought to protect fees in its area of medicine. While that self-interested process is not atypical in policymaking, it undercuts the notion that the RBRVS was based entirely on a scientific method. In fact, the notion that payment reform had achieved goals to redistribute resources from primary to specialty care far overstates the extent to which it was actually realized.

The last section of the chapter reviews the problems that were anticipated with a physician-led update process. Analysts of proposed payment reforms in the early 1980s consistently argued that the update process would need to be carefully managed. After the legislation was passed, concerns continued to be expressed about the need for an objective process.

The Lead-up to Physician Payment Reform

In the 1950s, rapid growth rates in health expenditure reached double digits (Somers and Somers 1961). In the early 1960s, expenditure growth temporarily dipped to an average annual increase of 2.6 percent, but in the three years after Medicare passed, expenditure increases surged to an average of 6.4 percent a year (Klarman 1969). Perhaps to build support for the bill, President Lyndon Johnson's administration did not reveal the true expected cost of Medicare (Blumenthal and Morone 2009), and almost immediately the fiscal impact of the program was unexpected and troubling.

Medicare "set fees such that almost all physicians would willingly see Medicare patients" (Newhouse 2002, 11). Soon, payments to physicians were identified as a major cause of increasing health care expenditure shortly after Medicare passed (Klarman 1969), which put pressure on Congress to do something. Congressional control over expenditure was more limited in Part B than in Part A because under Medicare legislation, Congress could not directly dictate physician payment levels. It could, however, adjust the "screens" that were used, which had the effect of reducing the payment below the submitted charge. The first cut put payments at the 90th percentile of customary charges; the level was reduced to the 83rd percentile in 1969 and to the 75th percentile in 1971 (Klarman 1969).

In amendments to the Social Security Act in 1972 (P.L. 92-603), Congress mandated a report on physician services in Part B. Under the law, the Health Insurance Benefits Advisory Council would report to the Social Security Administration on the program. Its lengthy and sophisticated econometric analysis showed that the introduction of Medicare had increased the rate of physician price increases by between 0.5 and 1 percent a year from 1966 to 1969. Inflation had increased during that time also, but these findings showed that the increases stimulated by the program were beyond these economy-wide inflationary effects (Health Insurance Benefits Advisory Council 1973). This may have been the first—or at least one of the earliest—detailed investigations into expenditure growth in Medicare.

Restraints on the growth of prices were introduced in 1974: carriers could increase fees only by a percentage change in the newly created Medicare Economic Index (MEI), a Consumer Price Index of sorts for Medicare. The Medicare Economic Index, based on price changes in physician fees, employee compensation, rent, and medical equipment, did not, unfortunately, succeed in containing costs. Expenditures grew around 17 percent a year between 1970 and 1984 (Helbing, Latta, and Keene 1991).

Policy experts increasingly recognized a dynamic relationship between the supply and availability of health care services and their use, that is, that supply and use were not necessarily related to "need." When the number of hospital beds increased, more beds were filled and more services were provided ("Roemer's law"), thereby also increasing the use of physician services (Roemer 1959, 1961).

Researchers found very different treatment patterns when comparing similar populations (Wennberg and Gittelsohn 1973). The idea that the delivery of medical care services is not determined by the health of patients alone was reinforced in studies using increasingly more sophisticated methods to link changes in physician behavior to changes in financial incentives. The evidence that physicians were influenced by subtle—and not so subtle—financial incentives was increasingly solid. Partly in response to these concerns, a variety of health policy approaches emerged in the 1970s, including health maintenance organizations in 1973, regional health planning organizations, and more research, such as the RAND Health Insurance Experiment on how efficiency in health care could be improved.

Another concern was the state of the primary care workforce. According to McMenamin, an Institute of Medicine report in 1978 linked declines in the number of primary care physicians to payment rates and recommended increases in fees (McMenamin 1981). In 1979, the Department of Health, Education, and Welfare proposed replacing Medicare's charge-based system with a fee schedule (Delbanco, Meyers, and Segal 1979). But for the most part, on these larger issues such as payment equity or efficiency of expenditure, one former official described how, generally speaking, Medicare was not essentially managed from Washington, DC, but a program governed at the local level:

> The issue of payment equity or payment policy or how things are defined, other than coverage issues which we could deal with, essentially we would say, "Well, that's a local prerogative," because there was no federal legislative or regulatory standard to say the Chicago Blue Cross/Blue Shield, hypothetically, well, they're paying too much for cataract surgery relative to something else. Essentially the system was built off their local policies that evolved over many years, and became sticky and hard to change. And Congress tried to deal with various issues such as the deal with inflation of customary and prevailing charges by putting in a cap on Medicare Economic Index Limited prevailing charges. So that prevailing charges could not go up faster than some rate of inflation that was considered acceptable.
>
> But it was a very different role that the government had with respect to the reasonable charge system. Because there was not all that much that could be done because of the way the system was constructed, except to enforce some legislative changes that Congress started to develop over time to deal with both the cost issues and some equity issues. (Interview Subject 24)

Greater regulation of the program was seen as necessary and came into use more readily during the 1980s (Brown 1992). One policy expert who served in various roles at the time said that the same strategy was used across different parts of the program, so that each part was targeted, such as home health payments:

> So it's been a very, over time, a sort of a reaction to cost trends that has led to kind of provider-by-provider payment regulation for cost-containment purposes. We were sort of knocking down one . . . one hurdle at a time. So we'd get hospital payment through DRGs [diagnosis-related groups] and then we did physician payments through RBRVS, and it was pretty widely accepted. The physicians accepted it. And policy makers accepted it. It did reduce the rate of growth in physician expenditures. And so it was a policy success, politically acceptable, reduced physician payment down-wise. I mean, you know, what . . . there's nothing wrong with that picture. (Interview Subject 14)

As noted by the interviewee, a major turning point for the Medicare program was the adoption of a new way of paying for hospital care using DRGs in 1983. It was also called the prospective payment system because it prospectively defined a set of service bundles (and theoretically a cap on the charges associated). This major change in hospital reimbursement, which, like the RBRVS, was later adopted by the private sector, acted as a trigger for reforming physician payment as well, since it was only a matter of time before Medicare turned to Part B (Mayes and Berenson 2006). With physician payments showing no signs of declining but without a clear plan forward, Congress passed the Deficit Reduction Act of 1984, which froze Medicare physician payment rates for 15 months (Helbing, Latta, and Keene 1991). Legislators later extended the law through April 1986 for participating physicians and through December 1986 for nonparticipating physicians (Helbing, Latta, and Keene 1991).

Following the payment freeze, Congress continued to take an aggressive stance toward expenditure growth. Congress initiated a series of incremental changes rather than fundamental reforms, because there was uncertainty about the plans for future reform (Iglehart 1988). Under the Omnibus Budget Reconciliation Act of 1987, Congress cut fees for overvalued surgical and other procedures. The AMA viewed these and prior fee cuts as "punitive" and "ad hoc" (Todd 1988, 2439), but the cuts unified a diverse but unhappy coalition of physician groups. Procedural and surgical specialties became allies with a common interest in creating an alternative to the CPR or UCR system (Todd 1988). Primary care physicians joined with these specialties because they felt their own fees were disproportionately low. All physicians were dissatisfied, to different degrees, with the administrative hassles of the payment system. Some felt that UCR resulted in arbitrary fees, significant variation in fees across specialties for the same work performed, and widespread variability across geographic areas (American Medical Association 1993). In sum, UCR was "complex, confusing, unpredictable, and unrelated" to the cost of providing services (American Medical Association 1993, 5). The AMA believed payment reform was imminent.

Congress debated extending Medicare's use of DRGs to hospital-based physicians, which included radiologists, anesthesiologists, and pathologists. The AMA "devoted enormous energy to fighting this proposal, which was supported by the Reagan administration," and the proposal failed in 1987 (Iglehart 1988, 865). The AMA helped unite the House of Medicine against reform proposals based on DRGs for physician services and "mandatory capitation." These two options, according to the head of the AMA, were "dubious" and "frightening solutions" (Todd 1988, 2439). Instead, the AMA proposed a resource-based relative value system. Surgical societies disagreed and wanted a fee schedule based on charges (American Medical Association 1993; Monk and Burger 2001).

The AMA believed that a relative value–based system would likely mean that physicians would have to accept restrictions on balance billing. Even so, the association decided that even if it had to give that up, it was preferable to capitation or DRG-type payments (American Medical Association 1993). The AMA Board of Trustees and the House of Delegates decided to support the "indemnity principle whereby the government decides how much to pay and the physician how much to charge" (Todd 1988, 2439). The expectation was that an RBRVS would operate much like a market-based pricing system:

> An RBRVS will simplify and rationalize physician payment. If it is implemented as part of an indemnity system, its simplicity will enable market forces to work their magic, helping to restrain both patient demand and physician charges. At the same time, the AMA recognizes that controlling expenditure increases will require a continuing focus on the volume and intensity of the services provided by physicians to patients . . . the AMA will be in the forefront of efforts to evaluate the RBRVS and to develop parameters of quality care. These decisions will not be made parochially or politically, but in the best interests of our patients. With a genuine sense of restraint and responsibility, the medical profession must respond to the RBRVS experiment in a manner worthy of our profession. (Todd 1988, 2441)

The AMA's immediate strategy was to try to retain fee-for-service payment by lobbying Congress for changes to the CPR system and to explore fee schedules based on relative value scales. The association reviewed the long-defunct CRVS as a model (American Medical Association 1993), but since it had not been updated since 1974,[1] its usefulness was limited.

Meanwhile, two congressional committees were addressing Medicare physician payment reform: the Health Subcommittee of Ways and Means and the Senate Finance Committee (Smith 1992, 128).[2] In the executive branch, the Health Care Financing Administration's Office of Research, Demonstrations, and Statistics (ORDS) allocated $2.1 million for extramural research on physician payment in 1981 alone (McMenamin 1981). The Health Care Financing Administration solicited various studies of relative values that explored, among other topics, a fee schedule based on existing fee distributions, ways to measure physician work using time and motion studies, the societal and individual benefits from various procedures, and how other countries paid physicians (McMenamin 1981). Hsiao completed another study for the agency in 1984 on physician pricing behavior. Staff at the Health Care Financing Administration knew that Hsiao had found large discrepancies between the fees for office visits and surgeries (McMenamin 1981), and in 1984, an Urban Institute report, commissioned by the agency (Hadley et al. 1984), proposed modifying it partly based on William Hsiao's earlier work.

In the Deficit Reduction Act of 1984, Congress mandated from the Office of Technology Assessment (OTA) a report on physician payment, which was published in 1986. The OTA report framed its investigation along four alternative models: (1) modifications in Medicare's traditional customary, prevailing, and reasonable method of payment; (2) payment based on fee schedules using relative value–based payments; (3) payment for packages of services; and (4) capitation payment (US Congress Office of Technology Assessment 1986, 5).[3] The OTA defined an RVS as an exhaustive list of physician services in which each entry is associated with one specific numerical value that expresses the value of the service in question relative to an arbitrary numeraire (US Congress Office of Technology Assessment 1986, 121). The OTA and Congress wanted a fee schedule that would reduce the disparities between specialists and primary care physicians.

Paul Ginsburg, former executive director of the Physician Payment Review Commission, saw the initiative for payment reform largely coming from Congress, whereas hospital reform had come from the administration:

Unlike hospital legislation, they saw little prospect of leadership by the administration. What was happening in the administration is there seemed to be about four factions. There was one that was supporting a fee schedule, one that was supporting greater use of capitation, one that wanted to do something like DRGs for physicians, and the White House just wasn't interested in resolving what its policy would be. There was support in Congress for rationalizing the payment system. Another thing that led to it was after TEFRA [Tax Equity and Fiscal Responsibility Act of 1982] and then the DRG legislation, come 1984 they had another round of budget legislation and decided it was the physicians' turn to take the hit. They didn't have many policy ideas. They wound up with a freeze that they were all very unhappy about, and also they were hearing from the internists and family physicians about distortions in the payment system which were starting to hurt more under an era of constraints on fees than they would have when fees were more generous. They were hearing from the rural physicians that they were being underpaid. So there was a lot of interest in a restructuring of the payment system and clearly not much expectation that the Administration would propose something. (Ginsburg 2002, 321)

The Consolidated Omnibus Budget Reconciliation Act of 1985, passed in April 1986, established a new payment commission to advise Congress solely on Medicare physician payment. The law gave Congress its own independent think tank focused on Medicare Part B. Previously, in 1982, Congress had created a commission to advise it on hospital payment, called the Prospective Payment Commission (known as ProPAC; both were later merged into a new advisory organization, the Medicare Payment Advisory Commission, which blended responsibilities for advice on physician and hospital payment).

The Consolidated Omnibus Reconciliation Act of 1985 directed the secretary of Health and Human Services to work with the Physician Payment Review Commission and OTA on a relative value scale (US Congress Office of Technology Assessment 1986).[4] The legislation itself mandated how a relative value scale might be constructed, based on characteristics such as the range of clinical settings, variations in "skill levels and training," and "the time required, and risk involved, in furnishing different services." Measures of time and risk subsequently formed the basis of the RBRVS.

The creation of an organization dedicated solely to Medicare physician payment added momentum to payment reform. For its part, Congress was apparently relieved to have an alternative source of policy advice, given its reliance on the AMA (Iglehart 1988, 867). Its rapid emergence as a "major participant in fashioning policy" was noted as being partly related to the expertise of its staff and leadership (Iglehart 1988, 867). Its quick entry into the physician payment world was no accident, because the organization was immediately under pressure to produce results due to the belief among some in Congress that it should be a temporary organization: "The House Appropriations Committee, which didn't like the idea of all these Congressional commissions, wrote in its first report that this should be viewed as a temporary commission not to exceed two years. Certainly there was a lot of pressure on the commission to produce quickly, feeling that if it didn't produce quickly it wouldn't survive" (Ginsburg 2002, 324). A deliberate decision was made to make much of its decision-making process open to the public once a year for a day or a day and a half of hearings. "We had a fair amount of outreach to talk to the interest groups. What we would do each year is tell them, 'Here are the issues we're planning to write on for our annual reports. Why don't you come in and tell us about which ones are important to you and what your views are'" (Ginsburg 2002, 324).

In early 1986, soon after it was set up, the commission was asked to find additional money in the budget by Congress and it identified procedures that were overvalued (Ginsburg 2002, 327). The staff found procedures to cut, but all but a few were surgical procedures, except a handful performed by internists that were gastroenterology procedures (Ginsburg 2002, 328). This immediately posed a potential problem of political opposition, and staff were "told that surgeons were the most powerful and they would be able to quash this, but Congress bought that approach. Initially they didn't alter our list at all" (Ginsburg 2002, 328). To their surprise, "in fact Congress has never involved itself in the details of this stuff" (other than one requested by Senator Heinz who added a service), but after that "the law was enacted" (Ginsburg 2002, 328). The success of this approach gave the Commission credibility and a higher profile, in Ginsburg's opinion, and it "paved the way within the Congress. This was a test vote that the surgeons lost, and this surprised people. This was a victory for the internists and the family physicians over the surgeons" (Ginsburg 2002, 328).

In short order, in March 1987, the Physician Payment Review Commission released its first report, agreeing with the OTA's earlier recommendation that the best option would be a relative value system. A year later, the commission endorsed a resource-cost approach as the basis for the new fee schedule (US Senate Special Committee on Aging 1988). As former head of the Physician Payment Review Commission Paul Ginsburg recalled,

we discussed the notion that a resource-based fee schedule was a useful approach. We actually didn't see much potential in capitation as a physician payment mechanism by Medicare. We also did not see much potential for a physician DRGs, which had been raised right after the hospital DRG proposal. A physician DRG proposal, which was only suitable for in-patient use, would be to make a payment to the physician based on the case, and the reason we weren't enthusiastic about physician DRGs was that first of all, given the lack of limitation on balanced billing, we felt that going to a payment system that diverged greatly from fee-for-service would wind up mostly affecting the beneficiaries rather than the physicians. A lot of physicians would simply say, "This is my bill," and the difference between that fee-for-service bill and a DRG-based bill would wind up in the patient's lap. Hospitals have had mandatory assignment from the beginning of Medicare, so that if you decided to pay hospitals a different amount, well all they can do is decide whether they want to drop out of the program or not. It doesn't affect the liability or cost sharing that the beneficiary has to deal with. (Ginsburg 2002, 325)

Defining Work: The Hsiao or "Harvard" Study and the House of Medicine

As said, the Health Care Financing Administration had already initiated a research program relating to physician payment in the early 1980s. What followed later was the study that sketched a method to develop relative values based on resource inputs. The blueprint for the new payment system— also known as the "Hsiao" or "Harvard" study—was led by Professor William Hsiao at the Harvard School of Public Health.

According to Hsiao, the RBRVS grew out of a project on competition in the market for physicians' services. "This small component, RBRVS, was really minuscule and was a detour I took in the main research" (Hsiao 1995, 390). Hsiao estimated how long surgical procedures took (called "skin-to-skin" time) using the 1975 Study of Surgical Services, and he calculated office visit times from the National Ambulatory Care Survey. Then Hsiao worked with a cardiologist, William Stason, to elucidate the concept of physician work. The article, published in the *Health Care Financing Review* in 1979, proved to be influential.

To understand the nature of physician work, Hsiao and Stason interviewed 25 board-certified physicians in Boston from five specialties (five each from general surgery, obstetrics and gynecology, ophthalmology, orthopedics, and urology). Physicians were selected "nonrandomly" from the Boston area to represent different practice locations and payment models and included teaching and community hospitals. They represented a range of ages and years of experience (Hsiao and Stason 1979, 25). The researchers measured both times and complexity of service. They found operative times (skin-to-skin time) to be fairly reliable, but pre- and postoperative times varied. The researchers concluded that it might be difficult for physicians to distinguish adequately between time and complexity, since the two were correlated.

The construct of the complexity of service recognized that "not all time is equal; rather, the degree of skill and intensity of effort required per unit of time vary widely from one service to another" (Hsiao and Stason 1979, 24), and therefore complexity was defined as "(1) the risk of intraoperative complications; (2) the diagnostic skills and clinical judgments required to choose the appropriate therapeutic procedure; and (3) the technical skills required to perform the procedure" (Hsiao and Stason 1979, 24–25). Complexity was considered to vary from procedure to procedure and from patient to patient, but the expectation was that an average overall complexity of one procedure relative to another could be established. To estimate the content of work, respondents were asked to rank (on a 10-point scale) the complexity of procedures they performed relatively frequently. Next, after choosing a procedure falling near the middle of the scale and assigning a value of 100 to that procedure, they were asked to estimate the complexity "per unit of time," from the least to the most complex, and compare that to an initial diagnostic office visit. The researchers then used a modified Delphi technique[5] whereby each physician was provided with his or her own rankings compared to the average of other physicians in their specialty, and changes were made to the final estimates.

The first unexpected finding was that there was much consistency between physicians in the same specialty (perhaps due to the Delphi process). The rank orders by complexity of service differed very little, meaning that physicians in the same specialty agreed on the order of ranking by difficulty.

The comparability of difficulty estimates ranged much more widely across specialties. In the exercise where specialists gave complexity per unit of time a number (with 100 being the middle of the scale), there were widely different estimates of the complexity of an office visit. Specialties had very different views of the magnitude of the complexities of services. Orthopedics, for example, put an office visit at 78, whereas ophthalmology gave it a score of 20. The variability of the range is notable, with obstetrics and gynecology, for example, giving a radical abdominal hysterectomy a rating of 360, and its lowest level procedure, diagnostic dilation and curettage (41), a rating similar to an office visit (40).

These absolute numbers were later transformed into measures of relative complexity, which corrected variations across specialties—for example, from 1.0 (bunionectomy) to 2.6 (total hip replacement) for orthopedics and

1.0 (removing a chalazion) to 10.2 (lens extraction, intracapsular or cataract surgery) for ophthalmology (Hsiao and Stason 1979). The next transformation allowed the researchers to take these estimates and develop a standardized scale, with a range from 1.0 to 4.0, that would be comparable with general surgery.

The researchers found that time was highly correlated to complexity, because the surgeons argued that procedures requiring more complexity per unit of time take more time. Some also said that fatigue as operating time increased contributed to the effort or concentration required. The specialists ranked pre- and postoperative complexity per unit of time equivalent to a routine office visit (1.0) (Hsiao and Stason 1979).

The researchers acknowledged that the estimates were based on a small sample that was nonrandom, but they defended the method by saying that "there is no reason to think, however, that responses were systematically biased unless physicians in Massachusetts see the world differently from their peers elsewhere" (Hsiao and Stason 1979, 36).

Hsiao and Stason found that relative values based on resource costs differed both from current fees based on Medicare charges and from California Relative Value Study values, particularly for office visits compared to surgical procedures. On average, office visits were undervalued two- to fivefold relative to surgical procedures, and "the hourly reimbursement rate in 1978 ranged from $40 for a general practitioner to $200 for surgical specialists" (Hsiao and Stason 1979, 23).

Massachusetts was a fertile location for Hsiao's work for two reasons. First, the Massachusetts Rate Setting Commission, responsible for setting rates for Medicaid services, adopted a revised version of Hsiao and Stason's approach in its fee schedule. The new scale, introduced in December 1983, increased payments for office visits while reducing or freezing payments for other procedures (Hadley et al. 1984). Second, physicians were particularly energized at this time because the Massachusetts Medical Society was fighting a new policy introduced by Blue Shield that limited annual increases of fees. The medical society opposed Blue Shield's pricing and mandatory assignment policies. Physicians wanted the state legislature to abolish mandatory assignment to encourage "price-conscious shopping" and "conservative patient evaluation of the need for recommended services" (Law and Ensminger 1986, 21).

The interest in Hsiao's method from several medical specialty societies and the Massachusetts Medical Society suggests that they saw it as a way to improve payment policies or at least propose policies that might be more favorable. They started to "take a much stronger interest in the theoretical concept [Hsiao] developed" (Hsiao 1995, 390). To Hsiao's surprise, specialty societies "read that article and then picked up the idea. Some medical organizations, particularly the internists, felt that my method was a rational approach to judge whether the price is fair or unfair. . . . The medical profession itself began to pick up this idea and pushed it" (Hsiao 1995, 389), including the AMA. According to Hsiao, the Massachusetts Medicaid program in 1984 asked him to do some more research on the idea (Hsiao 1995).

The Health Care Financing Administration commissioned researchers at the Urban Institute to review and advise them on a resource-cost approach. They were less optimistic that there was an objective way to develop estimates of physician inputs: "The process is fundamentally a judgment-laden task for which there is no objectively correct solution. Developing a formula for calculating relative costs gives the appearance of removing judgment from the process, but in fact does not remove judgment from either the construction of the formula or the measurement of what goes into it" (Hadley et al. 1984, 104). They proposed asking panels of specialty physicians (face-to-face and by mail) about the profitability of specific procedures and the right price for inducing them to provide them. Physician panels would estimate whether a frequently performed set of procedures was a "'winner' or 'loser,' taking into account limited data from cost studies, and perceptions and estimates of profit margins for specific services" (Hadley et al. 1984, 104).

One interpretation attributes the AMA's support for Hsiao's approach to the benefits that the organization expected to gain from it. When interviewed almost two decades later, Hsiao opined that the relative value approach helped the AMA to address its waning power. The division of physicians into smaller categories of subspecialties and competition between specialties posed a problem for the AMA that, he said, was neatly solved by the RBRVS. "AMA was wise enough to see actually a splinter of organized medicine into specialties, and also to have set off a competition among specialties." In Hsiao's own between-the-lines reading, the AMA saw organized medicine as "torn asunder both by not only different training and professional interests but also by the difference in income between specialties. They tried to bring in some kind of reunited medicine" (Hsiao 2002, 11).

In January 1985, the AMA proposed to the government that it could do a study of relative values, but the AMA was rebuffed by the Health Care Financing Administration (reportedly due to antitrust concerns) (American

TABLE 3.1 Chronology of Events, Harvard Study

Date	National study of resource-based relative value scales for physician services activities
1986	
June–July	First technical consultant group meeting
September	Pretest pilot survey instrument
October–December	Pilot survey
December	First cross-specialty panel meeting
1987	
February–March	Pretest national survey instrument
March–June	National survey
June	Advisory panel meeting
June–July	Second technical consultant group meeting
October–November	Pre- and posttime resurvey
December	Second cross-specialty panel meeting
1988	
January	Advisory committee meeting
February	Third cross-specialty panel meeting
March	National consultative conference
September	Physician Evaluation Committee meetings

Source: Reproduced from Hsiao, Braun, Becker, et al. (1988, 82).

Medical Association 1993; Rubin, Segal, and Sherman 1989). The House of Medicine asked Congress to fund research on a study of relative values, and Congress "attached an amendment to some legislation requiring" the Health Care Financing Administration to fund a study (Hsiao 1995, 390). The request for proposals issued by the Health Care Financing Administration "specifically excluded medical professional organizations (including the AMA, the American College of Surgeons and their related research organizations) from submitting responses to the request for proposals. That is, the study was to be performed by an independent, i.e. disinterested, research organization" (Braun and McCall 2011b, 2). The agency chose Hsiao's team at Harvard University to develop a resource-based physician fee schedule. The contracted research period ran from early 1986 to September 1988, with a final report due in July 1988 (extended later to July 1989).

A timeline for the project is shown in Table 3.1. Hsiao began the project with some apprehension about whether he would be able to deliver a product that the Health Care Financing Administration wanted. He had a theory about resources, but "we were not sure we could produce anything useful" (Hsiao 1995, 390). Unlike the 1979 project, however, this time the project was fully staffed. The research team of 12 professors from Harvard and other universities included clinicians, economists, statisticians, health service researchers, and political scientists (Hsiao 1995).

The team was charged with developing resource-based values for anesthesiology, family practice, general surgery, internal medicine, obstetrics and gynecology, ophthalmology, orthopedic surgery, otolaryngology, pathology, radiology, thoracic and cardiovascular surgery, and urology. The project selected these specialties after consultation with "representatives from the federal government and organized medicine." Hsiao and his authors said that specialties are those "with high numbers of physicians and Medicare and Medicaid dollars expended" (Hsiao, Braun, Becker, et al. 1988, 46).

Hsiao is greatly respected and admired by those in the health policy community for his work on the RBRVS (Interview Subject 14). One policy expert noted his experience as an actuary in the Medicare program before he went to graduate school, as well as his persistence and intention to effect policy. The project required the team to work this out very

> laboriously, and he had a way of cross-walking, normalizing across different specialties, and then working from there. And, my impression is that it was a huge, complicated, careful effort that was . . . you know, that had a huge effect on, we're now 30 years—that had a huge effect on how physicians, and a huge effect on how value service was calculated. Now you may think it was a good effect or bad effect, but it did put to rest some of the conflict about what the right way to pay physicians was. If you weren't going to capitate, then you had to have some rational way of assigning the relative value of different services. And he said, "Well, the amount of work should be what we use." And people kind of said, "You know, I guess that's okay." (Interview Subject 14)

The selection of the 12 specialties created problems, however, since societies not picked for the study wanted to be included. Six additional specialties requested that they be added to the study and were funded independently: allergy and immunology, dermatology, oral and maxillofacial surgery, pediatrics, psychiatry, and rheumatology. As the project grew, the funding expanded to include independent nonprofit foundations, the National Institute of Mental Health, and corporations (Hsiao, Braun, Becker, et al. 1988).

Given the politics of physician payment, the research team was careful to distance itself from charged debates around how much physicians should be paid or how to contain costs. Hsiao and his colleagues believed that their job was to conduct the project with maximum rigor and scientific validity. After they completed the project, the "political world would decide whether politically it was feasible to adopt the results for reform" (Hsiao 1995, 399). Hsiao and his team thought, "We have to do [*chuckling*] whatever we can to make sure our results are credible" (Hsiao 1995, 397).

However, Hsiao likely feared that the study would not be received well if organized medicine was strongly opposed to the project. Hsiao's team therefore signed a subcontract with the AMA, which would link the researchers, organized medicine, and practicing physicians. The organization helped design the surveys of physicians, commented on survey results, and "worked with national medical specialty societies representing the studied specialties to secure physician nominations to the study's Technical Consulting Groups" (TCGs) (American Medical Association 1993, 9). Survey samples of practicing physicians were provided to the researchers from the AMA Masterfile, a comprehensive database of physicians in the United States. When the letters requesting survey participation were sent out, they were accompanied by a cover letter from the AMA's executive vice president.

AMA staffers later said that this arrangement allowed for "extensive involvement by organized medicine" (Rubin, Segal, and Sherman 1989, 896). The organization's involvement would have given staff important insight into the RBRVS method and its core assumptions at a very formative stage. It gave the AMA a window into the data collection methods used by the researchers that was likely helpful later in the establishment of the Update Committee.

Using random samples of physicians researchers used telephone surveys to ask physicians how much work was associated with different services (Table 3.2). One person interviewed by the author said that attempts to select scientific methods may have been countered by efforts of physicians to overestimate the values of their services, although there is no specific evidence to suggest that others also did this. The interviewee, who later served on the Update Committee, recalled receiving a survey while he was employed at an academic medical center. Unsure if he should participate, he asked his department chairman for advice and what he should say. The chair said, "Make surgeries harder and office visits easier" (Interview Subject 5). The interviewee doubted that the survey could have been valid if, at this early stage, respondents were already gaming the level of work associated

TABLE 3.2 Example of Telephone Survey Question

Survey question for internal medicine

Scenario: "If a follow-up visit of a 55-year-old male for management of hypertension, mild fatigue, on beta-blocker/thiaridae regimen has a rating of 100, what number would you assign to the level of mental effort and judgment required to do . . ."

1. Management of a patient in acute pulmonary edema in emergency room, who subsequently is admitted to hospital, established patient
2. Office visit, sore throat, fever, and fatigue in 19-year-old college student, established patient
3. Aspiration of synovial fluid from knee
4. Rigid sigmoidoscopy, without biopsy, in office
5. Urinalysis with microscopic exam in office lab under your supervision, excluding collection
6. Initial office evaluation for diagnosis and management of painless gross hematuria in new patient, without cystoscopy
7. Emergency hospital consultation, 72-year-old, new patient, with possible bowel obstruction

Source: Extracted from Oral Survey for Internal Medicine; Hsiao, Braun, Becker, et al. (1988, 134–136).

Note: A total of 24 examples were given; seven are shown here.

with procedures. He assumed others took a similar specialty-protective approach: "If I did it, I'm sure that any number of other people did it" (Interview Subject 5).

Work estimations were based on a method called "magnitude estimation" that is designed to measure different aspects of work in relation to each other. Hsiao's team used it to compare how much work was involved for each service on a list of services that their specialty commonly performed. For example, if an uncomplicated indirect inguinal hernia repair had a work value of 100 and another procedure required half the work, the other procedure was rated at 50; if it required three times as much work, it was rated at 300 (Kahan et al. 1992).

Some specialty societies questioned the magnitude estimation approach to measuring work. Radiologists later wrote that magnitude estimation was appropriate for some questions but not others. For example, asking people to rate the brightness of light was acceptable, because researchers could then validate the numeric ratings using an instrument that could measure brightness independently. In such a case, the ratings made by individuals would be matched and calibrated to the scientific measurements to create a valid scale for use outside the research laboratory. Applying magnitude estimation to physicians was different, because one could not validate the rankings by an objectively measured standard (Moorefield, Macewan, and Sunshine 1993). Perhaps this is why the Update Committee chose not to use magnitude estimation in its surveys, although the method they chose, which is to ask physicians to name absolute relative value units, was not necessarily better (see Chapter 5).

The list of services that would be included in the survey was developed by surveying a group of 100 physicians who commented on the most common services or procedures they performed; questions on these services were pretested before the telephone interviews (Hsiao 2002). Much to the surprise of the researchers, the level of agreement was 70 percent or more, and when they made a preliminary presentation of the findings to psychologists, they told Hsiao's team, "You better go back and reexamine your data" (Hsiao 2002, 15).

In phase II, researchers used least squares regression to develop common measures of services to standardize those used by more than one specialty (Kahan et al. 1992). The researchers formed a number of specialty-specific technical consulting groups. Later, specialty societies complained to the Physician Payment Review Commission that members of the groups were not "official" representatives of specialty societies. Some societies objected to the fact that the research team had not always selected physicians from two to three nominations made by the AMA (which had consulted with other specialty organizations) for each slot on the panel (Hsiao, Braun, Becker, et al. 1988, 64–65). Nominees had to meet certain criteria: professional expertise, experience and stature in the specialty, capacity to listen, fair-mindedness, willingness and ability to seriously consider contrary views and evidence, and an ability to digest conflicting information, express good judgment, and offer constructive criticism. Panelists were expected to be representative of a broad range of practice settings (community practice, academic centers, HMOs), functions (chief of services, patient care), and geographic regions. Each TCG for each specialty had one to four members; it is unclear why some TCGs had fewer members than others.

Rumors later surfaced that "representatives of specialty societies contacted Harvard study panelists before meetings to impress on the panelists the consequences of different types of judgments," but there is no concrete evidence that these gaming activities occurred (Kahan et al. 1992, 22).

Despite efforts to develop representative samples, some specialty groups, such as vascular and thoracic surgeons, complained that the researchers "simply did not understand our specialty" and that AMA lists of thoracic and cardiovascular surgeons (Miller 1991, 399) included people without experience with their specific procedures. The specialists argued that no one asked "do you or have you ever performed this procedure" (Miller 1991, 400). Radiologists were disappointed that half of those chosen were radiation oncologists, a group that does not generally perform diagnostic radiology procedures (Moorefield, Macewan, and Sunshine 1993).

Some specialties were unhappy with the procedures that Hsiao's team used as the reference services, which influenced the overall values of the services they provided. Cardiothoracic surgeons were particularly dissatisfied that their specialty benchmark was insertion of a single-chamber pacemaker, a procedure mainly done by cardiologists, not cardiothoracic surgeons. More commonly performed procedures such as "coronary artery bypass using the internal mammary artery" and/or "redo valve operations" would have been more appropriate, they argued. Use of the pacemaker, a lower-value procedure, ran the risk that it would "pull down" all their values (Miller 1991, 400). Likewise, some orthopedists criticized the use of carpal tunnel release because they said it was a low-value rather than a mid-value procedure, and this dragged down their values (Filler 2007). Some groups complained that the amount of time they had to prepare for the meetings was too limited, that they did not receive material prior to the meetings, and that the meetings were too short (Miller 1991). Vascular surgeons complained; they "hadn't had a representative on there and they felt they got the short end of the stick as a result" (Interview Subject 13).

Some societies were concerned that the Hsiao study would harm payment rates. The American College of Surgeons (ACS), according to Hsiao, tried to convince Congress to "pull the rug out from under us" and mobilized the different surgical specialties to pay close attention to their team's work. The ACS created what he described as an industry of sorts; "more than twenty specialties that had their own independent technical consultants watching over us . . . we were monitored closely." Fearing budget cuts, the ACS "right away, worked with Congress and created two separate budget caps, one for surgery and one for non-surgery" (Hsiao 2002, 13).

The American College of Orthopedics commissioned a study similar to Hsiao's and published their study ahead of his. Hsiao contended that their methodological modifications resulted in biased results and that their preemptive publication was "to try to force us to say why, to put us on defense." Another strategy was to turn up to meetings. The research team did not allow hired consultants of medical societies to sit in on the technical panel meetings, but consultants got around this rule. At the coffee break, Hsiao's staff could not "keep other people out of the coffee break rooms. And it was swamped by consultants of surgical specialties" (Hsiao 2002, 13).

The research project was focused first on 460 services described in the AMA's billing code list. Researchers sent surveys of 400 vignettes of commonly performed services to groups of specialties. Of the 4,000 services under consideration in the first part of the study, 60 percent were excluded because they occurred fewer than 200 times per year in a large sample of Medicare claims. The researchers thought these services might ultimately be left out of the fee schedule (Hsiao et al. 1992). Nevertheless, the team then developed a method to extrapolate findings to the 6,000 billing codes (Hsiao 1995, 2002).[6]

The Hsiao report, finished in 1988, argued that reform was necessary due to the "downward stickiness of fees whereby physicians continue charging their old fee, regardless of changes in technology, risk, and time input" (Hsiao, Braun, Becker, et al. 1988, 29). The authors briefly reviewed some existing proposals, including ones based on a consensus or negotiation approach and that used a committee of stakeholder interests to negotiate rates (Roe 1985); a private-sector negotiation approach used by Caterpillar, Inc.; and the Urban Institute report mentioned earlier (Hadley and Berenson 1987). The authors did not agree with the so-called political negotiation approach, because it would require consultation of all interests. If the rates were based on "political solutions or compromises among the participants" and any interest was excluded, "any negotiation or consensus will fail to resolve underlying conflicts and disagreements" (Hsiao, Braun, Becker, et al. 1988, 37). A political approach also would need an "objective analysis of technical information, consensus or negotiated solutions," but the political negotiations would likely maintain the status quo (Hsiao, Braun, Becker, et al. 1988, 37).

The authors proposed a resource-based approach that would move away from charges as the basis for determining the relative values of services. A charge-based system would be unsatisfactory, because the historical price basis would "simply institutionalize whatever price distortions already exist in the imperfect marketplace. To be more equitable and rational, a payment system should rest on a method that gives the system independence from existing charges" (Hsiao, Braun, Becker, et al. 1988, 39). Three kinds of resource inputs should determine physician payment levels: a physician's time or work associated with providing a service, the costs of running a practice (including professional liability insurance premiums), and the opportunity cost of training, amortized over a career.[7]

The research team invited 120 stakeholders (including medical societies, government and third-party payers, and a panel of national expert discussants) to a national conference in March 1988 to review the study (Hsiao, Braun, Dunn, et al. 1988). Having reviewed the study, the Physician Payment Review Commission found it to be sound and drew heavily on it to develop the Medicare fee schedule (Lee et al. 1989). The AMA commissioned reviews of Hsiao's work by two consulting groups and, based on those reports, endorsed both the study and the RBRVS.

Physician Payment Reform Legislation

When physician payment reform legislation was debated in Congress in 1989, the question of whether the RBRVS would be the basis for fees was already largely determined. Not everyone supported the approach: William Roper, former administrator of the Health Care Financing Administration, who served in the White House during 1989 and disliked the idea of administered prices, said the administration decided to "swallow hard" in exchange for "real cuts in the rate of growth" along with limits on the expansion of the program over the long term (Scully 2002, 16).

The focal point of disagreement in the debate was a cap on Medicare physician expenditure to which the House of Medicine strongly objected. "They made little buttons that went around that said 'No E.T.'s,' and they were trying to kill it. . . . The AMA was lobbying like crazy and saying they were going to get us fired and they were going to kill us. . . . This was a big war with the AMA for about 5 months" (Scully 2002, 3). The priority of the AMA was to prevent expenditure targets: "The AMA supported the fee schedule, opposed the expenditure targets and opposed the balanced billing limits, but their fervor seemed to be focused on the expenditure targets, not on the balanced billing. They knew there had to be balanced billing limits for this to pass" (Ginsburg 2002, 325). In the bill proposed by the Committee on Ways and Means, the expenditure target formula "would have provided for unlimited and complete recoupment of the amount by which actual expenditures exceeded the target. Fee rollbacks would have been a distinct possibility" (Rubin, Segal, and Sherman 1989, 901).

Many legislators in Congress were supportive of the resource-based payment system and wanted to get it passed, even if it meant removing the cuts. An archival source indicates that the Physician Payment Review Commission worried that the AMA would withdraw its support and therefore advised Congress to support the bill without expenditure cuts. If cuts hit in 1990, that would compromise the entire fee schedule and the RBRVS, which the commission likely meant would result in loss of political support: according to staffers advising Senator Heinz, the Physician Payment Review Commission wanted to ensure "the doctor's buy-off on the reform package" (Memorandum to John Heinz from GLA 1989).

The fee schedule was closely tied to the other parts of the package, because the key question people were asking, according to Paul Ginsburg, was how was this going to save us any money? Expenditure targets combined an incentive mechanism, as a "way to allow the government to set a budget for spending for the Medicare program. Basically what it involved was setting a target for spending for physician services and then comparing that target with what spending actually was and then increasing or reducing fees in a subsequent year to reflect whether spending came in over or under the targets" (Ginsburg 2002).

In return for softening the targets, the AMA pledged to support greater use of outcomes research and practice guidelines (Laugesen 2009).[8] Ginsburg and others believed that physician organizations would see there was a collective incentive to reduce expenditure and work on policies to reduce expenditure, such as "developing practice guidelines, providing political support for an effort to reduce fraud and abuse. They can affect costs. The incentive was to the physician organizations, not to the physicians" (Ginsburg 2002, 329). The government expected the AMA and other medical societies to increase their use of practice guidelines as a way to reduce Medicare expenditures (Ginsburg, LeRoy, and Hammons 1990), and the federal Agency for Health Care Policy and Research would help physicians understand how to better provide appropriate services and reduce their use of inappropriate or ineffective services (Gray 1992).

Payment reform also required the Health Care Financing Administration to make a budget neutrality adjustment if the agency anticipated that changes to relative value units would cause expenditures to increase or decrease by more than $20 million from the amount that "would have been made if such adjustments had not been made" (Payment for Physicians' Services 2013). In practice, the use of this adjustment does not seem to have limited average increases in relative value units, as discussed in Chapter 6.

Congress chose to protect the Health Care Financing Administration from lawsuits relating to the relative value unit rates, which § 1395w-4(i)(1) prohibits from judicial review. Subsequently, court challenges to the Health Care Financing Administration (and later CMS) processes and rules were rejected (*American Society of Dermatology v. Shalala* 1996; *Fischer v. Berwick* 2013). Legislators wanted the 1989 Omnibus Budget Reconciliation Act to achieve multiple "wins": reduce growth in Medicare expenditures, develop equitable prices for Medicare physician services across specialty types, and protect Medicare beneficiaries from paying higher fees for physician services (Hsiao et al. 1992). Resource-based fees were intended to redistribute income from overpaid to underpaid specialties.

The AMA was pleased with the bill, which, it said, was reasonably consistent with the association's policy (Rubin, Segal, and Sherman 1989). In theory, the law had two cost-restraining strategies: an expenditure target (which became the now-defunct sustainable growth rate) and a requirement for annual revision of the payment base rate (called the conversion factor) depending on progress in meeting annual expenditure targets. If Medicare spending increased beyond targets, fees would be cut.

The first expenditure target, called the Medicare Volume Performance Standard, was used until the end of 1997 and then replaced by the sustainable growth rate in 1998, until it was abolished in 2015 by the Medicare Access and CHIP Reauthorization Act (Oberlander and Laugesen 2015). Initially, the Medicare Volume Performance Standard contained just one service category, but between 1991 and 1993, specialists advocated that there be two: one for surgical services and one for all other services. The Omnibus Budget Reconciliation Act of 1993 added a primary care services category. According to Ginsburg (2002), the surgeons supported the payment reform legislation in 1989 on the condition that they be given their own target.

Targets are based on factors that are considered to lie outside physicians' direct control and that might expand Medicare expenditure but cannot be related to physician behavior. For example, under the sustainable growth rate (1998–2015), expenditure might increase or decrease if fees paid for physicians' services changed, if the number of Medicare beneficiaries enrolled in Part B increased or decreased, and if new laws and regulations increased or decreased Medicare expenditures. Forecasted changes in real per capita growth in the gross domestic product (GDP) also influenced the sustainable growth rate.

The Health Care Financing Administration's formula was based on data that overestimated Medicare fee-for-service enrollment, which was in flux as more people chose Medicare managed care policies (Part C). The inclusion of GDP per capita in the formula (under the Balanced Budget Act of 1997) created additional room for discrepancies between estimated and actual indicators. The AMA took the Health Care Financing Administration to court in 1999 to recoup payment losses allegedly caused by faults in the calculation of the formula, which the AMA argued underpaid physicians by $300 million in 1998 and 1999 (American Medical Association 1999).

The expenditure targets defined the parameters for expenditure growth. The update was reduced or increased depending on a "performance adjustment," which was calculated based on the difference between expenditures above or below the target expenditures and actual expenditure increases or decreases two years prior.[9] If the actual expenditure fell below expected growth, conversion factors could increase. If physician expenditure grew faster than expected by the target, the conversion factor would be cut. Primary care services were cut by 2.3 percent in 1996 and nonsurgical services were cut by 0.8 percent in 1997. Then, in 2002, they decreased for all services for the first time as the Health Care Financing Administration announced a 4.8 percent reduction in the conversion factor. However, it is important to remember that the original expenditure target had a safety valve for both the government and physicians, since the performance adjustment factor was limited to a range within −7.0 and +3.0 percent.

Following the introduction of the conversion factor, the only major change (before 1997) was a provision of the Omnibus Budget Reconciliation Act of 1993, which changed the maximum negative expenditure target from −2 percent to −4 percent, limiting the size of potential fee cuts. The payment system appeared to be working. Indeed, expenditure averaged 4.4 percent per beneficiary from 1992 through 1997 (Mayes and Berenson 2006). Physicians believed Medicare patients' access to care had not declined (Iglehart 2002). Medicare beneficiaries were shown to have had fewer access problems and less hardship in paying medical bills than the privately insured (Schoenman, Hayes, and Cheng 2001).

Implementing the RBRVS

The Hsiao study was complete and physician payment reform had become law, yet significant work had to be done to implement the RBRVS (US House of Representatives 1989). Between the release of the report in 1988 and implementation of the RBRVS in 1992, four major actors wrestled with the distributional and budgetary implications of the new approach: Congress, the Physician Payment Review Commission, the Health Care Financing Administration, and the House of Medicine. A multitude of issues needed resolution, including improving the coding and payment classifications for office visits (Braun, Hsiao, et al. 1988) and making the payments relative across specialties (Braun, Yntema, et al. 1988), but the most difficult and visible issues related to cuts in fees.

The Physician Payment Review Commission was one of the few organizations that remained mostly above the fray, and its opinions appear to have been influential. The commission had "quickly become the most important influence on the direction that Congress pursues in changing Medicare's physician-payment methods," especially given the small staff devoted to Medicare reform inside the Health Care Financing Administration (Iglehart 1989, 1157). The commission also had some credibility with the House of Medicine, with six of the 13 members being physicians. Furthermore, there was good communication between the commission and congressional committees, as well as a degree of compatibility in thinking on the major policy issues relating to physician payment (Iglehart 1989).

The Physician Payment Review Commission was supportive of the Hsiao study and endorsed its approach and method. Paul Ginsburg recalled that while it was not closely involved in the study, "if history had been different, probably he would have been doing the study for us. But instead we took an arm's length approach" (Ginsburg 2002, 329). Staff recognized and sought to remedy various problems after the Hsiao study was published. Specialty societies told the commission about technical issues in the Hsiao study, and physician organizations were given the opportunity to "refine" its results. Thus, the Medicare fee schedule implemented in 1992 drew on three sources of data besides the Hsiao study: relative value scales, the refinement process conducted by the Physician Payment Review Commission in consultation with specialty societies, and Medicare administrative charge data (Levy et al. 1992). These sources were useful because the Hsiao study had only produced a subset of codes and other sources of data were used to "validate" some of the fees.

The Physician Payment Review Commission made changes to the values recommended by Hsiao's team due to some flaws it identified. As such, one observer cautioned that the original Harvard projections regarding the financial impact of the RBRVS should be disregarded (Berenson 1989). The commission's changes resulted in a redistribution of fees to primary care physicians about half as large as that projected by the Harvard group

(Berenson 1989). Whether intentionally or not, however, the commission's corrections to the fee schedule possibly inoculated payment reform against broad criticism: the medical community could not "use such errors as a means for invalidating the whole RBRVS approach" (Berenson 1989, 351).

The Physician Payment Review Commission's refinement process was lengthy. The commission asked physician groups to advise them on "clinical reasonableness" (Physician Payment Review Commission 1991) and to help standardize values for services performed by more than one specialty. In December 1990, the commission sent a survey to 62 societies and other organizations representing physicians and other professionals. Societies proposed alternative relative value units for 38 percent of the 341 services under review. The commission reported that societies thought that 59 percent of the Hsiao study values were "too low," but only 4 percent were thought to be "too high" (Physician Payment Review Commission 1991).

Hsiao's team, in turn, critiqued the Physician Payment Review Commission's approach, because (said the Hsiao team) the commission did not specify its review method, and only three of the 85 relative values questioned were said to be too high (Hsiao et al. 1992). The approach used by the commission was said to be problematic because physicians had been allowed to review the ratings of services in their own specialties in an "unconstrained manner" (Hsiao et al. 1992, 11).

Charged with writing new regulations that would translate these values into a working fee schedule, the Health Care Financing Administration proceeded in three stages: in September 1990, the agency sent to Congress the model fee schedule it had required the agency to devise. Nine months later, on June 5, 1991, the Health Care Financing Administration published its Proposed Rule and, on November 25, 1991, the Final Rule. Each stage expanded the number of services with relative value units attached, moving from a "tentative" list for 1,000 services to the Proposed Rule with "markedly less tentative levels for about 4,000 services" and the Final Rule encompassing 8,000 services (Balla 2000, 173). Simultaneously, phase II of the Hsiao study was continuing, and codes were being refined.

Each of these tweaks created new political controversies, because the values differed from those of Hsiao's original study. The Health Care Financing Administration's first model national fee schedule included 1,400 commonly performed medical procedures, one of which predicted likely reductions in fees for cataract operations in most parts of the country from $2,000 to $1,300 (Rosenthal 1990). When the fee schedule was first proposed, the Health Care Financing Administration received 290 comments in response to it, 89 from professional associations and the remainder from individual practitioners (Balla 1998). The model fee schedule also included an overall cut of 5 percent, which physicians were able to avoid when President George H. W. Bush's 1992 budget removed that item (Bell 1991).

Changes in projected specialty income, reported at every stage of the rulemaking process, were closely followed and analyzed by the House of Medicine. The greatest controversy occurred after the Proposed Rule, published in June 1991, cut the fees proposed in the model fee schedule (Balla 1998) and reduced revenues for the specialties listed in Table 3.3 by $1.1 billion compared to the model fee schedule. The Health Care Financing Administration then proposed payment reductions of almost 6 percent for 1992, the first year of the operation of the fee schedule.

The proposed rule caused outrage within the House of Medicine. Ninety-five thousand physicians sent letters, some of them in a standard format crafted by specialty societies (Balla 1998). Primarily, people who sent comments discussed the reduction in the conversion factor. The conversion factor reflected assumptions in the Health Care Financing Administration's model that fee reductions would be accompanied by increases in service volume by physicians, so the agency argued it needed to adjust the conversion factor by imposing a "behavioral offset." That assumption was based on economists' research showing that physicians increase the quantity of services when prices are cut, which economists call the volume-offset effect.

Unfortunately for the Health Care Financing Administration, the behavioral offset included in the Proposed Rule alienated both those thought to benefit from that offset (physicians whose fees would increase, such as family medicine) and those groups already opposed to payment reform who had already been told they would experience decreased fees (Balla 1998).

Committee hearings in June and July 1991 "generated a stream of grave remarks from the members of Congress responsible for Medicare policies," as well as letters of objection sent to the secretary of Health and Human Services (Oliver 1993, 165). Lawmakers complained that the administration had "clearly disregarded the intent of the law and, if necessary, legislators would repudiate the Health Care Financing Administration interpretation by enacting new statutory guidelines" (Oliver 1993, 165). The policy had failed to do what they intended—namely, reduce fees for overvalued procedures and improve primary care payment.

When Congress sided with physician groups and ordered the Health Care Financing Administration to eliminate the behavioral offset (Balla 1998), the agency retreated from its initial position, and the Final Rule increased

TABLE 3.3 Revenue Changes in Proposed and Final Rules

Specialty	Model fee schedule to Proposed Rule	Proposed Rule to Final Rule	Change from model fee schedule
Podiatry	−$13,662,000	−$24,439,000	−$10,777,000
Nuclear medicine	$5,171,000	$4,506,000	−$665,000
Neurology	$735,000	$10,225,000	$9,490,000
Pulmonary disease	−$15,185,000	$14,923,000	$30,108,000
Otolaryngology	−$16,140,000	$24,769,000	$40,909,000
Neurosurgery	−$17,887,000	$25,039,000	$42,926,000
Obstetrics/gynecology	−$17,520,000	$33,378,000	$50,898,000
Anesthesiology	−$25,718,000	$28,071,000	$53,789,000
General practice	−$22,856,000	$39,743,000	$62,599,000
Family practice	−$32,704,000	$47,575,000	$80,279,000
Radiology	$359,868,000	$449,789,000	$89,921,000
Dermatology	−$16,651,000	$103,511,000	$120,162,000
Thoracic surgery	−$80,339,000	$45,035,000	$125,374,000
Urology	−$117,359,000	$100,785,000	$218,144,000
Internal medicine	−$75,191,000	$146,650,000	$221,841,000
General surgery	−$189,787,000	$125,040,000	$314,827,000
Orthopaedic surgery	−$177,547,000	$177,619,000	$355,166,000
Cardiology	−$8,990,000	$477,580,000	$486,570,000
Ophthalmology	−$657,770,000	$258,972,000	$916,742,000
Total	−$1,119,532,000	$2,088,771,000	$3,208,303,000

Source: Data reproduced with permission and supplemented from Balla (1998, 667). Table 2.

Note: The amounts reported here track the impact on physicians first, relative to the model fee schedule and then relative to the Proposed Rule. The total amount in the last column is not indicative of the actual impact on physicians overall but reports the net change between the model fee schedule and the Final Rule.

the conversion factor to $31.001, up from the Proposed Rule rate of $26.873. The Final Rule also revised substantial cuts in fees for surgeons and other specialists ("Government Realigning Fees" 1991). Table 3.3 describes the impact of the changes between the Proposed Rule and Final Rule by specialty. Only two groups saw decreases. Podiatry suffered the biggest loss ($10 billion), and nuclear medicine was projected to lose revenue. All other groups gained, in some cases substantially. Fees for gynecology, vascular surgery, and chiropractic increased (Levy et al. 1992). Some procedural and surgical specialties found their fortunes almost reversed: the largest gain in the Final Rule compared to the Proposed Rule was for ophthalmologists, for whom the Proposed Rule projected a loss of $657 million compared to the model fee schedule but gained $258 million in the Final Rule.

An analysis of the comments using a regression model found that those submitted by high-income specialties exerted more influence on the Health Care Financing Administration's decisions than comments submitted by lower-earning specialties. The outcome of the rule reflected the needs of specialties such as cardiology and radiology (Balla 1998, 670). The AMA was upset about the conversion factor and launched a grassroots campaign that rallied members to protest what they claimed was a 16 percent decline in the conversion factor proposed in the Final Rule (Foreman 1991).

The rhetoric around payment reform was focused on the perceived benefits to primary care, but as Table 3.4 shows, even early analyses indicated that fees would increase for some specialties that were originally the target of reductions. Although the Health Care Financing Administration's early models assumed physicians would increase their volume, insufficient consideration was given to the fact that physicians could use higher intensity codes or exert pressure through the Update Committee to increase relative value units. Models that included not only price changes but also factors such as volume and intensity predicted that total Medicare expenditure would increase 74 percent between 1991 and 1996, ranging from a 50 percent increase for anesthesiology and thoracic surgery to 125 percent for family practice and 148 percent for optometry (Levy et al. 1992).

Measuring the impact of the fee changes shows that the regulatory process (and congressional intervention) counteracted the cuts that were initially proposed and that the hoped-for new fees were not redistributing payments to primary care specialties. Yet boosters of payment reform continued to forecast increasing payments for primary care. Pre-reform fee levels taken from Levy et al. (1992) show the payments for specific services (Table 3.4), although it should be noted that the data reported for a limited number of commonly used services selected by Levy may not be indicative of the aggregate impact of changes in payment by specialty.

Table 3.4 shows prereform levels, 1993 fees, and 1996 fee projections, which are compared to actual fees reported in 1996 using data from the 1996 Medicare fee schedule. Combining baseline fees with fees reported in the 1993 fee schedule (Table 3.4) shows that initially, the implementation of the RBRVS cut payments for surgical services by −22 percent, reduced payment for medical specialty services by −48 percent, and increased payment for outpatient and inpatient evaluation and management visits by 30 percent.

TABLE 3.4 Predicted and Actual Fees, 1992 to 1996

CPT	Description	Medicare fee			Predicted fee[a]	Change, actual (%)		Actual vs. forecast
		1992	1993	1996	1996	1992–1993	1993–1996	1996
	Surgical Services							
11100	Biopsy of skin, subcutaneous	$43	$45	$55	$38	5	22	45
19160	Mastectomy, partial	$428	$382	$475	$338	–11	24	41
20610	Arthrocentesis	$33	$42	$53	$41	27	26	29
27130	Total hip replacement	$2,105	$1,701	$1,923	$,1652	–19	13	16
29881	Knee replacement	$827	$673	$767	$653	–19	14	17
31500	Intubation, endotracheal	$97	$116	$147	$147	20	27	0
31625	Bronchoscopy with biopsy	$311	$241	$261	$241	–23	8	8
33207	Pacemaker insertion (ventricular)	$811	$577	$718	$561	–29	24	28
33512	Coronary artery bypass graft, three grafts	$3,178	$2,161	$2,828	$2,181	–32	31	30
35301	Thromboendarterectomy	$1,330	$1,096	$1,354	$1,056	–18	24	28
45300	Proctosigmoidoscopy	$44	$43	$46	$46	–2	7	0
45378	Colonoscopy	$337	$263	$285	$258	–22	8	10
47605	Cholecystectomy	$800	$701	$873	$634	–12	25	38
52204	Cystourethroscopy, with biopsy	$198	$163	$173	$180	–18	6	–4
52601	Transurethral resection of prostate	$981	$804	$1,000	$778	–18	24	29
58150	Total hysterectomy	$834	$807	$1,005	$779	–3	25	29
62270	Lumbar spinal puncture	$56	$61	$66	$60	9	8	10

Code	Description							
65855	Trabeculoplasty, laser	$780	$500	$456	$500	-36	-9	-9
66984	Cataract	$1,342	$943	$957	$913	-30	1	5
	Average, surgical services	$765	$596	$707	$582	-22	21	21
	Medical Specialty Services							
92235	Ophthalmoscopy	$121	$46	$86	$80	-62	87	8
92567	Tympanometry	$19	$18	$19	$18	-5	6	6
94010	Spirometry—global	$36	$28	$31	$29	-22	11	7
	Average, surgical services	$58.67	$30.67	$45.33	$42.33	-48	48	7
	Evaluation and Management Services							
99201	Initial patient visit	$27	$26	$28	$25	-4	8	12
99202	Initial patient visit 2	$34	$41	$44	$39	21	7	13
99203	Initial patient visit 3	$40	$56	$61	$54	40	9	13
99204	Initial patient visit 4	$61	$83	$91	$79	36	10	15
99205	Initial patient visit 5	$67	$104	$114	$99	55	10	15
99211	Established patient visit 1	$13	$13	$13	$13	0	0	0
99212	Established patient visit 2	$20	$22	$24	$21	10	9	14
99213	Established patient visit 3	$26	$31	$34	$30	19	10	13
99214	Established patient visit 4	$39	$48	$52	$47	23	8	11
99215	Established patient visit 5	$57	$76	$83	$72	33	9	15
99221	Initial hospital visit 1	$49	$58	$63	$57	18	9	11
99222	Initial hospital visit 2	$77	$96	$105	$92	25	9	14
99223	Initial hospital visit 3	$84	$122	$134	$116	45	10	16

TABLE 3.4 (continued)

CPT	Description	Medicare fee			Predicted fee[a]	Change, actual (%)		Actual vs. forecast
		1992	1993	1996	1996	1992–1993	1993–1996	1996
99231	Subsequent hospital visit 1	$28	$31	$33	$31	11	6	6
99232	Subsequent hospital visit 2	$34	$45	$49	$44	32	9	11
99233	Subsequent hospital visit 3	$47	$62	$49	$59	32	–21	–17
	Average, evaluation and management services	$44	$57	$61	$55	30	7	11

Data Sources: Pre-reform and 1996 predicted fee data from Table 1 in Levy et al. (1992), used under license; 1993 fee data from American Medical Association (1993); 1996 fee data from American Medical Association (1996).

[a] Predictions of likely fees in 1996 were made before payment reform was fully implemented.

TABLE 3.5 Medicare Dollar Conversion Factors, 1992–1995

Conversion factor type	Dollar conversion factors				Percent change
	1992	1993	1994	1995	1992–1995
Surgical services	$31.00	$31.96	$35.16	$39.45	27
Primary care services	31.00	31.25	33.72	36.38	17
All other services	31.00	31.25	32.91	34.62	12

Source: Reproduced from Physician Payment Review Commission (1995).

The numbers look different by 1996, after the committee had been established, when surgical services had increased from 1993, on average, by 21 percent; medical specialty services by 48 percent; and evaluation and management services by 7 percent. Forecasts made in 1992 predicted lower fees than the fees that were actually paid in 1996 across all services. Actual fees for surgical services were 21 percent higher than predicted, specialty services were 7 percent higher than predicted, and evaluation and management services were 11 percent higher than predicted.

One reason there were increases for surgical services was that surgical societies requested a separate conversion factor from Congress. Surgical services were paid at a more favorable dollar conversion factor. In other words, some of the changes to relative value units were softened by more favorable conversion factors (Table 3.5). Early gains made by primary care physicians were held in check by smaller increases in the conversion factor between 1993 and 1996. After 1997, the Health Care Financing Administration paid for Medicare services using a single conversion factor, after the Balanced Budget Act was passed in 1997.

An analysis by the Physician Payment Review Commission said that much of the activity during 1992 had been focused on "raising the values of undervalued services," with less effort made to correct overvalued services (Physician Payment Review Commission 1995, 40).

With the benefit of hindsight, the predicted versus actual impacts and price changes after the fee schedule was implemented showed what happened to payments after reform compared to the predictions. The Physician Payment Review Commission analyzed the causal factors in fee increases (Table 3.6).

One explanation is that politics intervened in the process. Predicted impacts were critical in the debates over payment reform, because they

TABLE 3.6 Causal Attribution of Fee Changes, 1992–1995

Type of service	Physician work[a]	Practice expense[b]	Geographic adjustment factor[c]	Conversion factor[d]
Primary care	0.35	1.65	0.00	0.56
Other	−1.27	1.36	0.00	−4.33
Surgical	0.04	−3.42	−0.04	9.06
Other	0.60	0.50	0.03	−4.35
Mean absolute change	0.55	1.65	0.02	4.60

Source: Reproduced from Physician Payment Review Commission (1995) simulations using 1992 Medicare claims, 5 percent sample of beneficiaries.

a. Compares 1992 fee schedule payments with those that would result if 1992 physician work values were replaced with those of 1995.

b. Compares 1992 fee schedule payments with those that would result if 1992 practice expense relative values were replaced with those of 1995.

c. Compares 1992 fee schedule payments with those that would result if 1992 geographic adjustment factors were replaced with those of 1995.

d. Compares 1992 fee schedule payments with those that would result if 1992 conversion factors were replaced with those of 1995.

triggered reactions by physician groups and subsequent adjustments made after pressure on Congress or directly through the rulemaking process. For example, Congress created a surgical conversion factor.

Reformers' Recommendations on Updating the Fee Schedule

Throughout this period, both the Health Care Financing Administration and the Physician Payment Review Commission were involved in the refinement of the Hsiao codes and the rulemaking associated with the first fee schedule rather than questions of how future updates would be performed. In 1991, the AMA formed the Update Committee, and as discussed later in the chapter, the Health Care Financing Administration delegated the RBRVS update process to it in 1992.

The delegation to the AMA of the code review process by the Health Care Financing Administration does not represent a lack of thought on the part of reformers about this critical detail. On the contrary, the need for an objective and structured update process had been anticipated years earlier. Most people involved in payment reform knew that the integrity of the RBRVS depended on having an unbiased and impartial review process. The question of how the RBRVS should be updated was always at the back of the minds of policy makers and researchers, and thus it did not appear from nowhere after payment reform was passed in 1989.

The Office of Technology Assessment report of 1986 laid out some of the problems of the updates to the CRVS, which was a physician-updated fee schedule, and some people would have likely understood that physician-based updates had disadvantages. Indeed, writing in the *New England Journal of Medicine* in 1985, one physician familiar with the pitfalls of the CRVS advocated a multidisciplinary commission focused on physician payment. He argued that members should include representatives from each medical specialty (including family practice), the American Hospital Association, the health insurance industry, the business sector, and the public (Roe 1985). In Roe's view, such an organization would act in the interests of consumers, taxpayers, and insurance buyers; it would reflect market forces.

Earlier, as said, the Urban Institute proposed an initial schedule of relative fees updated via negotiation between the Medicare program and physicians. This option included physicians meeting face-to-face and surveying individuals. Physicians would be asked about the profitability of specific procedures and to name the right price to provide them. Critically, however, panels of physicians would consist of practicing physicians, "rather than representatives of organized medicine," and a balance of physicians compensated in different ways, such as salaried practitioners and research and academic physicians. The authors hypothesized that "fee-for-service practitioners would have the greatest stake in the outcome of the process, and their potential conflict of interest would need to be offset by including disinterested physicians," and such a panel should include people expert in economics and physician payment, among other areas (Hadley et al. 1984, 124). "Special attention would have to be given to structuring the process to avoid 'capture' by self-interested parties and to promote consensus or majority approval" (Hadley et al. 1984, 125). Recalibration, according to the report, would need to be done perhaps every five years, due to changes in technologies and input prices, such as the cost of time for physicians, nurses, and other labor; however, more frequent evaluation of costs and efficiency could be done to build data for future reviews (Hadley et al. 1984). The Urban Institute report envisaged that an organization responsible for updating fees would have a small technical staff to collect data, obtain and review studies, and commission studies on resource costs.

Likewise, the architects of the RBRVS believed objectivity was an achievable goal for updates—even if it might be difficult. There would be potential for "problems of individual variation and potential bias when physicians review the ratings of services in their own specialties in an unconstrained manner," and therefore Hsiao's team recommended that the "relative value of each code should be carefully re-viewed by physician panels for validity and accuracy. Obtaining an unbiased and objective evaluation is not a trivial matter." They said there was a need for methods of review and modification that are "conceptually sound, validated, and resistant to bias and gaming," recognizing the challenges of balancing accuracy, flexibility, and objectivity (Hsiao et al. 1992, 125).

In its 1987 report, the newly created Physician Payment Review Commission suggested that it could provide advice to the government on the updates to the proposed resource-based fee schedule, given an "analogous" role advising on updates to the prospective payment system for hospitals (Physician Payment Review Commission 1987, 43). The commission thought that, while the conversion factors would be updated more frequently, the relative values would "be expected to change slowly to account for changes in medical practice" (Physician Payment Review Commission 1987, 42).

Prior to the payment reform legislation in the fall of 1989, the Physician Payment Review Commission issued a report to Congress suggesting that it would be involved in making technical fixes to translate the Hsiao study into a workable fee schedule (Physician Payment Review Commission 1989). The Physician Payment Review Commission would involve the medical profession in a structured way (Physician Payment Review Commission 1989). The Physician Payment Review Commission planned to collaborate with the AMA-sponsored CPT Editorial Panel on coding issues (Physician Payment Review Commission 1989).

Looking ahead, the commission made recommendations about updating the fee schedule. It also studied how fee schedules were updated in Canada, France, and (West) Germany to understand how the United States should approach the update process (including but not exclusively the relative value updates). On the basis of a study by New York University professor Victor Rodwin, the Physician Payment Review Commission said there were four options: a formula that updated the conversion factor to account for changes in practice expenses, rulemaking through the Department of Health and

Human Services, an independent commission providing technical information to Congress, and negotiations between physicians and the federal government. None of these options was chosen. Instead, the commission said elements of all of these would work best in the United States. One part of its review of overseas models did take root: the commission proposed working together with one or two lead organizations rather than try to consult all medical societies, and it suggested the AMA (Physician Payment Review Commission 1989).[10]

The Physician Payment Review Commission was going to take a central role in the update process—not physician groups (Iglehart 1989; Physician Payment Review Commission 1989), although it may have been meaning the refinement process (immediately after implementation) rather than updating. According to Paul Ginsburg, founding executive director, and Lauren LeRoy (who served after Ginsburg as executive director), the commission was not planning to be closely involved (Ginsburg 2016; Leroy 2016). Congress would set broad policies relating to the fee schedule, and the Physician Payment Review Commission would provide Congress with data, especially to help it review the annual conversion factor. The 1989 report suggested that groups representing physicians, beneficiaries, and others should participate "in both technical refinements and major policy decisions, the Commission being the principal forum for their input." The Health Care Financing Administration's role would be the principal implementing agency carrying out the policies of Congress through administrative and rulemaking processes (Physician Payment Review Commission 1989, 174).

The Physician Payment Review Commission viewed the House of Medicine as having an advisory role and that it would be one among several stakeholders. Updates to relative values would be "grounded in data and refined by the professional judgments of physicians" (Physician Payment Review Commission 1989, 174). The commission thus framed the role of physicians as a key *part* of the process—but physician groups would not be in the driver's seat.

Just over six months after the commission report was released, Congress passed the Omnibus Budget Reconciliation Act. The Physician Payment Review Commission would have an advisory role in updating the fee schedule. The law, as enacted, directed the secretary of Health and Human Services "to consider changes in medical practice, coding changes, new data on relative value components, or the addition of new procedures" no less than every five years. On the kinds of information required, Congress simply stated, "The Secretary may use extrapolation and other techniques to determine relative value units for physician services for which specific data are not available. In making extrapolations, the Secretary shall take into account recommendations of the Physician Payment Review Commission and the results of consultations with organizations representing physicians who provide such services" (Omnibus Budget Reconciliation Act § 1848).

Creation of the Update Committee

Meanwhile, the AMA was positioning itself as the "negotiator for all physicians in matters relating to an update factor and future revision of the relative-value scale" (Iglehart 1989). The AMA was cognizant of the need to be involved and was "attempting to secure an appropriate representational role for the profession in this process" (Donovan 2012).

Some say it was not just about payment: the update process might provide the AMA with a greater organizational role. As said earlier, Hsiao mentioned in an interview that a larger benefit of the AMA taking a key role in the update process was the opportunity to bring together the House of Medicine. Some viewed its decision to bring together the House of Medicine a ploy to increase the AMA's membership: "You got a seat on the RUC if your specialty group had a high membership in the AMA. And unofficially over the years, the way you get a seat on the RUC is, you know, if you're the gastroenterologist, you better have x percent of your members join the AMA or you're not in the RUC. If you took away the RUC, the AMA would probably implode. The way you get a seat at the table is by playing ball with the AMA" (Interview Subject 22).

Whatever the motivations of the AMA, what is striking about the history of its leadership of the Update Committee is both the lack of information about how the AMA came to be involved and the rapidity by which it occurred. The Update Committee assumed and expanded its role very quickly: "This thing was institutionalized in a year and a half" (Interview Subject 22). The committee quickly became CMS's "go-to" source for advice and developed a quasi-formal role in the Medicare policymaking structure. "CMS did not have the staff resources to replicate what the update process could do and over time, and the AMA and specialty groups became so vested in it" (Scully 2012, 3).

One interviewee said that the committee gained its position during a "void in time, never intended by the people who drafted it" (Interview Subject 22). Indeed, a group of former administrators of the Health Care Financing

Administration and CMS who were asked how the Update Committee was established at a Senate hearing in 2012 said they did not know exactly what happened (see US Senate Committee on Finance 2012). Former administrator Gail Wilensky said she left in February 1992, partly because the CMS lacked the staff resources to implement the fee schedule. One interviewee said that Wilensky likely left before the AMA was involved, and based on recollection, Wilensky would have had no intention of "leaving it to the AMA." The decision to involve the Update Committee was made by an acting head, who, "concerned about the complex assignment facing the agency, turned to the AMA for help" (Scully 2012, 2).

The acting head was most likely a career civil servant and regional administrator of the Health Care Financing Administration for New York, Bill Tobey. As interim director of the Health Care Financing Administration, he faced an unenviable task of implementing the fee schedule:

> So Tobey was in the final throes [of the RBRVS implementation]. The system started, I believe in '93, fiscal year '93. He was trying to finish the design and roll-out of it. So for about a year and a half, Bill Tobey was the Acting Administrator of HCFA [Health Care Financing Administration]. And he didn't know what to do about this, and the AMA volunteered to come in and do it for him. So he said, great. We'll have the AMA do it. And so by default, the AMA came in and put together this. . . . Somebody had to take out the relative values work, and CMS didn't have a lot of staff, so the AMA came in and said we'll do it for you. (Interview Subject 22)

Another interviewee described how the two organizations worked together:

> *Interviewer:* How would you have described your role, the RUC's role vis-à-vis HCFA?
> *Interviewee:* Partners in . . . trying to find your way through the muck and forest [laughs]. Partners in trying to understand the complexities . . . ways of working out fair evaluations and judgment. Not amounts, but . . . but ways that were intelligent and effective, fair.
> *Interviewer:* Was there ever any discussion at the time of HCFA doing its own valuations?
> *Interviewee:* No. They were smarter enough to know they didn't do that. No, there was no such discussions. (Interview Subject 15)

The scope of the committee's activities expanded over time. Like the proverbial camel's nose in the tent, the Update Committee worked at the edges of the process initially. Speaking before the Senate Finance Committee in 2012, Wilensky perceived the early role of the update process and the AMA as minimal: "It happened innocently enough . . . in its first year, the AMA approached the agency about whether it would allow it or like to have the AMA be the convener that would include all physician groups and make some recommendations, which initially were very minor adjustments that hardly affected the RBRVS at all" (US Senate Committee on Finance 2012).

One payment policy expert thought that policymakers were complicit in giving the update process to the profession because they viewed it as a potentially difficult process and were more concerned about the total budget:

> I think that Congress and the CMS cared, I think they had something of a plague-on-all-your-houses view of this. What they cared about was that the cost of physician care didn't go up as fast as they were, and if surgeons and generalists wanted to fight, that was their business. I don't think there was a perception that the long-term effect, or at least the perception that it could be implemented for political purposes, that stavering the procedure-oriented specialties led relentlessly toward more procedures, and toward the recruitment of more physicians into the procedure-oriented specialties. The underrepresentation of primary care in the workforce, the underprovision of primary care, and the situation we now find ourselves in, which is not having a sustainable primary care career for adults. (Interview Subject 14)

Another endorsed this view, suggesting that the assumption of budget neutrality meant that policymakers believed that physicians could be left to make these decisions: "Rather than have the government argue how to divide up the fixed pie, we don't care. There's a fixed pie, you physicians sort it out" (Interview Subject 4). Another possibility is that the AMA likely appeared to be uniquely qualified to engage in the update of the RBRVS: "The RUC had the authority now, with the Federal government sitting right here, to make relative value determinations" (Interview Subject 15). The AMA's involvement in the Hsiao study meant it was already familiar with the research methods, and they apparently met with the study researchers before or during the development of the Update Committee, according to one participant: "I think that the preliminary work was helpful. It was helpful. And we collaborated with them too actually, and met with them at times. So we had a little . . . a little groundwork to begin with" (Interview Subject 15).

The impetus for the committee came from the Board of Trustees of the AMA: "The AMA was intelligently anticipating it and responding to it" (Interview Subject 15). "They saw this move coming and were taking active steps to develop an administrative structure that would respond to the anticipated demands. And I think they hit it pretty well" (Interview Subject 15).

One argument in favor of the AMA leading was that Hsiao used the AMA's copyrighted billing codes, called the Current Procedural Terminology codes, to define services, which gave the organization an unrivalled understanding of and entrée into the RBRVS. Its role in defining billing codes meant the AMA was experienced in bringing together the House of Medicine; this, along with its understanding of the RBRVS, was likely critical for encouraging the Health Care Financing Administration to entrust it with the task. It is also conceivable that the AMA believed and/or created the impression that it would continue to use the same methods used by Hsiao, such as convening different consensus physician expert panels.

The committee's first meeting in 1991 included 125 people (including the staff of specialty societies). One interviewee recalled that it was in

a big hotel ballroom, on a wintery day, I think in November—God it was cold! . . . We had this big ballroom, and a lot of chairs obviously. But there was at least one chair, maybe two, between every person sitting in that room. . . . We developed an outline of what we were maybe expected to do and how we were expected to do this . . . . And the idea was that the people who were the members of the RUC were selected, not as representatives of a particular organization or specialty, but as to be judicious partners in the public good, public welfare, that when we put on our RUC hats . . . we sat down like Supreme Court judges in a certain sense. That is to say, we set aside personal interest and tried to hear and make judgments on the merits of the issues. So procedures, we developed procedures, which provided for widespread gathering of information, from the people who were involved in doing the procedures. (Interview Subject 15)

Former committee chair Grant Rodkey said "everyone understood that the nature of our work was to influence in some way what physicians were to be reimbursed for their services. Thus, the atmosphere of the meeting was, to say the least, somewhat restrained—reminiscent of a group of dogs on [a] leash eyeing a platter with a not-too-generous bone" (Parks 1997, 14).

In the early years the committee was "feeling its way through process and procedure" while under pressure to quickly develop a "process and procedure, and learn how to apply that both objectively and consistently," coupled with a sense of excitement because it was a "new frontier, it was a new way of looking at a new system of valuing services and procedures." From the beginning, it was also perceived as "extremely difficult for someone who didn't do something to rate how intense that was" and difficult to compare "how that intensity compared to other services." "RUC thought early on that that was something that could only be best provided by people who actually provided those services." Early and recent years were vastly different, with the committee of today being "a fairly fine-tuned instrument for doing what it does" (Interview Subject 18).

Conclusion

Professor William Hsiao published a landmark study on resource-based fees, and the AMA and other medical leaders, well aware of Hsiao's early work, saw it as providing a lifeline for fee-for-service medicine. Medical societies were behind the initiative to study these issues further and persuaded Congress to fund a report on relative value payment models (Hsiao 1995). After the contract was awarded to Hsiao's team, the AMA and specialty societies provided technical assistance, indeed "extensive involvement," in the study (Rubin, Segal, and Sherman 1989).

American physicians would have strongly rebelled against salaried compensation or per-patient subscription-based reimbursement models, such that policymakers likely felt they could not realistically explore the full range of policy options, and those options were therefore never seriously explored. The House of Medicine was an early proponent and sponsor of the resource-based system eventually adopted, and it encouraged the Hsiao study by lobbying Congress to fund a study of this approach.

The Hsiao study set the stage for the RBRVS, but Hsiao's relative values were tweaked and morphed over time. The Physician Payment Review Commission and specialty organizations reviewed services after his study was published and during the rulemaking process. Some changes were likely necessary, but the changes may have fundamentally reordered the original work of Hsiao's team.

The RBRVS was supposed to fit hand in glove with Medicare budget caps. The House of Medicine, active throughout the whole period, was influential in changing what later became the sustainable growth rate to expenditure "targets." The House conceded on balanced billing, but overall, the legislation largely conformed to the AMA's preferences. After the law was passed, the influence of organized medicine extended into rulemaking, where reductions in fees were reversed. Even the president intervened in the budgetary process to prevent one proposed cut. Fees for specialties increased and the principles of the 1989 legislation were constantly challenged. The evidence clearly shows that unpopular cuts to specialty fees were repeatedly mitigated.

Those who wanted to reform physician payment believed a new system would lead to a fairer distribution between specialty and primary care physicians, because payments would reflect the time and resources used. They failed to anticipate multiple levers available to reverse and bend payment policies, not only ones aimed at changing the distribution of payment across specialties but also those seeking to reduce the rate of growth.

The involvement of the Update Committee was viewed as helpful from the perspective of the agency administering the fee schedule but skeptically by others—including the architect of the RBRVS himself, William Hsiao. When interviewed two decades later, in 2013, Hsiao recalled his reaction to the involvement of the AMA: "And that was the point where I knew the system had been co-opted. . . . It had become a political process, not a scientific process. And if you don't think it's political, you only have to look at the motivation of why AMA wants this job" (Sweetland-Edwards 2013).

The Update Committee as formed increasingly took on a key role in updating the RBRVS. In the aftermath of payment reform legislation and the large-scale effort behind the Hsiao study (which required expansion beyond the original codes to the entire fee schedule), the decision to give the AMA its policymaking power through the Update Committee can partly be attributed to confusion and overload inside the agency. The legacy of these decisions is explored in Chapters 4 and 5, which consider the quality of decision making and the evidence used by the committee.

FOUR

How Doctors Get Paid

THE ADMINISTRATION OF THE RBRVS requires a system designed to fairly determine charges, the value of new services, and revision of services. The fee schedule, based on the RBRVS, is overseen by the CMS through the federal rulemaking process. CMS, however, relies heavily on advice from the committee to update and evaluate relative values in the RBRVS.

Update Committee members say that they see themselves as rigorous evaluators of recommendations made by specialty societies. Members of the committee see themselves as adjudicating among specialty societies who are vying for a share of Medicare expenditure. Committee members view Medicare expenditure as a fixed pie, due to the budget constraints they say Medicare imposes under the requirement for budget neutrality.

As one observer put it, the RBRVS gave "the medical profession a direct voice in determining relative values," and it is "difficult to find another situation where physicians have been granted as much influence in federal health policy decisions" (Doherty 2002). Likewise, some have also noted that the committee was created to reduce the payment differences between cognitive and procedural specialties, and the results have "sometimes been quite different, a striking testimony to the potential for physicians and specialty societies to influence the course of health policy" (Beyer and Mohideen 2008, 187).

How Medicare determines relative value units can be understood only by examining the institutional actors involved in updating the Medicare fee schedule. The House of Medicine plays a central role in shaping the RBRVS update process. The committee's structure and the nature of its membership are described. As the discussion shows, the committee is not "one committee": it is composed of different subgroups serving different purposes. The Update Committee, which is what most people mean when they talk about the committee, is one part, but a large "Advisory Committee" represents more than a hundred specialty societies and a committee of health professionals. A constellation of other participants, who are not formal members but involved in the process, also enlarges the scope of the committee.

The RBRVS

Medicare established a national fee schedule with rates for Medicare physician services based on the RBRVS. Each service has a total relative value unit associated with it, representing physician work, the price of liability insurance premiums, and practice expenses. As its name suggests, the fee schedule is supposed to reflect the resources used to provide the service. CMS and private payers calculate fees by adding the three units together and multiplying the total sum by a dollar amount, which is also adjusted for geographic variations in costs (Centers for Medicare & Medicaid Services 2013).[1]

Physician work is the biggest expense for most services, accounting for around 50 percent of the total relative value unit (Centers for Medicare & Medicaid Services 2013). The legal definition of physician work has not changed since 1992: it represents physician labor and time and intensity involved in providing a service (Payment for Physicians' Services 2013), with intensity defined as the mental effort, physical effort, technical skill, and psychological stress involved in providing the service.

The second largest portion of the total relative value unit is that for practice expense, which captures the nonphysician costs of providing services. Payments vary depending on whether the service is provided in a hospital facility or an outpatient setting; the practice expense relative value unit is higher for a service performed in an outpatient setting rather than in a facility such as a hospital, since facilities receive other Medicare payments for expenses, whereas practice expenses are borne by the physician (Smith 2012).

Professional liability insurance, or malpractice relative value units, were initially based on historical data but have been resource based since 2000. CMS calculates these based on differentials in malpractice risk. The agency uses average state malpractice insurance premium data to assess the expected premium associated with providing a particular service, based on the dominant specialty providing the service.[2]

Besides physician fees, the Medicare fee schedule is used to calculate payments to nonphysicians, such as nurse practitioners, physician assistants, nurses, occupational and physical therapists, optometrists, podiatrists, psychologists, social workers, audiologists, speech pathologists, chiropractors, and registered dietitians. Some services such as office visits to nonphysicians can be independently billed (at a lower rate), and others are provided under the supervision of a physician.

The Relative Value Specialty Society Update Committee

The AMA first convened the Update Committee in 1991, when the government was developing the first version of the new fee schedule. Prior to implementation of the fee schedule, most participants in the payment reform process had recommended an independent review process to update codes. Nevertheless, the Health Care Financing Administration accepted the AMA's proposal to review work values, and the agency published the first set of recommendations in the 1993 *Federal Register.* Former heads of the Health Care Financing Administration and CMS argue that the committee's original role was reasonably defined—namely, to review a small number of codes. Soon, however, the committee was conducting annual reviews and playing a key role in the determination of relative value units. Today, this committee also advises CMS on the practice expense and malpractice relative value units that also contribute to payments to physicians.

Table 4.1 shows the major components of the committee and the other organizations attending or participating in the meetings. The nucleus of the update process is the Update Committee, containing a chair and 30 members, which votes on and assesses relative value units. The Update Committee is the most important committee because it determines and votes on the relative value units.

Sitting outside the main committee is a second group of over 100 representatives of specialty societies called the Advisory Committee. Each specialty society has one representative, the members of which are called "advisors," who advocate for their specialty when bringing codes before the main Update Committee. Although called a "committee," the Advisory Committee has no leadership structure or formal charter.

TABLE 4.1 Participants in the American Medical Association's Specialty Society Relative Value Update Committee

The Specialty Society Relative Value Update Committee (31)
Chairperson (1)

Specialty society representatives
  Practice Expense Subcommittee representative (1)

  Permanent specialty society representatives (21): anesthesiology, cardiology, dermatology, emergency medicine, family medicine, general surgery, geriatric medicine, internal medicine, neurology, neurosurgery, obstetrics/gynecology, ophthalmology, orthopedic surgery, otolaryngology, pathology, pediatrics, plastic surgery, psychiatry, radiology, thoracic surgery, urology

  Temporary members (4): colon and rectal surgery, hematology, primary care, rheumatology

Non-MD members (2)
  American Osteopathic Association representative
  Health Care Professionals Advisory Committee (co-chair)

American Medical Association representatives (2)
  American Medical Association representative
  Current Procedural Terminology Editorial Panel representative

Specialty Society Advisory Committee (100+)
  Specialty society representatives, including societies represented on the Update Committee by other individuals

Health Care Professionals Advisory Committee (12)
  9 Non-MD members, 3 Update Committee members

Data Source: Relative Value Update Committee, American Medical Association (2016).

A third committee, composed of non-MDs, is the Health Care Professionals Advisory Committee (also referred to by members as HCPAC), which operates as part of the review process and shares members with the Update Committee. One non-MD health professional sits on the Update Committee (with voting privileges), and three committee members sit on the Health Care Professionals Advisory Committee.

Four different subgroups make up the Update Committee (Table 4.1). The chair, appointed by the AMA, votes only if there is a tied vote. Two individuals without voting privileges are appointed by the AMA: a designated representative of the AMA and one from the AMA Current Procedural Terminology Editorial Panel. The chair of the Practice Expense Subcommittee also serves but does not vote. Twenty-two members represent specialty societies and have permanent seats on the Update Committee. Some societies joined later than others, such as neurology (1997) and geriatrics (2012). All other societies have been represented continuously since the committee began (one threatened to leave, as discussed below). The list of permanent members parallels the list of specialties included in William Hsiao's RBRVS study or that of specialties that funded their own participation in that study. Each committee member has an "alternate" to represent the specialty society if he or she is unavailable.

Four term-limited "rotating" memberships offer societies the opportunity to be voting members for a brief period. Societies are nominated from the 100+ specialty societies serving on the Advisory Committee. Two seats are for internal medicine (added in 1999); only one of these can be an internal medicine subspecialty, and the other is for any non–primary care subspecialty. Primary care was granted a seat in 2012. Two non-MD representatives, one from the American Osteopathic Association and the other from Health Care Professionals Advisory Committee, form a third group.

The issue of which specialties or organizations can sit on the Update Committee is a topic of recurring debate. "The RUC was designed to be an expert panel, rather than a representative committee" (American Medical Association 2008). Over time, the committee developed rules governing eligibility for a permanent seat, although all existing permanent members were grandfathered. Any society can put itself forward for membership, but new additions have been infrequent. Before a society can propose itself, it must meet the following eligibility requirements: is recognized by the American Board of Medical Specialties (ABMS),[3] constitutes at least 1 percent of physicians in practice, accounts for at least 1 percent of Medicare physician service expenditures, and has Medicare revenue at least 10 percent of mean practice revenue for the specialty. In 2002, the committee added an additional condition that the specialty may not be already "meaningfully represented" on the committee by an umbrella organization as "determined by RUC" (American Medical Association 2010a).

Representation of primary care has increasingly become a focal point for more general dissatisfaction among some specialty societies. Critics have argued that because specialties are overrepresented, primary care physicians are disadvantaged by lower payment rates (Bodenheimer, Berenson, and Rudolf 2007; Goodson 2007). As a percentage of all Medicare charges, office visits account for the largest share. The Medicare Payment Advisory Commission has recommended that the committee should more accurately reflect the specialty composition of physicians billing the Medicare program (Medicare Payment Advisory Commission 2006a).

A report from the AMA Board of Trustees reported that primary care societies offered a motion to create a rotating primary care seat at the April 2007 meeting, and this was referred to the Administrative Subcommittee, which reported back the following September and recommended the creation of a new seat. "The Subcommittee had some difficulty getting agreement on the definition of primary care, but this was resolved through negotiation and compromises between primary care organizations and others" (American Medical Association 2008). Some members were concerned that the size of the committee would become "unwieldy" if it grew larger. When it was put to a vote, the proposal failed to obtain the required a two-thirds majority. The committee concluded that "the current expertise to review E/M services is sufficient" (American Medical Association 2008).

In 2011, the American Academy of Family Physicians (AAFP) threatened to leave if more primary care seats were not added. The AAFP presented its proposal at the September 2011 meeting, described by a representative of another specialty society as "a seminal one in the history of this committee" (Society of American Gastrointestinal and Endoscopic Surgeons 2011, 2). According to a member of the Society of American Gastrointestinal and Endoscopic Surgeons who was attending, the president of the AAFP (Roland Goertz, MD) addressed the meeting, arguing that the complexity of patients had disadvantaged primary care (Society of American Gastrointestinal and Endoscopic Surgeons 2011). Some members then expressed concern that if representation was proportional, significant antitrust implications would then occur (Society of American Gastrointestinal and Endoscopic Surgeons 2011). Nevertheless, in 2012, members voted to create a new permanent seat for the American Geriatrics Society and an additional rotating seat for primary care.

The Update Committee is nested within the larger AMA organization, which shoulders the cost of the meetings. The AMA reports that it costs an estimated $7 million per year to hold the meetings and staff the committee. The committee falls within a budget item called "Advocacy and Federal Relations" (American Medical Association 2011a).[4] The Update Committee constitutes one-third of this budget line, which is $21 million, the total of which is equal to 16 percent of the total expenditures by the AMA ($132 million) in 2011.

About six staff and a director are housed in the AMA Payment Policy and Systems Directorate in Chicago. The office manages the activities of the committee on a day-to-day basis and organizes meetings, assembles material for meetings, distributes agendas, coordinates conference calls, and works with specialty societies submitting code changes. Staff also respond to queries from outside organizations and individuals, as well as provide information on the AMA website.

During meetings, staff take a variety of roles, including recording and taking minutes of the meetings, coordinating electronic voting, staffing subcommittees, and answering questions from societies. The director of the unit usually sits beside the chair. Staff work hard to clearly document the rationales behind decisions and enforce a degree of consistency across committee decisions. Senior staff might, for example, point out inconsistencies even between an argument made in the morning and afternoon sessions. Participants speak highly of the staff, respect their professionalism, attest that staff members have a deep knowledge of the RBRVS and Medicare payment rules, and say staff have a detailed understanding of rules and norms.

All committee appointments are subject to approval by the AMA Board of Trustees. The Update Committee has its own set of bylaws and rules. Significant changes to policies and procedures are usually made via ballot or voice vote after a subcommittee report. Policy development around rules and other issues is delegated to three subcommittees, including a Research Subcommittee, an Administrative Subcommittee, and a Practice Expense Subcommittee, each of which mainly contains committee members but also has a handful of alternate committee members, Health Care Professionals Advisory Committee members, and Advisory Committee members.

The Advisory Committee

Theoretically, the Update Committee is an expert panel and separated from the advocacy role of specialty societies: "Specialties represented on both the RUC and the Advisory Committee are required to appoint different physicians to each committee to distinguish the role of advocate from that of evaluator" (American Medical Association 2005).

Recognized as advocates, advisors serve on their society's Relative Value Scale Committee (or similar), coordinate surveys of their specialty, and make presentations when relative value units are being assessed. They are also appointed to facilitation committees "to capitalize on their expertise and interest" (American Medical Association 2008).

The AMA distinguishes between the roles of Advisory Committee members and the voting members on the Update Committee: "While the role of RUC members is to exercise their judgment independent of their specialties, Advisory Committee members are permitted to advocate on behalf of their specialties" (American Medical Association 2008). Advisors act as a liaison between the committee and their specialty society reimbursement committee and staff. "Most of the specialty society and other health care professional representatives are supported by coding and socioeconomic policy committees within their respective organizations" (American Medical Association 2008).

Depending on the society's specialty, the workload of advisors can be high. The American College of Radiology, for example, typically sends out more than 50 surveys every year (Allen 2006), which means a presentation on each. Even if they do not have codes under review (which can be the case for many of the societies), the advisors attend meetings: A number of physician advisors attend each RUC meeting regardless of whether their specialty has an issue under review by the RUC usually with specialty society staff or reimbursement consultants. At the meetings, they gather information; network; monitor the meeting discussions to understand the interpretation of work, coding, and payment issues; and, most important, listen for changes in procedures or the statements and questions of committee members during each review. Advisors have been appointed to more committees and workgroups than in the past. Societies find this useful because advisors may eventually become members. Interviewees stress the learning curve of the committee and the need to be directly involved rather than just observing the process.

Physician organizations can only participate in the Update Committee or belong to the larger Advisory Committee if they have enough members of the AMA to be represented in the AMA House of Delegates, a parliament of US physician organizations and the official policymaking body of the AMA. The House of Delegates has more than 600 members representing 50 state medical societies and around 185 specialty organizations. To be a member of the House of Delegates, a specialty society needs a minimum number of AMA members, or the society must have 20 percent of its members (depending on the size of the organization) belonging to the AMA.

Therefore, societies with Advisory Committee members must maintain organizational eligibility for membership in the AMA's House of Delegates, which, as said, requires that a society have 20 percent of its members (or a minimum of 1,000 members) who also belong to the AMA (American

Medical Association 2005). The AMA audits the AMA membership of each specialty society every five years. In 2013, on average, around 24 percent of the membership of those societies audited also belonged to the AMA. Many societies fall below the 20 percent threshold but retain their status because they have at least 1,000 AMA members or have been grandfathered (American Medical Association 2013). When societies do not meet the threshold for membership, they may face a probationary status. Societies then encourage their members to "join the AMA to support retention of representation on the RUC" (Society of Vascular Surgeons 2013, 179).

Members of the AMA belong for a variety of reasons, and the organization provides a host of benefits to members, such as discounts on publications. While the motives of those joining the AMA cannot be deduced, some have speculated that many join to maintain eligibility to be represented in the update process. A participant interviewed by a journalist argued that specialty societies join the AMA largely, if not only, to participate: "No one cares about AMA. They care about the RUC" (Sweetland-Edwards 2013). Some have further speculated that representation of one group over another is determined by membership numbers, although there is no way to verify this claim: "The only reason their group as the urologists or the GIs or the surgeons are on there, versus some other urology group, or GI group, or surgery group, is because they had more of their percentage of their members join the AMA, and because they play ball with the AMA and they follow directions of the AMA." This means that, according to one interviewee, the AMA has considerable power: "The AMA uses it. Every specialty group is scared to death of the AMA, because if they screw with them, they lose their seat on the RUC, which is insane" (Interview Subject 22).

The Health Care Professionals Advisory Committee

The Health Care Professionals Advisory Committee has 15 members, three from the Update Committee and 12 others drawn from the major health professions in the United States: audiologists, chiropractors, dietitians, nurses, occupational therapists, optometrists, physical therapists, physician assistants, podiatrists, psychologists, social workers, and speech pathologists. Medicare and Medicaid require many professionals to bill for their services using Current Procedural Terminology (CPT) codes.[5]

The Health Care Professionals Advisory Committee does not operate fully independently: as said, three sitting members of the committee also serve on it simultaneously. The chair of the of the Health Care Professionals Advisory Committee is selected by the chair of the Update Committee, and he or she is always a committee member.

The Health Care Professionals Advisory Committee reviews work relative value units for codes provided by non-MD health professionals. For those services where non-MD professionals and MDs both use the same codes, the Health Care Professionals Advisory Committee members contribute to the review of relative value units through the main update process in conjunction with physician specialty societies, which usually take the lead. A precise estimate of the number of codes the committee reviews independently is difficult to make, because CMS previously separated Update Committee and Health Care Professionals Advisory Committee recommendations but does not do so now. However, between 1994 and 2011, there were only 43 services with separate reviews in over 3,000 recommendations submitted by the Update Committee. Between 2010 and 2011, 12 percent of all presentations included a non-MD organization appearing alone or with a physician organization, suggesting collaboration is not infrequent.

Other Participants

CMS staff have attended committee meetings "from the beginning" (Parks 1997, 14). The agency sends a small group of staff to Update Committee meetings, and two staff with medical director titles sit "at the table" during the meetings. CMS staffers sitting at the table do not participate in the discussions actively but monitor the proceedings and clarify points of CMS policy.

Representatives of other organizations attending meetings are designated as guests and/or observers. The Medicare Payment Advisory Commission sends staff to meetings, and periodically they give presentations on policy changes and other issues. Occasionally, staff from agencies such as the Government Accountability Office (GAO) and the Congressional Budget Office (CBO) attend meetings also.

Anyone who wants to attend a meeting needs permission from the chair. The AMA says it has never denied anyone access to the meetings (RUC Administrative Subcommittee Report in American Academy of Orthopedic Surgeons 2013, 310). Academics, overseas medical society staff, representatives of Medicare carriers, and a variety of other individuals observe the meetings as guests of the committee.

Committee Activities before Meetings

The Update Committee follows a set of steps, shown in Figure 4.1. Defining billing codes precedes the review process. Before services (also called codes, once they have a numerical identifier) can be reviewed by the Update Committee, they may need to be reviewed by another AMA-coordinated committee, called the CPT Editorial Committee, which defines and develops CPT billing codes. CPT is the "nomenclature" or language that defines physician services. The CPT coding system is essential for an understanding of Medicare and private payer payment systems (Kumetz and Goodson 2013) and is an integral part of how the Update Committee develops relative value units. The codes "translate the language of medical care into the jargon of accounting and payment" (Bean 2000).

Almost all US physicians and nonphysicians use the CPT coding system for billing; it is also used in many other countries. The AMA developed the CPT system in 1964; the codes are proprietary, and CPT is a trademark of the AMA, which sells coding software and other products for medical coding and earns royalties from the use of CPT by other organizations. A major coup for the AMA was the requirement that physicians use the system to bill Medicare in 1983; it was then extended to Medicaid. CPT is organized around a hierarchy of major organ and body systems and focused purely on the tasks performed, not the diagnosis. CPT codes emphasize what is done by the physician to the patient. Because CPT focuses on what is done, rather than why, insurers usually require that claims also include information about the diagnosis, which is coded using the International Classification of Diseases (ICD) system, a coding system maintained by the World Health Organization and not subject to copyright in the United States. The ICD system also has its own procedural codes, but the requirement to use CPT by Medicare likely encouraged the CPT system to diffuse more widely in the United States.

As one interviewee said, "The whole process begins going through the CPT. Once the CPT decides if they like the code, then they send it to the RUC" (Interview Subject 9). Between 1992 and 2007, the CPT Editorial Committee reviewed 3,163 new services, made 1,931 code deletions, and revised 3,161 existing codes (Duszak 2006). There are several reasons why these billing codes matter. First, they confer authenticity and credibility: CPT determines which services are recognized as "legitimate and compensable" and deserving of billing codes (Bean 2002, 4). Device and equipment manufacturers say that "their products are more likely to be used by physicians if a

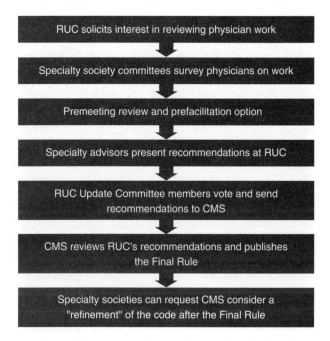

FIGURE 4.1 The review of new and revised codes by the
Specialty Society Relative Value Scale Update Committee.

separate CPT code for the product exists" (Bean 2002, 3). Second, after the
Medicare fee schedule was created, specialty societies realized that codes
were necessary and the segmentation might influence the income of their
members (Harris 1997b). Creating billing codes is not simply an administrative process but also one that defines what physicians do—definitions have
implications for payment. Interviewees repeatedly emphasized the close
connections between the Update Committee and the CPT process.

Generally speaking, requests for new codes or revisions are initiated by
specialty societies. As with the Update Committee process, some specialties
are more frequent participants than others. For example, between 2005
and 2007, the American College of Radiology alone proposed 85 new codes,
11 deletions, and 47 editorial revisions (Allen 2006).

In more highly procedural areas of medicine, specialty societies often
work with device or equipment manufacturers to present their proposal. In
many cases, a society has already had discussions with the manufacturer
during the process of getting a new CPT code approved before they request

review by the Update Committee. Sometimes the society will request a category III or "T" (for "tracking") code but usually it tries to get a category I code, which is the kind of CPT code that can be referred to the committee and has a work value attached to it. In other cases, the society said that it worked with the manufacturer, who was "comfortable with a category III code" (Interview Subject 9).

Code proposals assessed by the CPT Editorial Committee include minor and major changes in service descriptions, new codes that are created to replace existing ones, and new codes to account for changes in technology and medical practice. Sometimes changes are incorporated within an existing code by making only a minor change in its description. Minor changes "simply make the wording of the code easier to understand and more consistent" (Hassenbusch 2002, 36).[6]

In theory, new codes reflect changes in technology, such as a new test or device, or a change in practice. But not all new codes are truly "new"— sometimes specialties develop codes that are essentially "branches" from existing codes that further differentiate what physicians do. This increasing disaggregation of procedures seems to be a tendency of coding systems managed by physicians. As Chapter 3 shows, that has been concern since the late 1960s because it is seen as a back door to higher payment for physicians.[7]

The CPT Editorial Committee has many similarities to the Update Committee and operates in parallel. Like the Update Committee, the CPT committee has a nonvoting Advisory Committee, follows similar procedures and rules, and is funded and assisted by AMA staff. Each committee has representatives of the other. Many of the Update Committee advisors and members attend one or more CPT meetings, while CPT staff also attend the Update Committee meetings.[8] The committee can refer codes back to CPT if there are problems or ambiguities in how the service is described. The CPT Editorial Committee schedules are closely coordinated to ensure codes progress from the CPT to the Update Committee process.

After a CPT meeting, roughly half of all codes edited and defined are forwarded to the Update Committee. Of more than 6,000 code changes reviewed by CPT (not counting deletions or minor changes) between 1992 and 2007, approximately 2,800 were reviewed by the Update Committee (Duszak 2006). The CPT committee only refers codes to the Update Committee if the change (or a new code) requires a review of physician work and/or practice expenses.

Codes before the Update Committee sometimes are shown as having problems in their description, such as ambiguities. If the description has a problem, the Update Committee may refer the billing code to CPT or leave the work value unaltered but recommend a coding edit. Following review by the CPT Editorial Panel, codes are forwarded to the Update Committee.

Staff members at the AMA review the information and invite specialty societies to express their interest in reviewing its work value. If one society has shepherded the code through the CPT process, that organization is a natural participant, but the Update Committee allows multiple societies to work together on recommendations of work values. Specialty societies can simply comment on other societies' recommendations, decline to comment if they believe the work value does not change, or take no action because the codes are not used by physicians in their specialty.

Developing new codes and/or making work recommendations is not something societies take lightly, given the extensive work involved, and in some cases, societies make tactical decisions not to evaluate recommendations, for fear of a decrease. If the service is used by broader specialties as well as subspecialties, smaller societies may piggyback on their larger "parent" societies. Given the overlapping constituencies, larger societies have formal structures to coordinate with subspecialty societies. For instance, the American Academy of Orthopedic Surgeons has its own reimbursement committee, which includes their update Advisory Committee members, and it also coordinates a committee representing 12 musculoskeletal specialty societies concerned with representing "the interest of orthopedics on coding and physician payment issues" (American Academy of Orthopedic Surgeons 2014).

If the society or societies decide to get involved, they send out surveys that ask physicians about the time and difficulty associated with the service. Reference codes are provided for comparison purposes. These surveys are completed online (as discussed in Chapter 5). Subsequently, the society requests the Update Committee to review the code at an upcoming meeting.

In the past, specialty societies would receive feedback from the Update Committee members immediately after their presentation. Today, two premeeting processes give societies feedback on their proposals before the meeting. The first is pre-review, which is automatic, and the other is prefacilitation, which is optional.

Premeeting review has changed the process: as one participant put it, societies find meetings easier because "the idea is that there are no surprises" (Interview Subject 3). The Update Committee chair assigns four reviewers who provide feedback to the society in conference calls between committee members and the society. Those calls can alert a society to potential problems and concerns. Alternatively, societies might bring questions to the committees about their proposal. Previously, there was stigma associated with admitting problems: five years ago, recalled one interviewee, "admitting you had a problem was kind of like the antelope going ahead and laying down and saying, 'Okay, I'm tired of running from the lion, they can eat me.' Now admitting you have a problem is going to a negotiation table with the lion and saying, 'You know, let's work something out'" (Interview Subject 6).

If significant problems arise, the Update Committee allows the society or the reviewers to request prefacilitation meetings. Before each meeting, the chair appoints approximately three ad hoc facilitation committees. These committees combine the Update Committee members and Update Committee advisors and number roughly 12 individuals. According to one society, they are used to focus on complex codes that would require an "inordinate" amount of time if presented to the entire RUC, and after the meeting, the committee members write a report and reject or accept the specialty society recommendations (American College of Radiology 2001). Often, prefacilitation is unnecessary, because "you may have formulated your code so well, and you're so confident in your data, that you say to yourself, I don't want to prefacilitate this, I'm confident in this, I'm happy to put it up to right off the bat" (Interview Subject 1).

One society described the meetings as "grueling and exhaustive" because the society had to explain their procedure to nonradiation oncologists. Not just one but multiple meeting sessions were needed to fully explain the technology. According to the society, the prefacilitation committee "worked closely with ACR [American College of Radiology] and ASTRO [American Society for Radiation Oncology] representatives as well as AMA and CMS staff." Those recommendations were accepted by the committee, and then the recommended values outlined in the facilitation committee's report were accepted by the Update Committee. (American College of Radiology 2001).

While the committees are supposed to be representative, the Update Committee members say they know what to expect: "We know their inclinations" (Interview Subject 7). The recent chair (Dr. Barbara Levy) is said to have done a better job of balancing the facilitation and prefacilitation committees and making them more mixed. Members say the assignment of people to facilitation committees and other committees better reflects the Update Committee as a whole, whereas in the past, it was possible to get "one group that you know is going to go in one direction as opposed to another" (Interview Subject 7).

Longitudinal data are not available on the use of prefacilitation committees, but 2014 data provided by the AMA (American Medical Association 2014) show that of 206 work relative value unit recommendations made in that year, just under half (99) were reviewed by prefacilitation committees. Of the 99 that went to facilitation, around one-fifth (21) were changed before the presentation. Of the 206 codes, societies changed less than 10 percent (30), with the majority of those (21) changed after prefacilitation.

Interviewees say they like the opportunity to have their proposals reviewed by these committees. Prefacilitation meetings are particularly useful if there are queries from the two pre-reviewers assigned to the code. "'Well, we looked at this and we had a problem with this, and da, da, da, da, da,'—you're better off having arranged that in advance" (Interview Subject 10). Given almost half of all services are reviewed by prefacilitation committees and societies make changes to one-fifth of those, the committees seem to serve as forums where societies can "road test" their ideas and/or adjust their recommendations.

A logistic regression with the dependent variable being whether or not the Update Committee made a recommendation that was higher than the current work relative value unit showed a statistically significant relationship (odds ratio, 1.82; $p > 0.049$) between having a code prefacilitated and seeing a code increased from the current year's value. Likewise, a simple bivariate linear regression, with the number of "yes" votes for work units as the dependent variable, showed a statistically significant and positive relationship ($p = 0.003$) between prefacilitation of a code and the number of "yes" votes recorded. But controlling for the magnitude of change in the work unit, the effects of prefacilitation disappear: the magnitude of change in the work value before and after review is more important than whether the code was reviewed by a prefacilitation committee (odds ratio, 17.18; $p > 0.000$).

The main goals of seeking prefacilitation, according to participants, are to minimize unexpected objections, address problems in advance of the meeting, and reach consensus. One interviewee described these meetings as a subset of the Update Committee in which the environment was more collaborative, and societies could get help with their recommendation. Update Committee participants like the prefacilitation process because it is lower pressure and more cooperative. The option is appealing if it seems "it's going to be hard to get up at the RUC" (Interview Subject 10). The prefacilitation process minimizes the risk of unexpected questions at the main meeting, especially the kinds of question that encourage a bandwagon effect:

> If you're really going for broke and you really want to get a good value on something, and you think you've got a good argument, then it can be easier to take that argument to a small, informal committee beforehand, rather than presenting it to the whole world, where anyone can put their hand up and say, "And about this." And then that can turn the whole . . . discussion. And suddenly, other people put their hands up, and then the code will go down. And then it'll have to go to [post]facilitation. (Interview Subject 10)

Sometimes the reviewers "hash out some way that the presenters can modify their recommendations so that we accept it. The committee will say, 'We don't think this is going to get through to RUC, so we'd recommend that you say, for example, that you recommend not the median work value but actually the 25th percentile. We think if you recommended that, we could support it, and, you know, it would get passed'" (Interview Subject 7). Prefacilitation can strengthen the overall presentation by identifying the right argument to use for the data or the recommendation: "Somebody looks at it and says, 'Look, you have a really weak argument here,' or . . . 'It's hard to understand this'" (Interview Subject 7). Yet, not all societies avail themselves of the opportunity, and in these cases, "certain societies will not present it in a fashion that the RUC will agree with it, so, they'll decline the code. And then it goes to a [post]facilitation committee" where they are negotiating "on what the value of the code should be" (Interview Subject 9).

Prefacilitation can be helpful when the values are controversial and/or because the society is presenting a large number of codes, especially ones that are difficult to explain. One Update Committee member said that "our society has 23 codes" that might be controversial, and by starting them off in prefacilitation, they start the process before going to the Update Committee. As a committee member, the interviewee would not participate in the prefacilitation (Interview Subject 7).

The key task of the specialty society advisors and their colleagues is to persuade Update Committee members that there is a logic underlying the work recommendation. But explaining the work involved in a procedure is difficult when only one or two panel members (or none) might understand the service. Societies face challenges due to the specialized nature of medicine, and it can be difficult for some subspecialties to adequately convey what happens during the delivery of the service. The prefacilitation process helps the society frame the presentation so that committee members understand the work involved in relation to the level of work value requested:

> Sometimes you have to educate the RUC on what the procedure is. Most codes that we present are procedural codes. And so it's important that the RUC understands, you know, what the code procedure is so that they understand that what we're presenting is reasonable, but if you have a number of codes being put forth, you'll have them prefacilitated so you can get the RUC input before you present it. And they'll give you some good tips on, you know, what to emphasize, what not to emphasize, and, you know, that sort of thing. And then once you present it, usually you do a lot better job. (Interview Subject 9)

At other times, the society needs to keep the work value at the same level or increase it, but the society anticipates problems related to the quality of the survey data: "We've had some codes that we prefacilitated just because we weren't as confident of the data as we should have been" (Interview Subject 9). The facilitation committee process helps the society interpret or better explain the data so that they are more convincing when they are presented at the main meeting: "We have a problem with that, we have a crappy survey, or we have data that doesn't make sense. Can you help us work through how we ought to deal with this?" (Interview Subject 6).

If there are problems with the survey data, getting a favorable work value increase is even more important when the service is a code that members bill frequently—described by interviewees as "bread and butter" codes. In one case, an Advisory Committee member presenting a code for a specialty society knew there were weaknesses in the proposal: first, the surveyed times seemed longer than what the society believed was accurate, and the reference code that had been selected was not the right code, according to the committee member:

> There was a certain strategy I wanted to use. What I wanted to do was I wanted to link the [redacted] code to one of the higher valued [redacted] procedures as a comparison. I think from memory, I didn't have a good comparison code. I thought this was very, very important, because there's going to be a lot of these procedures being done, and we wanted to get as good evaluation as we could, because it's . . . you know, it's difficult. So we took it

to prefacilitation, and . . . basically we facilitated to the point where it was . . . it was rubber-stamped. The whole thing was just perfect. We walk in, presented the procedures in reverse order, the prefacilitation evaluators said they had no problem with what we discussed; we would agree to reduce something there and change something there, and it was done. (Interview Subject 1)

In short, prefacilitation helps societies achieve valuations they want by minimizing uncertainty that could derail the success of the recommendation and provides societies with an opportunity to pretest the presentation and arguments. After facilitation, societies do revise their recommendation and/or change how they approach their presentation. There is a general consensus that presenters should follow the recommendations of the prefacilitation committee members. At the Update Committee meeting, the society will usually thank the committee and often peg its valuation at a lower level, and it may be accepted.

Meetings and Specialty Society Presentations

In-person Update Committee meetings are usually held in late September or early October, January or early February, and late April. At each meeting, the Update Committee reviews and makes recommendations on several hundred work relative value units. Over a long period, this means it has reviewed thousands of codes: between 1994 and 2011, more than 3,000 codes were submitted by the Update Committee to CMS. Around half of the services reviewed over this period were new services (Laugesen, Wada, and Chen 2012).

Registered attendees receive the meeting agenda on a CD-ROM in the mail before the meeting. The agenda and supporting documents can exceed 5,000 pages. Every code has a summary of survey results and details about the specialty society recommendations. Subcommittee reports are also included on the CD-ROM. People observing or participating in the Update Committee meetings must sign confidentiality agreements.

Update Committee meetings usually begin on a Wednesday and last three to four days, beginning with subcommittee and workgroup meetings. The main meeting starts with introductions of guests, and typically there is a presentation from the AMA lobbyist from Washington, DC, that outlines the political and lobbying goals of the AMA related to Medicare payment and the likelihood of specific laws passing.

Several hundred people participate in the meetings. Most of them are Advisory Committee members, since more than a hundred societies belong and each has an alternate and a representative attending. The meetings are held in a hotel ballroom. The Update Committee sits at tables arranged in a square U-shape. The specialty societies presenting codes sit at the open end of the table arrangement. Directly facing the presenters is the chair, and sitting next to him or her is the director of the unit overseeing the committee at the AMA, alongside the AMA representative, the CPT committee representative, and the Practice Expense Committee representative. Behind these officials are members of the Update Committee staff. Advisors, or "Advisory Committee" members and "alternates" (who fill in for voting members as needed), sit behind the Update Committee members on both sides. Also sitting with Advisory Committee members are staff and/or "consultants" who have been contracted by the specialty societies to advise them on coding and reimbursement; if the society is large, it may have full-time staff there as well.

At the opening of each day, an Update Committee member usually begins the meeting with a light-hearted review of sporting scores. Meetings are run according to parliamentary procedure. Presenters appear before the committee and must declare any conflicts of interest at the start (American Medical Association 2010b). If presenters have multiple codes under discussion, they will often present them together. Sometimes practice expense units are considered in packages. The time estimates from surveys influence practice expense levels.

Prior analysis indicates that most services considered by the Update Committee are surgical (Laugesen, Wada, and Chen 2012). The participation of surgical specialty societies is therefore high. Content analysis of publicly available meeting minutes (using two coders) for 514 codes at the April 2010, October 2010, February 2011, and April 2011 meetings shows that 64 percent of specialty society presentations were from surgical specialties. The data provide an impression of the participation of different specialties in the process (but do not add up to 100 since more than one specialty can present at a time): 27 percent of presentations included procedural specialties, 13 percent included radiologists, 12 percent included nonphysician groups, and 9 percent each included pathology and emergency room. Family medicine and general and internal medicine participated in 10.5 percent of the presentations, interdisciplinary groups in 9 percent, and nonprocedural specialties in 6 percent. General and internal medicine presented at 5 percent.

Most societies present either alone or with one other society: 35 percent of codes were presented by a single society, and 29 percent of presentations were by two societies. Ten percent were presentations by three societies, 7 percent included four societies, and 14 percent of presentations had five societies. One percent of the presentations included six or more organizations.

Analysis of the relationship between the number of societies presenting and the value of the work relative value unit sent to CMS shows a small negative effect of the number of societies presenting and the committee's work recommendation. The effect, however, is not statistically significant. When CMS determines the final work value, however, there is a small and statistically significant positive effect on the likelihood of CMS accepting recommendations as the number of societies increases.

The Update Committee established rules that require societies to prove that the service is over- or undervalued when they seek to change codes, because the committee's stated presumption regarding the RBRVS is that the current values are correct (American Medical Association 2010a, 76). The society must convince the Update Committee that "the existing values are no longer rational" (American Medical Association 2010a, 32).

Presenters describe the service and walk committee members through the process of providing it. The presenters may review a clinical vignette for the service. A vignette usually describes a patient scenario, such as "an infant born at 35 weeks. . . ." The presenters typically break their description of the service into three parts, each of which reflects the RBRVS division of work: preservice work, intraservice work (face-to-face patient time), and follow-up or postservice work. A key part of the work description is establishing the level of intensity and complexity of the procedure. Factors that influence intensity and complexity include the urgency of decision making, such as whether it is performed on an emergency basis; the risks of the procedure; and the kinds of patients treated. Where the services are usually provided (inpatient setting, emergency room, clinic, or office) is typically mentioned, and committee members have summaries of Medicare utilization data available to them in their own database.

Having described the nature of the service, presenters move to the centerpiece of their presentation—usually the results of a survey sent to physicians asking them to rate the work associated with the service. By this stage, most people at the meeting will have turned to the appropriate section of the meeting documents or scrolled to it on their laptop, focusing particularly on the "Summary of Recommendation" for the code. The summary of recommendation contains extensive information about the survey findings and the society recommendation. Societies discuss how they sampled their respondents. Samples are not always randomly selected, with many drawn from society membership lists, rather than from lists of all physicians practicing in the specialty, or provided by a device manufacturer.

The process of decision making and the evidence used are discussed in Chapter 5. In brief, the standard survey asks physicians to estimate how long services take to provide and the difficulty of the work. At the start of the survey, respondents are presented with a patient vignette and are asked to say how "typical" that vignette is for the service described.

Generally, participants say they cannot predict outcomes. "Sometimes you go in thinking, 'Oh, this is a slam dunk,' and then you get tripped up in the process. Or sometimes you think, 'There's no way those codes are going to pass, it's way too high,' and, you know, by golly, they pass anyway, and it's just like, 'Well, how did that happen?' So it's . . . not an exact science" (Interview Subject 2).

Committee Decision Making

The process of the Update Committee's decision making is discussed more in Chapters 5 and 6. Reviewers assigned to the code or group of codes will make a statement on the society's proposal, and the Update Committee member will describe the outcome of a prefacilitation meeting, if one was held. Then, other members have an opportunity to ask questions, but much depends on what the primary and secondary reviewers say: "So if the primary reviewer and the secondary reviewer say, 'You know, I've reviewed the methodology, I agree with its submitter. I think their request is appropriate or it's reasonable,' and the secondaries [secondary reviewers] say, 'Sounds good,' deal with a couple other questions, it's going to go through" (Interview Subject 3).

In the past, participants say that they could not be certain of what would happen after the presentation. The use of review panels has decreased but hardly eliminated the level of uncertainty for specialty societies. Presenters might arrive at the meeting thinking the data supported their recommendation, but "after many questions you have the sinking feeling" (Interview Subject 3). There are particular risks associated with the bandwagon effect mentioned earlier, whereby a single question leads to others asking more questions: if one Update Committee member identifies a weakness, others join in "like the Roman chorus" (Interview Subject 3). Participants say that if one of the reviewers starts saying, '"I really question your methodology or . . . these numbers really seem to be out of whack with our procedures that your society performs,' or whatever, then, I said, then it's pile on methodology . . . and someone on the panel says 'I don't think that your values are correct,' or 'You use the median and I think the twenty-fifth percentile should have been appropriate' or 'that valuation, it's going to cause a rank order anomaly with another code' then the panel starts piling on" (Interview Subject 3).

Opinions vary on how difficult it is to persuade committee members that the work values are appropriate, with some asserting that the process is rigorous. On some occasions, voting members of the committee begin drawing on personal experience in the discussions of specific procedures. At one meeting, for example, a member mentioned how someone in the member's family had a surgical procedure and recalled the pressure on the physician to not fail due to the stress associated with making a major mistake (Author's meeting notes, April 2012).

Some interviewees say that if the information presented is consistent with the data presented by the society, the committee will be "comfortable with the recommendations, [and] things go well" (Interview Subject 3). Committee members do not always call out inconsistencies between survey data and recommendations, however: participants say that despite discrepancies or questions, the codes can go through without difficulty. Such discrepancies were noted by CMS in its review of committee recommendations in 2010.

When asked why society recommendations fail to be accepted by committee members, societies overwhelmingly refer to the characteristics and perceived quality of the survey. Societies try to avoid situations where the committee assails their data and recommendations. The only insurance against such setbacks is deep knowledge of the process, which is honed during repeated exposure to it—and sometimes lessons learned from a past humiliation before the committee. The process is complex, and it has its own folkways and norms. Therefore, participants say that experience-based expertise is highly valuable.

Those who feel the process is rigorous say that proposals to increase work values receive more careful consideration: "People's eyebrows kind of go up and you probably get a little more scrutiny" (Interview Subject 2). Such inquiries do not always result in code reductions, however, since many of the problems with the survey are resolved during postfacilitation committee meetings.

Many presentations are clear and polished, demonstrating a facility with the material and an understanding of the most important information that committee members want to hear. At other times, society presentations are sometimes inaudible or poorly organized. A poor presentation can doom the society's chances. A presenter might respond inappropriately to a question, such as the time when a radiologist was asked why utilization was increasing, to which he responded, "Because there are more machines" (Anonymous observer notes, 2008). In some cases, a society might struggle to articulate what the service is or why it is time-consuming or difficult. When the work and the service are not described logically and clearly, committee members may underestimate the work involved. In such situations, committee members can get frustrated and express irritation. Such mishaps are more common with societies less accustomed to presenting before the committee, including non-MD organizations. To save face, sometimes presenters are given a second chance, and the service is referred back to the society for resurveying and resubmission at a future date.

When the presentation is not going well and it looks like there may not be a favorable vote, respondents say that the chair plays a vital role— provided he or she is sympathetic to the society. If the society is lucky, the chair "will take pity on you and will make a comment such as, 'You know, I'm going to entertain a motion for this code to go to facilitation' . . . good chairs will entertain motions rather quickly [*laughter*], and you will get out of the line of fire . . . it's a humbling experience when that happens. It is character building" (Interview Subject 3).

Budget Neutrality Adjustment

CMS has to apportion the changes to relative value units in such a way that increases do not trigger penalties required under law. The Omnibus Budget Reconciliation Act (1989) stipulated that changes to the fee schedule "should not cause expenditures to increase or decrease by more than $20 million from the amount of expenditures that would have occurred." If increases to relative value units will increase Medicare expenditures to exceed $20 million, CMS must make changes that reduce growth to $20 million, thereby ensuring that changes to the fee schedule do not increase expenditure by more than $20 million above the amount specified in targets. The agency calculates the impacts (in percentage terms) by specialty, based on the changes to the services that were reviewed and the decisions made in the Final Rule.

The original idea was that if units increased too much, then adjustments would be made across the board to the entire pool of units. The analysis underlying the adjustments is based on past utilization, but a detailed description of the methods used to calculate these estimates is not typically made available.

Each specialty has an interest in making sure its services are valued at higher "work" values in the RBRVS, but the countervailing pressure, in theory, is that committee panelists keep them honest because they do not want to suffer cuts. Fees can therefore only go up so much, or the House of Medicine will have its feet held to the fire. Indeed, it is unlikely that policy makers would have allowed physicians to play such a central role in the process without a budget neutrality adjustment. The hope was that specialties would fight among themselves to ensure the fairness of the process or, at least, that specialties would share the pain and gains of codes as they worked within the constraint of budget neutrality.

The problem with this portrayal of the committee is that generally speaking, codes go up rather than down. The assumption that committee decisions are budget neutral in their long-term impact and that this encourages or discourages prudent changes to codes is far from clear: "At a very fundamental level, the RUC is an example of the fox guarding the hen house" (Interview Subject 11). Budget neutrality adjustments might be made, but they act as an ineffective constraint in the decisions of the committee. Yet the idea of budget neutrality is so powerful and so readily taken at face value by committee supporters and even detractors as a real constraint that critiques of the update process as inflationary are often dismissed a priori.

In the early in the 2000s, specialty societies and the AMA argued that relative value unit adjustments were disruptive for private payers using the RBRVS and that the adjustment should instead be made to the update of the dollar conversion factor. Societies made this argument repeatedly over a number of years. Under this method, the conversion factor would be reduced instead of the relative value units. In 2008, Congress directed CMS to adjust the RBRVS for budget neutrality using the dollar conversion factor under the Medicare Improvement for Patients and Providers Act of 2008 (MIPPA).

Congress reduced almost all of the cuts proposed under the sustainable growth rate (Laugesen 2009). Between 2008 and 2015, the budget neutrality adjustment was applied using the conversion factor, so every time Congress declined to revise the conversion factor downward, it was also in effect removing the incentive for the committee to keep unit increases in check. Absent the cuts, units can increase without any penalty. Congress does not seem to take into account the growth in relative value units. On the other hand, there is evidence that CMS has applied the budget neutrality adjustment to relative value units within specific code families and for specific providers (such as chiropractic services) (Centers for Medicare & Medicaid Services 2011).

Thus, CMS can still make changes to specific code families through the relative value units but tends to do this only under certain conditions. The incidence of such cuts is ambiguous. CMS appears to only make budget neutrality adjustments if the unit goes up without a corresponding increase in work. If work increases, apparently the code is given a free pass:

> When the AMA RUC recommends work RVUs [relative value units] for new or revised CPT codes, we review the work RVUs and adjust or accept the recommended values as appropriate, making note of whether any estimated changes in aggregate work RVUs would result from a true change in physician work, or from structural coding changes. We then determine whether the application of budget neutrality within sets of codes is appropriate. If the aggregate work RVUs would increase without a corresponding true increase in physician work, we generally view this as an indication that an adjustment to ensure work budget neutrality within the set of CPT codes is warranted. Ensuring work budget neutrality is an important principle so that structural coding changes are not unjustifiably redistributive among Physician Fee Schedule services. (Centers for Medicare & Medicaid Services 2011)

> There was a code for a vaginal hysterectomy, and the GYN [gynecology] surgeons wanted to have two codes instead—one for a uterus that weighed less than 250 grams and one for one that weighed more. Because the ones that weigh more, they're harder, so they did that, and they got two values for the code. Both of those values were higher than the value of the original code. And, so what they ended up doing was saying, well, this has to be budget neutral, so the one that's greater than 250 grams will be slightly higher than the older value, and the one that's less than 250 grams will be slightly lower, so that when you multiplied the value times the frequency of those events, Medicare

would pay the same amount of money. So that's how budget neutrality was performed.

If it was in the five-year review, and the OB-GYN or the GYN physicians were able to indicate that the typical patient that had a vaginal hysterectomy had gotten older, sicker, harder, more difficult, some technology in the way that you did it made it harder, longer, who knows, then they would have had the ability for both of these codes to become higher than the original code from which it was split. And that money would then come from every other CPT code in the fee schedule. So it would be say it was a million dollars, well, that'd be a million dollars out of 90 billion dollars, and the 90 billion would stay the same, but an extra million would be put in . . . would be taken out of all the codes across the fee schedule for less than a penny each probably. (Interview Subject 7)

The fact that it is less than a penny for each is significant, as the impact may be imperceptible for most, yet with large impacts for those providing it. This example is helpful for understanding why expansion of the number of codes or increases at the top end of the distribution help physicians, because budget neutrality is based on current utilization numbers, not predicted utilization. Yet physicians tend to migrate to higher codes if they are available. When a code decreases by 5 percent, it increases the probability of the physician choosing the next highest code. A $1 reduction in the value of the Medicare next lower service intensity CPT code means a physician is 1.35 times more likely to choose a higher code, across all physicians, by a factor of 1.26 for internists and 2.31 for cardiologists (King, Lipsky, and Sharp 2002). Up-coding occurs: the greater the "marginal revenue, the more likely the physician's choice of the higher-paying code" (Brunt 2011, 838).

Other committee members say that they believe the Update Committee works to achieve budget neutrality, even if there are flaws in the process:

Well, the process itself, and I say this quite happily on the record, the process is arcane, unscientific, and highly politically charged, because in the end it's to do with the distribution of money, and in a closed revenue neutral system. So discussions can become, between perfectly civil and amicable people, can become quite heated if someone feels that what's being proposed is not well justified. Because if that's a net loss, or, a net addition to certain amount of work, then it's going to have to come from somewhere else. (Interview Subject 1)

Yet, it all depends on the utilization numbers for any given procedure: differential incentives for commonly performed services compared to those that are not: "If you get a 10 percent increase in something that has two billion iterations, that's a huge overall increase in the number of procedures. If you have a 10 percent increase in 200,000, well . . ." (Interview Subject 1).

This logic puts primary care specialists at a big disadvantage, because their codes are more widely used. There are ambiguities about how much budget neutrality is or is not taken into account. On one hand, everyone says that it is important; on the other hand, it is not something that is explicitly discussed or encouraged in the actual meetings, perhaps because the committee sees itself as a panel simply evaluating the technical merits of work. There is a strong presumption that therefore money is not to be mentioned. This was illustrated in an interview where the interviewee said that the issue of budget neutrality can only be considered implicitly, not explicitly. Members were taking into account "financial impact" (budget neutrality):

> And what happened when we got to the valuation was something that should never happen at RUC. RUC is not to consider the financial, ah, impact of its decision. Rather just, ah, is this value accurate? And so the survey medians for the E&M [evaluation and management] codes when they finally passed RUC, most of those settled way below the 25th percentile. Almost never happens. . . . Procedures typically end up on the 25th, the 50th percentile. In the last few years, [its] almost always the 25th. But the E&M values were hammered extremely low. And the reason that kept coming up inappropriate, I think, was, "What this'll do to the entire system?" Because it's a budget-neutral system. This is going to mean conversion factors will fall for everything, because there's so many E&M services.[9]

A five-year review, like all reviews of "potentially misvalued codes," addresses budget neutrality slightly differently than the annual reviews. As mentioned previously, in a review of services that might be under- or overvalued, any changes that exceed the statutory $20 million change are adjusted across the whole fee schedule. This means that in a review of misvalued services, the impact is broader and not confined to a set of codes, so as in the previous example of gynecological surgery, the impact is small for the whole:

> Well, the five-year process is completely different because when the five-year process goes on, there's the ability to provide compelling evidence that the code is misvalued. And if that compelling evidence is accepted and the

value is changed, the difference in the value is corrected for budget neutrality by the remainder of the fee schedule. If you change the value of code outside of the five-year cycle, it has to be budget neutral within the family that they code it in. (Interview Subject 7)

The fixed pie is at least partly a myth; because the differential impacts vary considerably depending on the utilization of services, not all services have the same effect on the budget neutrality adjustment. Second, when the cuts are being made within the same specialty family of services, the assumption is that physicians are not trading off services or that each has the same "value." There seems to be an assumption that utilization patterns or service choices are fixed, whereas in fact physicians do shift their utilization to more lucrative services. Although code reductions make both CMS and the committee look like they are enforcing the fixed-pie requirement, specialists can frequently redirect their work to services that have increased in value; presumably, physicians could also substitute similar codes when a code is removed or reduced.

The way in which losses are inconsequential is well illustrated in the following example, where 200 services saw reductions and 11 saw increases. The authors (one of whom served on the committee) show that the good news/bad news situation is mostly favorable, once you consider the frequency of using services along with changes in value. The net loss or gain is influenced by the utilization estimates, but the net gain or loss masks important trade-offs made among codes. On the one hand, the Society for Vascular Surgery said that there was a net gain of 0.5 percent (Zwolak and Trout 1997). The net impact masks substantial gains that the specialty reported to its members (Table 6.1), showing increases for some services as high as almost 45 percent and one with an increase of 39.9 percent, and the majority with increases above 15 to 30 percent. Therefore, society members would benefit from "substantially improved work RVUs of 11 commonly performed procedures" (Zwolak and Trout 1997, 1084). While 200 codes were cut, they were only cut by 3 percent. In this case, the cuts appear to have been small, but for many codes, the increases seemed significantly larger. Nevertheless, the outcome of the review was received cautiously: "Only the relatively high claims frequency of the 11 upgraded codes will prevent a substantial fiscal loss to the vascular surgeons as a result of this 5-year review process" (Zwolak and Trout 1997, 1084).

Physicians shift their practice to the services that "provide a more generous return, services that . . . are being paid less, physicians provide less of them; services that have higher margins, they provide more of them"

(Interview Subject 11). In theory, policy demands "payment neutrality and you don't necessarily make more money doing one procedure over another," but one interviewee who had researched physician responses to price changes believed the actuality was different: "Over the past decade, what we've seen is that there's been a great increase in some services relative to others. Imaging is one, various other diagnostic tests and so on and so forth. Some of that has to do with technology" (Interview Subject 11). This pattern influences primary care and specialty physicians differently: "The majority of what primary care physicians do is office visits." The interviewee acknowledged that "there are opportunities to increase or to alter the mix of services that [primary care physicians] provide," and that there was evidence imaging was an area practices had moved into, but he also noted that their ability to do this is "somewhat more constrained than a lot of specialists" (Interview Subject 11).

The assumption of equal impact is a significant flaw in the budget neutrality adjustment. The policy makers who created it assumed that it would affect all physicians equally, but if the services in question are specialized enough, large increases provide a net win for the specialty involved. The adjustment thus provides more gains to physicians who deliver services that are not widely provided, because budget neutrality may not be triggered for a small volume of services. Highly specialized services are more likely to be increased because they will not necessarily trigger the budget neutrality adjustment. A service used by all specialties is less likely to increase than one performed by a handful of physicians within one specialty. For subspecialties, the win can be great, even if the loss to Medicare program is small. Experts such as Bodenheimer, Berenson, and Rudolf (2007) note that small increases in office visit relative value units result in a large increase in total Medicare physician spending, which would trigger a budget neutrality adjustment. Yet "procedure increases are less contentious because no single procedure has sufficient volume to perceptibly increase total Medicare spending" (2007, 303). This important distinction gets lost in the platitudes of the committee working with a "fixed pie." However, in addition, the private sector can compensate for cuts to the values if they are made:

> *Interviewee:* Because if that's a net loss, or a net addition to a certain amount of work, then it's going to have to come from somewhere else. In the greater scheme of things, that's not so important because it's . . . there's a lot of other money that gets distributed based on these values as well.
> *Interviewer:* The private . . . private sector?
> *Interviewee:* That's commercial insurance. (Interview Subject 10)

How much budget neutrality acts as a constraint is ambiguous. Aggregate impacts (in percentage terms) on specialties are calculated every year based on the changes in the Final Rule. The analysis underlying these estimates is based on past utilization, but there is a lack of detail on how CMS makes its calculations and estimates. That, along with the inbuilt complexity of the committee process and the strategic selection of codes, makes scrutiny of budgetary impacts difficult.

Voting

After each presentation, committee members vote using electronic clickers. Observation of meetings for two years between 2010 and 2012 suggested that most codes passed. Lately, the committee has come under pressure to show that it does not "rubber stamp" recommendations.

For many years, information about the number of people voting and the number of people who supported or rejected a recommendation was tightly held by the AMA. Except when a staff member accidentally showed the tally (the author saw the vote tally flash on the presentation screen on one occasion), that tally was invisible to meeting participants—it was simply announced as having passed or failed. Under pressure for greater transparency, the Update Committee now releases data showing how many people voted and how many supported the society recommendations.

A quorum of 16 is needed for a vote to count, and there is a two-thirds favorable requirement for a work increase. Observation of meetings by the author suggests that few votes fail to meet the quorum, and this is confirmed by voting data from three meetings, which show almost 100 percent attendance—for only four votes out of 208 were any members absent (American Medical Association 2014). The only limitation of this count is that the total potentially includes votes that were held after the initial vote failed.

Views differ regarding whether voting members form voting blocs (an issue discussed in Chapter 5). Some participants are adamant that there are distinct voting blocs along specialty lines, others say the committee is an expert panel that makes decisions purely on merit, and still others contend there are blocs, but not everyone follows them consistently. One interviewee said that they disliked the "politics" and that they tried "to rise above it." "I try to do the right thing and vote my conscience." Some members had a reputation for being independent and "not afraid to be a maverick and break party lines" (Interview Subject 4).

Committee members generally see themselves as belonging to different subgroups, such as cognitive or surgical or procedural physicians. One description of the "cognitive" camp included neurology, psychiatry, pediatrics, internal medicine, and family practice or "people who basically are earning a living from seeing patients" (Interview Subject 5). The group described as surgeons includes thoracic, spine, ENT (ear, nose, and throat) and pediatric surgeons. In the middle are some specialties that are not aligned, including pathologists and dermatologists, and the Health Care Professionals Advisory Committee also is considered a swing voter (Interview Subject 5).

Specialty society members both lobby and are lobbied by their colleagues. Interviewees suggest there is a degree of "horse-trading," but they emphasize that horse-trading is too coarse a term—because the process of persuading voting members is subtle. "It wasn't beyond me to go up to somebody and say, 'Ah, you know, this code is coming up. I really think this is a fair number'" (Interview Subject 5). In any case, sometimes interviewees say positions taken reflect similar worldviews rather than blocs and that if the cognitive specialists are not successful, it is because they have not been willing to "spend the money," which refers to investment in staff and resources:

> Everybody else is reasonable. And when they look at the codes, they do so with honesty. But again, you see things through the eyes you have. The surgeons, they truly believe that surgery should be paid this much more. They truly believe that what they do is harder, and more important. And they work harder for it. And they should be paid more. And then don't forget, cognitive doctors are not as organized. They just have never been as organized. They've never been willing to spend the money. (Interview Subject 5)

The votes are by secret ballot, according to the AMA. However, some interviewees claim voting is not anonymous:

> *Interviewee:* So, here's the dirty secret: It's supposedly anonymous voting, it's up or down, give us the number. But everybody has a numbered ballot, right? And the AMA staff, they know. They know who votes which way. And at times . . . at key political times . . . information has been leaked. . . . About, you know, "Stop being so critical, you don't really know who your friends and enemies are." They'll tell you, the AMA will tell you, that they don't vote in blocs, and I don't believe that. I don't believe that for a second.

Interviewer: They . . . [the AMA] they say that they have analyzed the data [showing there is no bloc voting].

Interviewee: I don't believe it for a second. (Interview Subject 4)

Postfacilitation and Reconsideration

When a society's recommendation fails to get a two-thirds majority (required if a code is increasing), the chair usually gives the society some options, including resubmitting or resurveying the code. The chair can also ask for recommended relative value unit recommendations from each of the committee members present via paper ballot. Each voting member writes down his or her recommended relative work value on a piece of paper. Some people are critical of this approach, because it averages the opinion of each committee member's suggested work value: "There's a near-complete abandonment of any kind of scientific guise for the proceedings. There is no way to know how members arrive at these figures. So when the initial 'ask' is rejected, the specialty society can just count up the votes it will get at each relative value unit valuation and make its next request accordingly. RUC composition and internal politics therefore dominate all other concerns on resubmission" (Anonymous observer notes, 2008).

After a failed vote, societies have the option of a postfacilitation meeting to review their recommendation. The goal of the postfacilitation meetings, according to the AMA, is to "reach consensus." Postfacilitation meetings are held between meeting sessions and allow committee members to ask questions about the service and discuss how the society can best explain how that service works. In postfacilitation meetings observed by the author, the facilitation committee members discussed the arguments in favor of the value the society had recommended and the data the society was presenting. Facilitation committee members generally worked cooperatively and tried to help the societies to justify their argument and at times debated whether a different relative value unit request would be appropriate. In some cases, the discussion centered on what kind of recommendation would be likely to pass muster. At one facilitation meeting, the author observed a discussion about whether the relative value unit should be a rounded number or set at a .99 level. One facilitation committee member believed it would be better to have a number just below a round number (Author meeting notes 2012). But respondents generally agreed that the facilitation process was helpful:

[Post] facilitation is where the chair has said the society needs help because the RUC can't come to a decision or there's a failure to obtain agreement. And it's not quite a time-out, but facilitation is sort of a time-out where, you haven't done your job, you haven't gotten a recommendation through, and you're going to try to sort it out. Not necessarily of your own volition. Facilitation is not necessarily something you want to have to go to, because it means you're having problems with your recommendations. (Interview Subject 6)

According to one participant, at these meetings, "you just, fight it out for what's going to . . . what's going to happen. And, usually there's some compromise" (Interview Subject 7). The committee presents a brief report of the meeting to the larger committee, and then members vote again. These meetings can entail clarification, as voting members develop a better understanding of the specialty's work and the code in question:

It forces you to make some tough decisions in that hour. Either sink or swim. And you have to decide whether you're going to compromise and kind of accept what they suggest. Do I think it works well? I'm not sure that the work process is evidence based at all. So what it certainly does is it forces people, and they use the term, to think very quickly on their feet, to make some very quick decisions, that, do they think the numbers work, or do they think the numbers don't work. And you support the suggestions, or can you live with what's being suggested? Or can't you live with it? And, there are some people—you know there are people who will tell you that when you come out of facilitation, no one's happy. And I have a personal philosophy that is that if no one is happy coming out of a negotiation then you did a good job. (Interview Subject 3)

Postfacilitation is not necessarily perceived positively: "There's some horse-trading, and usually the horse-trading is not particularly . . . I want to say beneficial to the society—that's not the right way to say it. Usually it doesn't tend to work out in the society's favor" (Interview Subject 6).

Services that are not accepted in the first round and end up in postfacilitation are generally higher than those accepted. The codes reviewed by postfacilitation committees had an average unit level of 4.65 compared to a mean work relative value unit of 3.77 for codes that were not reviewed by postfacilitation committees. Once the process is completed, the facilitation committee sends codes back to the committee. After facilitation, the average committee-recommended work relative value was 4.59 for those not sent to facilitation and 4.60 for those that were. At least for the final vote, postfacilitation seems to also result in greater consensus among the committee members: a simple bivariate regression shows that for those codes that were sent to postfacilitation, there was a statistically significant increase (significant at the 0.001 level) in the number of "yes" votes for those codes, suggesting that the process does lead to greater consensus by the time the final vote is held (American Medical Association 2014).

When the societies return to the committee after facilitation, they need to win its support to get the code passed, and it may help if they show some deference to the postfacilitation committee and its input. According to one interviewee, a society will thank the members for their feedback and say they will propose a different value from the one they proposed initially.

Postmeeting: The Rulemaking Process

The Update Committee submits recommendations to CMS after its meetings. Each November, CMS publishes in the *Federal Register* a Final Rule with new fee schedule relative values for implementation on January 1. In the Final Rule, CMS provides the rationale for its decisions and usually includes a discussion for each Update Committee recommendation or group of similar recommendations. The agency may also reference evidence presented by the specialty society at the committee meeting, society data, and/or comparisons to reference codes.

An analysis of committee work relative value unit recommendations and CMS decisions for the period between 1994 and 2010 by Laugesen, Wada, and Chen (2012) showed that CMS accepted 2,419 (87.4 percent) of the 2,768 work values proposed by the Update Committee. CMS decreased 298 work values (10.8 percent) and increased 51 (1.8 percent). Similarly, a subsequent analysis for the period from 1993 to 2012 comparing whether relative value units were the same or greater showed that in 93 percent of codes, CMS matched or increased the value of work recommendations made by the committee (Hirsch et al. 2014). On average, recommended work values were higher than those of CMS values, and this difference was statistically significant (Laugesen, Wada, and Chen 2012). The difference between the committee's recommended work values and CMS's work values was greatest for surgical services and smallest for pathology and laboratory services.

The fee schedule values are implemented almost immediately, on January 1, as published, but societies have an opportunity to request changes in the values in the next cycle, which would be the following fall. Despite being called a Final Rule, CMS describes work relative value units as "interim." Therefore, specialty societies have an opportunity to question the work values published in the rule. While physician groups and others can send comments on the work values, CMS says it will only review information pertaining to "the clinical aspects" of the physician work associated with it.

If CMS believes the request for review is warranted, the agency refers the request to a "refinement" panel. Refinement panels usually have eight to 10 physicians from the specialty performing the service, other related specialties, primary care physicians, and medical directors who work for Medicare contractors. CMS officials say that societies tend to use the refinement process to object to situations where CMS disagreed with a committee recommendation and sometimes simply repeat information that was presented or decided by the committee (Centers for Medicare & Medicaid Services 2012).

Historically, refinement panel recommendations were based on an F-test of variance in panel ratings, but the agency changed this approach in 2012 because panel members would simply recommend a previously discussed value instead of a new unique value. After 2012, refinement panel recommendations were based on the median work values from all panel members. Unless CMS decides it needs more time to review the code, the agency typically publishes its response to the comment the following fall. At that point, the CMS decision is final.

Publicly available evidence from specialty society documents and articles over the past decade confirms the tendency for codes to increase as a result of refinement. Specialty societies have traditionally viewed the refinement panels as arenas where they can exert influence (Allen 2006). As one society remarked, "You might look at this as an appeal process" (American Society of Anesthesiologists 2014, 2), and some specialty societies report that they are able to persuade CMS to change the unit values (Congress of Neurological Surgeons 2009). Even if CMS does not follow the society-requested recommendation and does not match the original committee recommendation, the value is still typically higher than the pre-review payment level (Society of Vascular Surgeons 2013).

Specialty societies can also seek to change work values when they go through the five-yearly or misvalued code review processes, which have proposed values published. When there is a Proposed Rule, specialties have the option of commenting on the decision to CMS directly after the Proposed Rule is published. In 2006, a Proposed Rule would have cut orthopedic procedures, but the American Association of Orthopedists countered the move:

> Orthopaedists joined for another successful political mission in 2006. In June 2006, as part of the current five year review, CMS proposed to cut work RVUs for total hip arthroplasty by 21%, work RVUs for total knee arthroplasty by 10%, and work RVUs for hip fracture treatment by 18%. The orthopaedic community unified under the leadership of the nonpartisan Orthopaedic Political Action Committee, worked together, and presented data driven arguments to CMS. On November 1, 2006, CMS announced that would not implement these reimbursement cuts. This victory underscores the importance of an orthopaedic political presence in Washington. (Hariri et al. 2007, 244)

CMS's annual process raised concerns among legislators, because of a lack of opportunity for the public to comment on Proposed Rules outside of the committee process until the publication of the Final Rule in November, and the fee schedule is introduced on January 1 every year. Agencies have the discretion to issue Final Rules if there is a good reason to do so (in this case, to allow immediate implementation into the fee schedule). If people comment on the valuations, the changes would not take effect for one year. In April 2014, House Democrats argued in a letter to CMS that the practice lacked transparency and that CMS should issue Proposed Rules before introducing revised work values (Levin et al. 2014). As a result of the letter, CMS changed its practice in 2014 and said it would issue Proposed and Final Rules.

Conclusion

The RBRVS was introduced as part of the Omnibus Budget Reconciliation Act (OBRA) of 1989, which created a national fee schedule to replace a system whereby pricing decisions were determined by the organizations processing claims, rather than by a consistent set of rates. The creation of the RBRVS involved establishing a brand-new administered price system that required expert judgment to ensure relativity for thousands of services. The AMA brought the House of Medicine together and created the Update

Committee, which now has 30 members. Since the RBRVS was established, the House of Medicine has played an important role in determining the relative value units used in the Medicare fee schedule. The committee has developed a comprehensive set of rules and processes that are designed, at least in theory, to standardize and formalize the process.

The process by which recommendations are made to the government based on specialty society recommendations is complex. The committee is charged with developing work values for new services and revising existing services, but billing codes are the starting point for much of its work. There is extensive premeeting preparation, including a process for pre-review where societies get feedback on their recommendations. At meetings, around the U-shaped arrangement are more than 100 specialty society members who sit before the committee and present their proposals for work values. Another committee of other health professionals reviews codes pertinent to their members and presents proposals before the committee. Specialty societies make presentations to the committee, and the response to presentations can be highly negative at times, and at other times the Update Committee almost "rubber stamps" the proposals. There is some evidence of voting blocs as well as premeeting lobbying to ensure that a society's recommendation goes through. The process allows some leeway, however, because if a proposal fails, a small committee negotiates a revised value, and it is put back to the committee for a vote.

A variety of ad hoc and standing working groups and subcommittees address specific issues. Facilitation committees help broker solutions, when the committee has failed to agree on a society proposal, or before the presentation, if the service is challenging to explain or there are large numbers of codes. In this case, a society needs to get input before the presentation to help structure the rationale for its proposal.

Much emphasis in this process is put on survey data and justifications that relate survey findings logically to other codes and show that the work value should be changed or maintained. Presentations are opportunities for the societies to provide interpretations of their survey data in relation to the codes they are comparing the service to, from which societies make recommendations. Some people say the committee provides an effective way to evaluate work; others disagree and say that voting blocs and alliances reduce its credibility as an independent expert body.

Interviewees hold contradictory views of how rigorous the committee process is. Rigor is difficult to measure quantitatively because of the multiple stages in the process and the lack of long-term data. Committee processes are more transparent today than in the past, however. Increasing scrutiny of the process generates more effort by the organization to challenge (or seem to be challenging) specialty society recommendations. On the other hand, it is possible that societies modulate their requests to meet the expectations of the Update Committee.

FIVE

Conflicts of Interest and Problems of Evidence

FROM THE VERY beginning, the RBRVS "was wrapped in the imagery of science, technical proficiency, and objectivity" (Oberlander 2003, 128). That reflected, in part, the conscientious efforts made by William Hsiao and his colleagues to study resource-based inputs using transparent and well-documented methods to sample, collect, and analyze the data. Since its creation, the Update Committee has developed ways to estimate work, based on Hsiao's model of expert judgment and consensus panels of physicians as its template, although this chapter shows that its approach differs.

The one thing that people usually know about the committee, if they know about it, is that medical societies hold voting seats. At face value, the claim that there is a potential conflict of interest seems to make sense. The organization has two main responses to this charge and what it calls other misperceptions about its process. The committee has recast itself not as a body of representatives but as a panel of experts that relies on evidence-based decision making. Second, the committee stresses that it has no incentive to overestimate physician work values, because increases are cancelled out by the zero-sum nature of the process.

This chapter assesses whether the committee is an expert panel. Having a better understanding of the roles of members and their relationships to specialty societies that they serve is essential for determining whether they are experts or advocates. The view of the committee as an expert objective panel does not find credible support when we examine how members represent their societies and the extent to which they are autonomous individuals or society representatives. The efforts to validate committee time estimates and the documented problems with their estimates are reviewed based on available sources. This is followed by a discussion of the potential causes of the committee's tendency to overvalue and increase (rather than decrease) work values. Previous research has touched on some of these questions regarding why this occurs, especially relating to the quality of the data used to make decisions, but a deeper understanding of why the committee's estimates are flawed is necessary.

Three explanations or causes of inaccurate work values are identified. First, the committee's claims that it is a panel of experts cannot be substantiated. Evidence of how committee members are linked to their specialty societies and how decisions can and are affected by their affiliations demonstrates that their claim of independence is not as credible as it first appears. Committee panel members are too embedded in their societies that both objective and subjective factors weigh against considering them impartial judges of physician work. Second, there are methodological issues with the data and surveys used by the committee. The committee has developed its own rules of evidence and uses surveys that rely on apparently poor sampling methods and thus are subject to biases. Third, using evidence from the scholarship on research methods and cognitive psychology, the problem of inaccurate estimates may potentially be explained by biases and group effects observed by psychologists and behavioral economists in other settings. Combined, these explanations contradict the Update Committee's claim of scientific rigor and independent evaluations, as well as point to the underlying causes.

Problems in the Estimation of Work, Time, and Intensity

Many organizations have raised the alarm regarding potentially overvalued services and repeatedly recommended that CMS change its approach to valuing services. Multiple reports were completed by Nancy McCall, Jerry Cromwell, and other research teams at various points starting as early as 2001 for the Department of Health and Human Services and the Medicare Payment Advisory Commission. These investigations showed that committee survey times were "systematically different, and typically higher, than the times measured by the original Harvard study" (McCall et al. 2001, ES-2). Compared to the average times recorded in the logs of surgical operating rooms, the researchers found that Medicare times (which largely are based on specialty survey time estimates) exceeded actual times by a few minutes to almost two hours. Around half of the procedures exceeded the actual times by 30 minutes or more (McCall et al. 2001, ES-7). Time estimates for some longer office visits were excessive compared to the actual times spent with patients, given that more than one-quarter of all office-based CPT consultations billed to Medicare by general and orthopedic surgeons and two-thirds of cardiologist consultations coded by these physicians were 60 minutes or more. This billing pattern is not supported by the National Ambulatory Medical Care Survey, which showed there are relatively few visits over 40 minutes. Likewise, the researchers suggested that medical and surgical specialties also appear to consistently bill Medicare using CPT codes based on 25 minutes when 20 minutes would be more likely for these visits (McCall et al. 2001, ES-5).

These findings created an interest in understanding why there were time discrepancies, and some of those efforts critiqued the committee's method at a time when primary care physicians were beginning to agitate about what they described as a specialty bias on the committee. Both of these factors likely culminated in changes later included in the ACA. The committee itself responded by reviewing services that were "potentially misvalued" and changed its minimum response size from 30 physicians to 50 (for high-volume services) in 2014.

Physician work represents both time and intensity, and there is the possibility for errors in either of these components. Most efforts to assess the accuracy of work values have focused on time estimates rather than intensity errors, since time is more easily compared to measurable data. It is particularly difficult to estimate intensity across services, and one respondent said while the committee had done a "pretty good job," it had much work to do on this issue (Interview Subject 18).

Accurate physician time estimates are important, because time is usually the largest component of the work value. If physician time is overestimated, the fee is likely to be too high. Due to the availability of data, much of the existing research on physician times focuses only on time in the operating room (typically derived from surgical logs), as well as national surveys that collect data on the length of office visits. While some researchers suggest physician times estimated by the update committee are accurate or even underestimated (Krupinski et al. 2015, 5; Little et al. 2006), the preponderance of studies comparing committee-recommended time values with real-world surgical logs find that actual operating times are shorter than committee-estimated times; in short, physicians provide services more quickly than the committee has estimated. For some services, the time estimates of physician work have not changed since the original Harvard study was completed. In other cases, it appears that societies have successfully increased the times estimated by Harvard. One study found that intraservice time estimates (the time spent with the patient) for the same services are approximately 14 percent higher than those measured by Harvard, while total service times are 20 percent higher (Cox et al. 2007, 11). Over the last decade, a degree of consensus has developed that RBRVS time data are flawed (Braun and McCall 2011a; Cromwell et al. 2010; Maxwell, Zuckerman, and Berenson 2007; McCall, Cromwell, and Braun 2006; Medicare Payment Advisory Commission 2011, 13). In response to these studies, the Update Committee has reviewed physician times identified for some services, but fee schedule times still remain higher than actual times. Table 5.1 shows the percentage difference between Cromwell and colleagues' actual operating room times and physician times estimated by the committee and in use in the 2013 fee schedule. Fee schedule times (which, as said, are based on update committee time estimates) remain higher than actual times. For most procedures studied, time estimates that form the basis for payments used by Medicare substantially exceeded observed times.

One study tested the hypothesis that higher work units predict longer operative time across a variety of procedures, which is what we would expect if the units were accurate. However, researchers found that units did not predict variability across services in recorded times. Only 15.6 percent of the differences in operative times were explained by variance in relative value units (Nguyen et al. 2012). A study completed in 2015 for CMS reinforced earlier findings, even though researchers used a different method to estimate times. Researchers found that for 83 percent of the procedures, the times they estimated were longer than the fee schedule times. They found that the greatest differences occurred for procedures performed on patients outside the hospital and without anesthesia, where the valuation was off by 20 percent, whereas inpatient procedures were only 6 percent overestimated, on average. Some substantial discrepancies were found. Medicare's fee for colonoscopy, for example, assumes it takes 51.5 minutes to perform a colonoscopy, but researchers found that it takes 16.9 minutes (Wynn et al. 2015, 141,158).

To be sure, the update committee has acknowledged such problems, especially in recent years, and has been revising time estimates for a number of services. Yet, at the time of writing, it remains unclear as to whether ef-

TABLE 5.1 Percentage Time Differences between Medicare and Observed
Times for Selected Procedures, 2013

Procedure	Percent greater than times recorded in operating theaters
Deviated septum surgery	127
Transurethral resection prostate	92
Upper gastrointestinal endoscopy, with biopsy	88
Radical abdominal hysterectomy	74
Cataract removal	63
Hip replacement revision	57
Neuroplasty	56
Laparoscopic cholecystectomy	45
Bronchoscopy	36
Implant pacemaker	36
Lung removal	34
Cystourethroscopy	30
Aneurysm repair	30
Carotid artery endarterectomy	29
Abdominal hysterectomy	21
Craniectomy	15
Colectomy	7
Dilatation and curettage	5
Knee replacement	2
Total hip arthroplasty	1
Coronary artery bypass	0
Breast reduction surgery	−16
Upper gastrointestinal endoscopy	−17
Vaginal hysterectomy	−24

forts to make the times more realistic have translated into changes in physician work times.

If times are overstated, there is also the possibility that other components of physician work might be overstated—such as estimates of higher levels of difficulty and case complexity (also called service intensity). Some of the assumptions made by the Update Committee are in line with received wisdom about health care services, such as that services provided in a hospital are likely to require more work, or that patients of greater age justify higher work values. However, some research has found that the factors that we would expect to be related to work difficulty do not track relative value units on average. For example, factors such as the age of the patients receiving the service may be less important than is often claimed: "The total work was also similar for visits with patients in different age groups: 40 or younger, 41 to 64, 65 to 74, and 75 years of age or older" (Lasker and Marquis 1999, 341). Furthermore, "among interventional cases, no correlation existed between ranked RVU value and case duration, radiation dose, or adverse event probability" (Lasker and Marquis 1999, 340).

Services considered risky because of high complication or mortality rates would be expected to have higher relative value units. For services with high relative value units there is a degree of consistency and a stronger relationship between complication and mortality rates and relative value units than the other characteristics mentioned. For services with low- to mid-value units, unit levels are not consistently associated with differences in factors such as median length of stay and median operative time for services, where we would not expect such variations (Shah et al. 2014). Relative value units do not correlate with certain metrics of surgeon work while moderately correlating with others (Shah et al. 2014). In the area of pediatrics, some of the most technically challenging procedures are paid the same as a short and more straightforward service (Bergersen et al. 2013, 258). This reinforces critics' perceptions that reimbursement is more off-kilter for services that are shorter in minutes.

Indeed, as more research emerges, the evidence suggests that the committee is not necessarily always wrong for all services, but that mismatched physician work estimates of time and intensity are not distributed uniformly across primary care physicians and specialists or different kinds of physician work. Committee time estimates for procedural and surgical services are likely more inaccurate than they are for other services (McCall, Cromwell, and Braun 2006), whereas time estimates made by the committee for office visits are more similar to times measured in actual office visits. However, that is only true for primary care providers: specialist visits are shorter and therefore are further from the committee's time estimates (McCall, Cromwell, and Braun 2006). This suggests that there is a bigger gap between estimated and real-world times for surgical and procedural services and specialty office visits.

Findings such as these lend support for claims that the committee is more likely to overvalue surgical and procedural services and, to a lesser extent, the work of medical specialties. Like time, estimates of physician "difficulty" depend largely on self-reported estimates. Indeed, the issue of relativity between services has been a concern of physician groups whose members spend most of their time engaged in face-to-face visits with patients and providing "evaluation and management" services—for example, services such as care for patients with Alzheimer's disease who require complex processes of care (Brunt 2011, 839).

The fact that surgical and procedural services are prone to have time estimates that are too generous raises questions about the relativity of the payments made for different kinds of services in the RBRVS. Overstated time estimates provide additional advantages to physicians that perpetuate primary-specialty fee differentials. The benefits accruing to physicians providing some surgical and imaging services are compounded because many of these services can be provided together or repeatedly on the same day, such as imaging studies of different but related body parts, which previously were paid separately. The GAO drew attention to the time and other efficiencies when physicians furnish multiple services for the same patient on the same day (United States General Accountability Office 2009). Changes in recent years to both reduce payments for so-called same-day services or services provided together have tried to address this.

Sometimes inaccurate times also develop because the estimates are simply out of date. Times that were estimated long ago are likely less accurate and therefore overcompensate physicians providing those services. Among many surgical and procedural services, service times fall the longer the procedure has been in use, because physicians become more familiar with the service, and also small efficiencies are gained as the technology itself may be improved (Medicare Payment Advisory Commission 2006b). At the same time, the fact that times are outdated has not led to reviews of those services, at least until CMS began looking at the issue more closely. If there were better methods of monitoring service times and physician work differences, that would be helpful, but unfortunately, specialty societies often resist reviewing services that that are generously compensated because they are based on historical time data, as shown in Chapter 6.

Advocates or Experts?

The problems described above lead to overpayment of physician services. When payments are higher than might otherwise be justified, it is understandable that the most persistent criticism of the committee is that physicians have an incentive to increase the value of services for their own specialties and, more generally, have a fundamental conflict of interest.

Even interviewees who speak favorably about the committee admit that there is no question that every society is looking for advantages.

Skepticism regarding the committee's ability to impartially value physician work is countered by members who argue that voting members (not the Advisory Committee) are members of an expert panel rather than a committee of organizational representatives. They argue that its function as an expert panel allows it to successfully avoid the perception of a conflict of interest. Indeed, over the past decade or so, rules have changed, and some of the past specialty-oriented habits have been discarded. Update Committee members do not present services to their colleagues or vote on their own specialty society services—that role is taken by Advisory Committee members. Granted, they may belong to the same specialty society, but members point to the fact that the panel is tough on specialty societies. On the other hand, Advisory Committee members do serve on committees such as facilitation committees, and are sometimes counted by the leadership as part of the "expertise" of more than 100 specialty organizations, even though these members openly serve as advocates for their specialty organizations.

The committee's self-designation as an expert panel is less credible if its mission and goals are examined. It was created by specialty societies for specialty societies. From the start, the committee has claimed that it gives the House of Medicine the means for specialties to influence government policy and a body that "provide[s] a unique and valuable forum for specialties to work together to affect Medicare payment policies" (American Medical Association Board of Trustees 1999, 41). A review of the committee for the AMA Board of Trustees in 2001 described the committee as also representing "organized medicine well in the countless number of days spent preparing, attending, and participating in meetings to ensure a fair review of material presented by specialty societies" (American Medical Association Board of Trustees 2001, 1). In the AMA organization, the committee formally sits inside AMA's larger political and advocacy program, as evidenced by the fact that its funding is allocated under the category of "advocacy" in the AMA's budget. At committee meetings, there is the opportunity for specialty societies to be brought up to speed on larger policy and political issues. The AMA's lobbyist from Washington, DC, typically provides a keynote presentation, although this is only a small portion of the overall meeting time.

In the following, other evidence is reviewed showing that the committee's members clearly serve as representatives of their specialty society. The argument of objectivity and independence therefore falters, based on the information presented. Coalitions among members challenge the idea that they are autonomous experts with no political or specialty goals. Finally, members cooperate through a détente and essentially quid pro quo arrangement, whereby societies work together on code presentations. Evidence of commensurate opportunities to reduce the codes of other societies is lacking; instead, some evidence suggests that societies avoid calling out overvalued codes.

Representatives or Individuals?

The committee's official name is the Specialty Society Relative Value Update Committee, and its bylaws explicitly refer to its members as representatives of specialty societies. The committee is composed entirely of physicians who belong and sit at the table by virtue of their association with a specialty society or are appointed by the AMA. Members are not autonomous physicians acting as free agents or attending their meeting under the auspices of their employers, such as academic medical centers. In comparing the Update Committee to the coding or CPT committee, one society said that, unlike the "CPT® Editorial Panel, which has no designated seats for specific specialties, the RUC does have seats for the major specialty organizations" (American College of Radiology 2016).

One illustration of members' representational role is that for many years, until more critical scrutiny was directed towards the committee, committee members sat behind cards with their specialty organization's name displayed. More important, members were permitted to present codes from their society to their colleagues, and members viewed their role as serving their specialty society: "Overall our success in defending the values for our services was excellent" and, with regard to the 2007 five-year review, "values of major services successfully defended" (Allen 2006).

Policies were revised after the Medicare Payment Advisory Commission published a report critical of CMS's reliance on the Update Committee's recommendations in 2006. The committee made some changes to its rules in October 2006 so that voting specialty society representatives could no longer present on behalf of their society. The official committee policy dating from 2006 is that committee members are not supposed to "advocate" for their specialty. According to a committee document published by a specialty society, committee members are not allowed to be involved in surveying or serving as a reviewer of an issue that affects their specialty (American Academy of Orthopedic Surgeons 2013, 309).

After the removal of official society labels, a former chair of the committee would tell members at the beginning of the meetings to metaphorically take off their specialty hat and "put on their RUC hat." The author was told by several interviewees and by a former chair that at one point, the committee also distributed hats with "RUC" prominently emblazoned on them.

Changes to rules such as disallowing members to vote on their own services and possible changes in the culture of the committee suggest that the more visible accoutrements of specialty representation have shifted over time. Yet, the interlocking and deeply embedded relationships between specialty societies and committee members remain. It is not possible, from a practical standpoint, to delineate update committee members from their role as society members, beginning with financial ties. Their travel to meetings is paid for by their societies (understandably it would likely be unattractive for individuals unless they had financial support from the specialty societies). Some committee members also say they receive stipends from their specialty societies (Kerber et al. 2014). Others privately indicated to the author that they received generous travel per diem payments but declined to give on-record numbers. However, one society stated that its per diem reimbursement totals $9,000 per meeting (Burtless and Milusheva 2013) or $3,000 per day for a three-day meeting. A similar amount was mentioned by the American Academy of Dermatology, which debated paying a stipend (plus travel expenses) of $2,500 per day for attendance at meetings and other meeting-related activities. The society decided not to, at least partly, because it would need to also compensate other officers of the organization (American Academy of Dermatology 2010).

Financial support of Update Committee and Advisory Committee members is an irrefutable indicator of society sponsorship that reflects the importance of the process to each society and its members. Specialty societies describe their participation in the coding and reimbursement process as essential for the health of the specialty and necessary to improve the economic position of its members. Even when societies are not presenting code changes at the Update Committee, the society will send representatives. There are tangible benefits to the society in engaging in the process. When there is a favorable change in a work or practice expense value for a code, most organizations will readily take the credit as a way to show the effectiveness of the organization to members. Newsletters, reports, society annual reports, and reports of board meetings reveal societies' efforts and involvement in the Update Committee's activities.[1]

Another indicator of the representative, rather than expert, role played by Update Committee and Advisory Committee members is that members are closely connected to the internal leadership structure of a specialty society. Typically, they serve on or chair a coding, reimbursement, or economic issues committee that comprises society members who are usually full-time practicing clinicians—for example, the American College of Surgeons. In teleconferences and in-person meetings, reimbursement committee members discuss what codes are going to be presented to the CPT committee and also, if they are approved by the CPT committee, "how we're going to survey the codes and then present to the RUC" (Interview Subject 9). Some societies have consolidated their coding and RBRVS update functions within one committee to coordinate, expand, and support the combined activities (Bean 2000). Coding and reimbursement committees, depending on the size of the society, may also have staff support on a day-to-day basis. The American College of Radiology has a 22-member Coding and Nomenclature Committee, supported by a staff team that works on economic issues.

Update Committee members serving on these committees are at least aware, if not directly involved, in the larger advocacy agenda surrounding coding and reimbursement issues. Naturally, such committees are central to societies' government relations and reimbursement policy strategy, and committees coordinate with their government affairs unit, or government affairs staff may oversee update issues.[2] The American Association of Neurological Surgery/Congress on Neurological Surgeons, for example, has a Coding and Reimbursement Committee and a budget for specialty society participation in the update and CPT processes, which is coordinated with the Washington Committee (Bean 2000). Sometimes societies try to strengthen the links between their coding and reimbursement activities and their government relations work (Society of Nuclear Medicine 2010a).[3]

If having a society seat on the Update Committee has little value due to the fact that members cannot vote on their own codes, the eagerness on the part of societies to be part of the process suggests that overall it is advantageous for the society to be represented. Every specialty society appointed to the original Update Committee in 1991 has maintained its voting seat, and new seats have been added. There are continuing calls by some societies to increase the number of cognitively based specialties with voting privileges. If offered a seat, a society would be unlikely to decline the offer. The number of organizations represented on the Advisory Committee also has grown. Even the smallest societies that do not serve on the Update Committee (but are members of the Advisory Committee) benefit from participating in the process. And in recent years, greater scrutiny of the committee by government agencies may have increased the value of having representation on the committee, after greater attention was given to misvalued codes:

- SNM [Society of Nuclear Medicine] is considered to be an expert in the area of coding and reimbursement for nuclear medicine not only by our members, but by other specialty societies, CMS, AMA (including CPT and RUC).
- Based on increased pressure from government agencies, AMA and RUC have significantly increased the review and revaluation of current CPT codes. Similar to what happened with the myocardial perfusion imaging (MPI) codes another series of high volume nuclear medicine procedures will be sent back to specialty societies for review and bundling or resurveying. By having a seat at the table, SNM is able to give a much better review of our own codes, (and not only influence but lead these activities) as opposed to other societies who would otherwise be responsible for our codes but whose expertise lies in other areas. (Society of Nuclear Medicine 2010c, 56)

This quote illustrates how the delineation of roles for smaller sub-specialty societies is significant. Yet it also shows that the separation of societies from one another is not necessarily clear when there are sub-specialties and specialty organizations that are connected to one another. Update Committee members and others serve overlapping roles, such as serving on related but independent specialty organizations. Therefore, they can be involved in subspecialty organizations even if they are not officially representing them as members on the Update Committee. The following is from an announcement of a webinar:

And don't miss this opportunity to hear from James Blankenship, MD, MACC, FSCAI, who serves as Cardiology's RUC Panel representative and will present our spotlight topic: "The RUC Process, the RUC Survey and the Benefits of Coalition Building." Dr. Blankenship will describe and take your questions about the impact of the RUC on you and your practice, why your participation in the process is essential, and how SCAI [Society for Cardiovascular Angiography and Interventions], ACC [American College of Cardiology], and HRS [Heart Rhythm Society] band together and engage other[s] in our efforts to protect the values for the services and procedures you provide to your patients. (Society for Cardiovascular Angiography and Interventions 2012)

In this example the Update Committee member is advising the members of a related specialty society. Typically, update committee members serve on their own society coding and reimbursement committees before beginning as an advisor or alternate member. The complexity of the process means societies need to groom people to serve, as it takes a long time to be proficient. As one specialty society put it, specialty societies need to have a long-term strategy for recruiting representatives, which often involves bringing people in the society up to speed on the process so that there is a pool of potential representatives (American Academy of Dermatology 2011).

There are many examples of overlapping roles indicative of a high level of engagement in the specialty societies by Advisory and Update Committee members. Both kinds of members serve on committees that are closely involved in advocacy activities on behalf of the specialty. By virtue of belonging both to a society's coding and reimbursement committee and to the Update Committee, they have a role in advocacy for their specialty. Some are even employed by the organization they represent: For a period when she was chair of the Update Committee, Barbara S. Levy also served as a staffer and vice president of health policy at the American College of Obstetricians and Surgeons involved in "federal and state legislative policy and regulatory affairs" (American College of Obstetricians and Gynecologists 2014). One interviewee said, "It's not like she's independent. She's the Washington lobbyist for a physician group" (Interview Subject 22).

A representative for the American College of Radiology held various positions simultaneously during his service in 2006 (chair of the society's Diagnostic Carrier Advisory Committee Network, vice chair of the Commission on Economics) (Allen 2006). And due to the nature of sub-specialty medicine, some are actively involved in other societies that are closely related to their specialty or one of the organizations under a larger specialty parent organization.

After completing their service, members often assume prominent leadership roles in specialty societies, signifying the appreciation of their service, the esteem with which former members are held in their societies, and the importance of coding and reimbursement issues in specialty societies' missions. As one interviewee put it, "In most cases becoming the RUC guy in your specialty society is the pinnacle of your—and should be—the pinnacle of your career. You've been honored by your colleagues with your . . . you know, of the surgeon or of urologists, that you're at the top of your profession to be representing this group, and it's exciting and great and they should be very proud of themselves" (Interview Subject 22). For example, an American College of Radiology representative was a former chair of the specialty's Commission on Economics. After stepping down from the Update Committee, he was the vice chair of the American College of Radiology Board of Chancellors, chair of its political action committee (RADPAC), and a member of the American College of Radiology Budget and Finance Committee (American College of Radiology 2012). A representative of the American College of Radiology in 2014 served in 11 committee or leadership roles in the organization during his tenure on the Update Committee, including chairing its Reimbursement Committee and acting as vice chair of the society's Commission on Economics; he also served in a variety of leadership roles in a subspecialty society and a state medical society (American College of Radiology 2014). Another representative of the Society of Vascular Surgeons subsequently served as second vice president.

Specialty Society Coordination and Coalitions

Many members say that they approach their work on the Update Committee using impartial judgment and rigor and, above all, independence. Some members believe the committee members are fair:

> There is a perception that somehow being at the table, being on the panel makes, makes it easier to get your coding proposals through. And I would say that the panel is an equal opportunity torturer. They use the same degree of due diligence in evaluating any proposal. (Interview Subject 3)

Others, however, state candidly that their specialty codes would be adequately or highly valued only if they had supporters, which was changing as the atmosphere became more sensitive to primary care physicians. In a presentation to his colleagues, a representative discussing the future of reimbursement said the American College of Radiology faced a major challenge keeping its codes valued favorably. He said that "increases in utilization of MRI [magnetic resonance imaging] and CT [computed tomography] have put radiology squarely in the cross-hairs." The specialty could not count on the support of other societies because "radiology has no friends." Furthermore, "new alliances are forming at RUC" and the Update Committee has a "distinct leaning toward primary care physicians" (Allen 2006).

The importance of having "friends" goes to the core of the question of how impartial the committee is, although some might argue that friends agree because they tend to share similar views. Regardless of the motivation, however, it is clear that specialty societies have alliances, and voting members hint that many decisions are made outside of the committee process. One interviewee said that coalitions occurred through the mid to even late 1990s and that surgical specialists would meet at the ACS before the meeting: "They would review each and every single code, and their language was, 'Okay, how are we going to vote the bloc?' And they participated in bloc voting" (Interview Subject 4). The tendency to form alliances is not restricted to surgical or procedural organizations, however. The nonsurgical societies also organized their own meetings, and one interviewee described their success as owing to "similar organizational meetings in anticipation of the third five-year review" (Interview Subject 4).

Others say that voting blocs are rumored but unlikely. When asked whether there are different blocs, one member explained it more as an issue of familiarity or a comfort level that drives some kinds of organizations to support each other:

> I don't know there's ever been an official bloc. I think the surgeons tend to . . . to support themselves with the codes come up. Although that's not always true. I've seen some of the surgeons, you know, turn on their colleagues when the codes that are presented are way too high and tell them that, you know, they need to be lowered. But as far as I know there's no official bloc voting. But the surgeons tend to support each other and the . . . the cognitive physicians tend to support each other as well. And that may be a familiarity thing. Surgeons are more familiar with surgical codes than they are with the E&M codes. (Interview Subject 9)

Acknowledging that the AMA had worked hard to deny claims of collaboration, one interviewee also said that enough people "either participated in the process or inadvertently overheard parts of that process acknowledge and verify the veracity of that." By the time Barbara Levy became chair, "the AMA exerted significant pressure to stop those meetings because . . . they gave the appearance of bloc voting and cartel behavior. But the reality is, it was too threatening to the surgeons" (Interview Subject 4).

Others believe the divisions are not about specialists versus primary care, given there are "pathologists and radiologists and others who . . . and there were some very good people doing this kind of work and so it wasn't like a cabal that we're going to screw the primary care docs and we're going to keep the money for ourselves. It wasn't that clear, it was just a systematic or an inherent sort of bias towards procedures and a process that rewarded deal making" (Interview Subject 25).

Some involved over a long period described deal making as common: "It's politics. Some people got together somewhere, or whispered and a deal was struck, you know? I mean, it's it happens all the time. We strike deals, they strike deals. The official thing will be that no deals are struck, but it's a body. Of course deals are struck. Barbara Levy [chair at the time] will tell you there's not, okay? You can tell her I said . . . I love her dearly, but she's wrong" (Interview Subject 5). Furthermore, committee members say they request cooperation from other societies:

> It wouldn't . . . it wasn't beyond me to go up to somebody and say, "Ah, you know, this code is coming up. I really think this is a fair number." We can't really take less than that. And I've done it, okay? They'll say . . . no, they'll . . . they'll do something, like they'll come up to us and they'll say that "we don't want this code to go through like this," because we think it's going to be abused by, you know, ENT will say it's going to be abused by the audiologists, or something like that. We have our people we trust. I'll approach, and someone else'll approach someone who's an archenemy. The only one I won't . . . there's only one person that it's just hopeless to talk to, and I won't tell you who it is. And I think he's the partisan. But I think he's the only one that I . . . that I would say is partisan. Everybody else is reasonable. And when they look at the codes, they do so with honesty. But again, you see things through the eyes you have. They're surgeons, they truly believe that surgery should be paid this much more. (Interview Subject 5)

Some members make a similar argument, and they stress that the addition of one primary care seat would be unlikely to change the dynamics. One member's description of getting codes passed suggested that it required the same kind of vote counting that we would expect more in a legislative process rather than a panel of experts:

> It's about the money. It's about the power. And that's where the party line comes in because the way it is currently constructed, the proceduralists can do what they want basically. Unless someone breaks party lines, and I would

include anesthesiology and radiology and dermatology as part of the proceduralists. That group with the surgical specialists, and that could comprise
two-thirds. And so they can push through anything they want, and the others
around the table cannot block. So if I were to advocate for one change it would
not be one primary care seat. Because one primary care seat doesn't change
the math to allow more than a third block the proceduralists. It requires two
or three seats. So you give those three medical specialty societies each a seat.
Or you give two of 'em and have one dedicated geriatric seat. Because this is
about Medicare . . . after all, and geriatrics is primary care. I would give one
seat to geriatrics, one seat at the table to pulmonary, which also represents intensive care and arguably allergy as an umbrella organization. And one to
the combined specialty of hem-onc [hematology and oncology], rather than
gastroenterology. And with those three seats, you change the balance such
that there really needs to be goodwill partnership and compromise. Because
the proceduralists can't push it through since the cognitive and primary care
can block. Cognitive and primary care aren't in control so it wouldn't be a
threat to the surgeons. It would allow them the ability to produce a bloc and
a stalemate, forcing compromise in negotiation. (Interview Subject 4)

The most notable example of bloc voting occurred in 2007, when an effort
by cognitively based physicians to increase office visit codes was fought by
procedural and surgical societies. The story of this event was told to the
author from people on different sides but consistently. "The surgeons didn't
want to increase the E&M values very much, if at all" (Interview Subject 19).
Those who did not want office visits to be increased refused to acknowledge the evidence presented by the cognitive societies that patients were
more difficult to treat today:

The primary care groups came in and said "we want a substantial increase
in E&M payments" and a number of the procedural specialists basically said
"we're not giving it to them." In more recent years, it's become more overtly
political, you know what was sort of less overtly political dealing, has now
become sort of overtly political . . . primary care and some of the cognitive specialties were posing a direct threat to the big pool of RVUs and
the specialists really saw that as a primary care attack. At the same time,
I believe, people were talking about the need for more primary care
representation so that was the one time it was clearly primary care against
specialists. (Interview Subject 25)

They certainly deserved increases. So then they . . . then the surgeons attacked the cognitives when the cognitive codes came up. They attacked them on the basis of compelling evidence—compelling evidence means what's changed? Well, the simple truth is, that medicine is much more complicated than it was 20 years ago. You've got a hundred different medicines; you're treating sicker people. So there was compelling evidence. But, they just wouldn't stop. And that's when the RUC almost fell apart. I'm sure you've heard of that. (Interview Subject 5)

Supporters of the primary care societies argue that the evidence was fairly clear and that the societies used a variety of sources to demonstrate that:

both the average time of visit and the average complexity of a visit, which would be measured by a number of prescriptions written, number of decisions made, number of diagnoses made per visit, was increasing. And then the confounders that led to that reduced length of stay, higher complexity of patients' conditions at discharge. . . . So the compelling evidence argument actually flew fairly easily and quickly. The issue that resulted in prolonged . . . prolonged facilitation were the values . . . survey medians for the E&M codes when they finally passed RUC, most of those settled way below the 25th percentile. Procedures typically end up in the 25th, the 50th percentile. In the last few years, almost always the 25th. But the E&M values were hammered *extremely* low. And the reason that kept coming up inappropriately, I think, was, "Do you know what this'll do to the entire system?" Because it's a budget neutral system. This is going to mean conversion factors will fall for everything, because there's so many E&M services. (Interview Subject 18)

After the showdown between the organizations, Interview Subject 3 described how the process was taken behind closed doors:

Interviewee: There was a big executive meeting and it almost fell apart. [In] Executive session. The surgeon bloc was not allowing any increases at all for . . . for cognitive work. They finally allowed increases for level 3 and 4 visits, 5 visits. A little bit for level 3. They kept 2 and 1 the same, and it was enough to prevent it from falling apart, but it didn't translate into much. Now this past year, on account of Congress I think, ordered a 10 percent increase in cognitive. And then the people who get the real proceedings are the panel members. The real proceedings? Like. . . .

Interviewer: What do you mean?

Interviewee: What happened in executive session.

Interviewer: Oh, I see. What happened behind closed doors?

Interviewee: Right. Who made what comment that led the panel to making a certain recommendation or not. It's all part of the game. (Interview Subject 3)

If societies believe other societies are cooperating against them, each area of medicine seems to believe other areas are working against them, or at least not helping them. Procedural and surgical specialties feel that other specialties are biased against them. They say that they face organized opposition to their codes:

If we had a procedural code that was submitted for valuation, what you would see is four or five individuals on the RUC would have talking points that they had established in a meeting prior to the RUC meeting as their methodology to not permit this value to be accepted. I mean, we would hear people speaking at the table using exactly the same language. It was just like watching, you know, a politician talk on TV. (Interview Subject 7)

Cooperation is perceived as problematic (when being done to your society) but understandable otherwise. In general, there is a perception from the outside that societies are engaging in a zero-sum conflict, but that is to mischaracterize the incentives. One observer of the process said that budget neutrality was not an incentive for societies to sabotage each other, even if on the surface this would appear to be

an obvious incentive to achieve maximal achievable RVU values for codes that one's own society members perform, and to critique (where possible) other societies' attempts to maximize their code values. This potentially antagonistic situation is tempered by the frequent need for cooperation between societies to present codes together in frequently shifting alliances. Furthermore, voting members of the RUC itself are specifically barred from advocating for code valuations presented by the societies they represent; they are charged with sitting as impartial judges of valuation. These checks and balances tend to dampen intersocietal conflict. (Donovan 2012, 425)

This quote suggests organizations are incentivized to work together, but Donovan suggests that the independence of the voting members is assured because they cannot vote on their own services. It also demonstrates how the Update Committee's processes and group dynamics are subtle or not always immediately obvious.

Voting data suggest a high degree of consensus overall among voting members, or at least in the 2014 year, for final votes (excluding votes that failed the first time and were revised by a facilitation committee). The committee voted on 206 work values in 2014; multiplying these by the number of people voting for each code equals 6,044 total votes cast. 97 percent of these votes were favorable, and just 3 percent were "no" votes. Of the 206 votes, societies had complete consensus on almost 70 percent (143) of the codes. For those votes where there was not 100 percent agreement, most had just one or two dissenters. Only in a handful of cases did a larger group of members oppose the code recommendation: there were 10 votes where five or more people voted no. However, these numbers, as noted above, do not include the votes that failed to pass the first time and so do not likely reflect the true universe of votes cast (American Medical Association 2014).

Identifying Overvalued Services

If societies gain more from working together, they also benefit more from focusing on their own codes and not policing payments that are already too high. Donovan (2012) suggests that there is more to be gained from working together than from reducing the codes of others, a view that was shared by an interviewee:

> The RUC has used a series of what they call are screens to try to identify procedures that should be valued but haven't been valued, or haven't been going through. They talk a lot about the Harvard Valued Codes, and they make a number of comments about how we should go back and look at the Harvard Valued Codes. But the reality is, you're not looking at the codes that should be looked at. They're not looking at procedures that have not been reviewed in a long period of time, because there's no incentive or interest in doing so. Why would you want to challenge the reimbursement of your bread and butter codes? The answer is you wouldn't. (Interview Subject 3)

According to the interviewee, societies ignore overvalued services performed by other societies, because to do so would invite retaliation and scrutiny of the codes their members use:

> There are a number of bread and butter procedures in the RUC database, for which there is no incentive by the specialty societies to have those codes resurveyed, because it would result in a revaluation downward of reimbursement.

[Interviewer: Now, devil's advocate would say, "But you all know that each other, that you're all doing this. So why wouldn't you draw attention to each other's lack of review of bread and butter codes?"]

Because it's the House of Medicine. The House of Medicine to a certain degree protects the members of the House. Because it's like . . . the Russians and the US all possessing nuclear arms. Why would we bomb Moscow if we knew that once we launch the rockets, they were going to bomb Washington, DC and New York? So if you live under a fear of mutual assured destruction, or madness . . . no one challenges the status quo. So therefore, if you live under that philosophy in medicine, why would the surgeons want to tattletale on the primary care physicians? Well, I can give you another reason. Forgive me, please. I'm not telling you this one. (Interview Subject 3)

The interview transcripts suggest that societies prefer détente over conflict, and that there is more to be lost than gained from policing the codes of others. Asked if a society had any incentive to propose changes, one interviewee said, "Oh, absolutely not. If we were . . . if we were to write a letter saying, the CMS, saying 'We'd love for you to please direct the RUC to look at these [specialty] surgery codes,' we'd be blacklisted" (Interview Subject 4).

Methodological Problems Relating to Evidence

To make recommendations about physician work values, the committee needs estimates of time and intensity of physician work. Specialty society recommendations to the committee are based predominantly on surveys of its members that ask questions about how much work is associated with the service.[4] As far back as 1995, the Physician Payment Review Commission recommended changes to the process, and "at a minimum, the data should be verifiable, nationally representative, and collected uniformly" (Physician Payment Review Commission 1995, 42).

On occasion, the committee claims to have used the "same methodology as Hsiao/Harvard" (Levy 2012) since 1992. In fact, there are a number of ways it deviates. The original estimates of work in the study led by William Hsiao and colleagues in the 1980s used standard survey research methods and the researchers documented their methods and results extensively. Methods were transparent and reported in detail. Researchers recruited relatively large samples and tracked nonrespondent characteristics.

The reliance on physician-completed surveys is problematic, because the data collection does not follow scientific protocols such as those used by Hsiao and colleagues. Granted, the Harvard team recognized that its large-scale randomized samples were too time-consuming and expensive to be used for the update process. Problems include shaky sampling methods, small samples, low response rates, and inconsistent usage of data in the decision-making process. The methods used by the committee can be assessed by evaluating their surveys, using theoretical and empirical evidence drawn from other contexts.

Survey Question Design: Reference Codes

The survey instrument is standardized for all societies, as it was in Hsiao's study. However, the society has some discretion regarding the choice of clinical vignette (if the code has not been reviewed before) and also a list of reference services against which to compare the services. Respondents are asked to rate the intensity for each component of the surveyed code against a "reference" code. Societies provide a wide range of codes and are warned by staff not to bias the results by their choice of reference codes. In interviews, participants say societies do better if they use a reference code from outside their own specialty. Respondents are given a choice of responding 1 to 5 (low to high) and instructed to base evaluations on "the universe of codes your specialty performs" (The AMA/RUC Physician Work Survey 2013). Some societies say that they make an effort to develop a reasonable list of comparison codes and describe their strategy as allowing systematic evaluation:

> It's good to have several codes from other specialties to show that this particular work value is, in the greater scheme of things, not undervalued or overvalued in relation to similar amounts of work. And by that I mean, if there's a [specialty] procedure, [specialty] procedure, [specialty], something like that, that takes place in the similar sort of patient group, the same operating time, same hospitalization, same number of postoperative visits . . . then really, the only thing they're talking about in terms of valuing the procedure that . . . our index procedure that we have just surveyed, and the one that we're using as a comparison is the intensity of the work. If the work is the same, and all the postoperative visits are the same, the postoperative work is all predefined, they're all a fixed amount, so that the, the only variable

here in the end is the operating time and the intensity . . . if we can find a procedure code out of our specialty that resembles ours in terms of these various parameters that I've mentioned, and we align our value with that, that's a very powerful sort of point of comparison. (Interview Subject 1)

In other cases, the reference code choices are considered biased, although there are also situations where members seem to recognize when this happens. One person interviewed recalled a meeting where for "nine of the eleven measures, the reference code wasn't just more intense, it was significantly more intense." The society that was presenting was asking for "a higher value, the key reference service took twice as much time as the code they were surveying. It makes no sense. Just based on intensity and time, this code should be valued half what they're asking" (Interview Subject 18).

Societies trying to boost a relative value can face problems finding a suitable reference code, but there are strategies that can help. To address one case where the reference services "were believed to be undervalued," the society added "several general surgical procedures to a short list of vascular operations" (Zwolak and Trout 1997, 1080). That was a successful strategy for the society: the services in question increased substantially, including one that was given a 44 percent increase (Table 5.2).

Sample Size and Nonrespondents

Good sampling methods and adequate sample sizes are absolutely essential for accurate time data. The fact that the committee consistently overestimates physician time indicates that there are problems with the method or process.

The Hsiao study researchers initially used a pilot survey of 18 physicians, which was used to estimate the standard deviation of the population for every specialty surveyed in the pilot, and each gave responses to the questions. That number was estimated to be 50 physicians, but the researchers decided to use samples of 100 to allow for an ample margin. To ensure a 60 percent overall response rate, researchers drew at least 185 names for each specialty from the AMA Masterfile (Hsiao, Braun, Becker, et al. 1988). Hsiao study researchers also tracked nonrespondent characteristics. That is not done by the committee.

TABLE 5.2 Vascular Surgery Procedures Evaluated in the Five-Year Review of Work Relative Value Units

CPT	Description	1995 Fee	Society of Vascular Surgery	7/1995 Work group	8/1995 RUC	11/1995 CMD	4/1996 HCFA NPRM	1997 Fee schedule	Percent change from 1995
35081	AAA, sleeve	22.15	28.50	26.23	26.23	25.23	26.23	26.23	+18.4
35082	AAA, ruptured[a]	28.82	37.00	34.20	34.20	34.20	34.20	34.20	+18.7
35091	AAA, suprarenal[a]	28.10	36.50	33.16	33.16	33.16	33.16	33.16	+18.0
35102	AAA, AI or AF	23.44	31.50	28.80	28.80	28.80	28.80	28.80	+22.9
35301	Carotid endarterectomy	15.95	18.00	17.79	17.79	17.79	17.79	17.79	+11.5
35556	Fern-pop w/vein	15.47	22.00	18.00	19.37	19.37	19.37	19.84	+28.2
35566	Fern-rib w/vein	20.21	26.25	22.80	24.45[b]	23.55	24.45	25.00	+23.7
35583	Fern-pop in situ	15.97	24.00	19.60	20.03	19.43	20.03	20.50	+28.4
35585	Fern-rib in situ	19.05	27.00	23.60	25.92[b]	24.96	25.92	26.47	+39.0
35681	Composite graft add-on[a]	8.05		3.93	3.93	3.93	3.93	8.05	0.0
35875	Remove clot graft[a]	9.07		8.19	8.19	8.19	8.19	9.07	0.0
35656	Fern-pop synthetic	13.86	18.00	17.84	17.84	15.96	17.84	18.42	+32.9
36830	Dialysis graft	7.78	11.25	7.78	11.25	9.36	11.25	11.25	+44.6

Source: Reproduced under license from Zwolak and Trout (1997). Table 1.

Note: All codes represent physician work expressed in relative value units. AAA = abdominal aortic aneurysm; AI = aortoiliac; AF = aortofemoral; Fern-pop = femoropopliteal; Fern-rib = femorotibial; CMD = carrier medical director; CPT = Current Procedural Terminology; HCFA = Health Care Financing Administration; RUC = Relative Value Update Committee; NPRM = notice of proposed rulemaking.

a. Codes submitted as potentially overvalued or undervalued by other societies.

b. Work values determined as interim at the August meeting, finalized in February 1996.

Societies frequently struggle to get enough surveys completed. Committee rules require a minimum of 30 individuals to respond, and 50 for services with higher use. Participants admit that "it's not a scientific process, the number of responses is often . . . certainly in scientific terms is modest in a way. We can't do much with less than 30 responses, and frequently we have somewhere between 30 and 60 responses" (Interview Subject 10). Smaller societies have problems obtaining adequate data, and larger societies are perceived as having better quality surveys and skilled staff that lead to favorable outcomes:

> We always have lousy surveys. But the bigger, well-organized specialties (and I'm not talking about the cognitives) [name of society redacted] has spent a fortune, hiring [society staff name redacted] to run their numbers, and to do their surveys. We do a survey and it's like, what do we do with these numbers? They don't make sense. The [name of society redacted] does a survey and [society staff name] makes sure it comes out tight. Whether it's the way [society staff name] poses the questions or whether it's the . . . you know, you don't have to turn over your raw material. (Interview Subject 5)

Analysis of 849 codes reported in the summaries of recommendations at four different meetings between 2005 and 2012 by specialty societies shows a wide variation in survey sample sizes, from 15 people to 29,250, with a median of 240. But the average survey achieved a median response rate of around 16 percent, and some had no responses. The median survey response number was 43 people. Societies bemoan the lack of responses, and indeed getting completed surveys would seem particularly challenging given the length and intricacy of the survey instrument, which is likely to pose challenges for those not familiar with the underlying basis of the fee schedule. Societies are frustrated by the lack of response by members, and to address the response rates, they even encourage board members to complete the surveys:

> It's very embarrassing for the Society as well as those making the presentation. The Board of Directors needs to figure out a way of doing this in the future. Dr. Conti suggested that we connect the survey to the CME [Continuing Medical Education] credit sheets. Dr. McKusick stressed that every Board member should fill out a survey, and they don't. We need to explore what the key points are, what the training is, what are the crosswalks, etc. We need 50 doctors at 50 hospitals doing these surveys. (Society of Nuclear Medicine 2003, 2)

Certain cognitive biases may encourage committee members voting on code changes to believe each survey, no matter how small, is a valid source of data, because psychological research shows that people believe sample size is not important if they believe the survey is conducted from a random sample (Tversky and Kahneman 1982, 24). They are overconfident about the representativeness of data from small samples and expect two samples drawn from the same population to be more similar than sampling theory would suggest. In small samples, people believe that due to random selection, errors are self-correcting. They use idioms such as "errors cancel each other out" when estimating the validity of results and, in doing so, are also unrealistic in their expectation that the results can be replicated (Tversky and Kahneman 1982, 24).

A problem is that society surveys of members, even if random, exclude practicing physicians who are not members, and not all physicians belong to their societies. In addition, it is possible for societies to draw their survey respondents from a convenience sample—such as asking physicians to fill out surveys at a conference—and some medical societies actively recruit physicians to fill out surveys to either supplement or replace a random sample of physicians or even members:

> To volunteer to participate in the survey process, email surveys@asge.org with your name and contact information. Based on the list of surveys below, please specify which procedure surveys apply to you. Additional information will be provided prior to the start of each survey. (American Society for Gastrointestinal Endoscopy 2016)

> Members may also volunteer to fill out the surveys. It is essential that orthopaedic surgeons fill out these surveys accurately. If the AAOS [American Academy of Orthopaedic Surgeons] cannot collect sufficient data to present to the RUC, certain undervalued services will not receive an increase in RVUs and other procedures deemed overvalued by the CMS may face declining reimbursements. (Hariri et al. 2007, 244)

> The AAOS is continuously trying to identify undervalued musculoskeletal services and is calling for members to help in collecting data to defend reimbursement rates. When you receive a survey to assess resources needed to perform a service, it is essential that you take the time to complete it honestly and accurately and return it promptly. The politics of the current five-year review underscores the importance of these surveys. Furthermore, orthopae-

dists can engage in economic studies quantifying the impact of present and future Medicare changes on the practice of orthopaedic surgery. Studies examining the costs of providing certain services are useful in identifying undervalued codes for future review. Concerted orthopaedic political activity is therefore essential to effect change. (Hariri et al. 2007, 244)

If you are interested in helping with the RUC surveys, please contact [staff name] at [website]. (American College of Radiology 2016)

Specialty societies might argue that these practices ensure greater consistency. But when the standing panel is drawn from the practice management section of their society, that is not a representative sample of members. Indeed, societies sometimes encourage reimbursement committee members to fill out surveys: "Staff will send out the gastric emptying survey soon. We hope all committee members participate" (Society of Nuclear Medicine 2010c, 2). In a small respondent pool, survey completion by committee members would likely bias the results. People serving on reimbursement committees are likely more aware of how these surveys work.

However, the author has been unable to obtain evidence, if it exists, of extensive investigations by societies or the AMA into how response rates could be improved and/or whether the survey should be redesigned. Independent survey research companies, which might be familiar with ways to boost response rates, are not generally involved in administering the surveys.

One constraint that Hsiao and his colleagues did not face in the 1980s is the task of estimating work values for procedures not known to many physicians—by design, the researchers picked commonly performed services. The original basis of the fee schedule was that these commonly performed codes would provide the parameters for the other services. That is not the case today, where every code is reviewed, yet with the hyperspecialization of medicine, this becomes more difficult. New technologies and procedures may be provided infrequently. There is no minimum requirement for how many people actually have to be familiar with the procedure. At meetings, the author observed that societies acknowledge that some people filling out the survey have no familiarity with the procedure. This is often for understandable reasons, due to low response rates or a lack of individuals who do the procedure (especially when there is a new technology and/or few people are receiving the service). On the other hand, to address the gap in familiarity, specialty societies can use data based on respondents selected who are "using the procedure"[5] as well as expert panels convened for the purposes of determining work values, but these samples may be drawn from lists provided by manufacturers. New technologies might be more likely to be provided at academic medical centers. If academic medical centers are overrepresented, this could be a problem, because physicians at teaching hospitals have overall longer times (although research suggests they were also more accurate in terms of being closer to the actual times that were self-reported). Unless the service is only going to be performed at teaching hospitals, samples drawing mainly from teaching hospitals "could be a major source of the longer surveyed times" (Cox et al. 2007, 15).

Anchoring and Self-Interest Effects

In addition to the sampling methods, some features of the surveys that societies send out may be subject to certain biases arising from "meta-level modes of judgment which may occur outside the awareness of the individual but, nevertheless, influence reasoning and judgment" (Cleaves 1987, 158).

One example of potential bias arises from the nature of the comparison of the reviewed service to other services, and respondents pick a work value they believe is appropriate. Psychological research shows that people are highly suggestible to or influenced by baseline numbers that anchor their responses. People are used to anchoring numbers based on a first approximation or natural starting point. Most famously, one experiment showed the profound effects that can arise from priming people with certain numbers. People were asked to write down their Social Security number and then estimate the number of doctors and surgeons in the Yellow Pages. The response was strongly related to the Social Security number (Wilson, Houston, Etling, and Brekke 1994 in Kahneman and Tversky 2000, 666).

If physicians fill out the survey with knowledge of the current value, that constitutes an anchor against which they may base their estimates. Indeed, the official committee policy is that all current values are assumed to be correct, and therefore all changes must prove that the current value is inappropriate. Expertise is no guard against anchoring. While people with higher cognitive ability are slightly less susceptible to anchoring, it is still appreciable and measurable (Furnham and Boo 2011). Experienced legal professionals are "influenced by irrelevant sentencing demands even if they are blatantly determined at random" (Englich, Mussweiler, and Strack 2006), and judges are also strongly influenced by sentencing guidelines that are inappropriate for the crime (Mussweiler 2001; Mussweiler and Strack 2000). Philip Tetlock declared that experts were no better than chimpanzees at throwing darts, and others have also asserted that experts vastly over-estimate their skill (Furnham and Boo 2011; Quirk 2010; Tetlock 2005).

Decision making is problematic, in general, when people have a vested interest in the outcome (Cleaves 1987). Self-interest bias would lead to an overestimation of relative value units. Indeed, CMS has found that the committee sometimes ignores data used in its own justifications for the values it has proposed to CMS, with the effect of upward valuations (Centers for Medicare & Medicaid Services 2011).

To some extent, the issue of anchoring is universal, however. Current prices are inevitably going to influence perceptions about the appropriate price. Even when other methods are used to evaluate work, similar effects are observed. In an interview, William Hsiao said that past experience had taught him that people were unable to separate the value of trading off one service against another without taking in consideration the current fee reimbursed (Hsiao 2002).[6]

One problem, however, is that problems occur with regard to the relativity of fees across the schedule, when the anchor services for shared or similar services are higher in one specialty than another. In one case, there was a service performed by both radiation therapists and obstetrician-gynecologists:

> So the obstetrician-gynecologist produced a pretty good survey—I forget the number—but it was a pretty good survey. And they ranked that code based on time and intensity right in the middle of a family of services that were GYN services. And radiation therapy, therapists, did the same exact thing. They put it right in the middle of a family of their services. However, the value for that code was dramatically different between the two. And I forget the skew, but it may have been a three- or four-fold difference. And when it came to the table it was insanely obvious to everyone that there is no relativity between these two families. To my consternation, RUC chose the higher value. (Interview Subject 18)

This suggests that specialties may anchor services relative to the parameters of existing families rather than a universal metric of physician work: each specialty has a different set of parameters.

Recall Bias and Recollection of Time Use

One interviewee admitted, "I think I spend more time doing things than I actually do. And when I self-report that, I think there's a potential reporting bias that's unrecognized" (Interview Subject 18). Compared to diary-based records, when people have to remember how long they work, they exaggerate their hours (Robinson and Bostrom 1994); therefore, diaries are more reliable (Bonke 2005). People are not good at estimating their time, especially when they have a stake in the outcome or there is a social desirability bias. "There are good reasons to be skeptical of individuals' self-reports of their time at work" (J. Jacobs 1998, 43). People are likely to provide normatively desirable answers rather than precise information, while exaggeration of working hours may be increasing, as people in dual-earner families who feel squeezed for time (Robinson and Godbey 1997 in J. Jacobs 1998, 43).

Physicians who work long hours may be particularly prone to overestimating how much work they do or how many hours they spend working because people who work more than the usual hours per week (which for many physicians is the case) may develop distorted perceptions about how long things take. Longer hours might involve less regular schedules with fewer anchor points or "time markers," because they work during times when others do not. They also might feel deprived by having to work hours that other people do not, especially if they are subject to unscheduled interruptions and distractions (Robinson and Bostrom 1994). People who work longer hours show a decrease in accuracy in terms of their time estimates compared with people working fewer hours: people who said they worked more than 55 hours per week usually overestimated their workweek by 10 hours per week. Among those who said they worked 60 hours a week, the actual workweek was 53 hours. The difference was two hours for the 40- to 44-hour category, but the gap increased to 25 hours for people who said they worked 75 hours or more (Robinson and Bostrom 1994).

Recollections of events or intense experiences and their duration can be inaccurate. Experiments designed to test whether the duration of pain makes a procedure a more difficult for the patient found that longer, more painful procedures were not judged more negatively than painful but shorter procedures (Redelmeier and Kahneman 1996). Duration only has an impact if the event is very salient or correlated with emotional intensity, as it is in the duration of childbirth. People tend to remember selected moments rather than an exact running total of the experience (Redelmeier, Katz, and Kahneman 2003).

The Health Care Financing Administration recognized some of the problems early on and warned people they should be careful not to "anchor" the value of the service when it is at its peak of intensity. Maximum intensity may be an inaccurate basis for estimating values, since "a lengthy procedure that is simple except for a few moments of extreme intensity is probably less work than one of equal length during which a fairly high level of intensity is maintained throughout" (Health Care Financing Administration 1994).

Survey Administration Effects

Surveys to physicians are done under the imprimatur of the specialty society. Survey respondents receive materials from the society such as coversheets and emails discussing the purpose of the survey. Across a variety of specialty society websites, a review of the publicly accessible information shows that societies describe the purpose of surveys in neutral terms, such as helping to improve the accuracy of Medicare payments rather than to increase reimbursements.

Even so, the administration of the survey by a specialty society raises questions about priming effects, due to the association of the survey with the society and its advocacy activities focused on gaining higher reimbursements. In the mind of a survey respondent, who might access the survey through a society website or click on an email link sent by the society, the survey is sponsored by the society. With some exceptions (such as a new procedure, where the device manufacturer may help select the respondents), survey respondents are almost always drawn from society membership, who have likely joined at least in part because they support one of the key missions of the organization, which is advocating for higher reimbursements and trying to influence policy.

Since the survey is long and detailed, not all respondents find the experience user-friendly. Most people say it takes around 25 to 30 minutes to complete, but it has been described as "long and difficult to answer," particularly because respondents are asked to rank more than eight items. A ranking of four or five items is more reasonable, because otherwise, "respondents to start giving arbitrary rankings just to get past the item" (Lavernia and Parsley 2006, 8). As one interviewee said, "the length of the survey doesn't help. Those surveys are multiple pages, and unless you've been exposed to it, it's not easy to grasp the first time you do one. So for the uninitiated it's like, it's a major investment in terms of time and thinking to . . . to fill one out. And if you're doing a family of codes, and you're asking to fill out multiple versions of that that, then it escalates from there" (Interview Subject 2).

No evidence suggests that staff prompt people who are filling out surveys or that website materials are designed in any way to influence particular outcomes. Training and assistance are permitted, but society members say that explicit directions are discouraged, such as sending an email before the survey is sent out with instructions such as the following: "when you're talking about operative time, you're including all that operative time, from the time you cut the skin to the time you finish the incision, and look back over your records and give us an idea of what that is, over the years, rather than just guessing it." The interviewee said this is "strictly frowned upon in the RUC process. Because the RUC members, RUC leadership, want the surveys to be completed by people who haven't been led, haven't been trained" (Interview Subject 1).

Societies are allowed to educate members on "how to fill out the survey," with societies conducting educational phone calls "to explain to people in a large group how to take the RUC survey" (Interview Subject 3), and some societies host webinars (American Osteopathic Association). Committee members themselves know surveys are not easy to complete, as demonstrated by one committee member's request for members to participate in a webinar:

> Interventional cardiologists who receive a survey this fall should make every effort to complete it accurately and return it on time. "There is no room for error in completing these surveys," Dr. Blankenship said. "SCAI recognizes the surveys can be quite complex, so we will be hosting a webinar to educate members about the process and the surveys themselves." To learn more about the RUC process and participate in SCAI's free webinar. . . . (Society for Cardiovascular Angiography and Interventions 2011, 2)

One society requested that the AMA train 70 members "in RUC surveys" (Pediatric Orthopaedic Society of North America 2012).[7] Societies have the resources (although not in all cases) to provide assistance one-on-one. A former specialty society staff member now working as a consultant said, "They get stuck on the whole thing about understanding times and how these different things correlate, you know. I can sometimes spend a half hour, 40 minutes with somebody that's having questions and not understanding how to complete the survey" (Interview Subject 19). The same interviewee said that "I always clean the data and I don't mean that I change the data, I mean that I go in and I look, and if I see somebody missed the point, like last time I was doing a survey, some guy, one of our prestigious medical schools in the country, he ended up putting five for everything. I spent an hour on the phone [laughs]. He said, 'I just didn't understand it, and I just, that's what I did,' you know. And they're all very busy people, and that's the problem, is that if they're not, you know . . . I do this for a living, so I mean, I'm very close to it, and I understand it" (Interview Subject 19).

Biases and Group Effects in Decision Making

CMS has criticized the committee's approach and has said it "does not rely on a single consistent methodology to value codes" (Centers for Medicare & Medicaid Services 2010, 73218). The agency has said that sometimes magnitude estimation is used in conjunction with survey data, but on other occasions, magnitude estimation is used to override the results of the survey data and justified as a way to maintain relativity to other services (Centers for Medicare & Medicaid Services 2010, 73218). One observer who attended a meeting and shared notes with the author observed that the use of survey findings in the process does not actually reflect survey data: "estimates are often tweaked during committee discussions because they say it wasn't quite right or something, but then others are viciously assailed if their surveys don't seem scientific standards" (Anonymous observer notes). One interviewee perceived that "sometimes RUC will buy that, many times they won't. And as a result, I think the RBRVS has developed some inconsistency across families when it comes to intensity measures" (Interview Subject 18).

The facilitation committees and prefacilitation processes may provide ample room for negotiating rather than objectively determining relative value units. Some societies believe the committee's decisions cannot be predicted, and they say that it is "a little bit of a crapshoot, you know . . . we've see things happen at the RUC that have just flabbergasted us." An argument that had been "absolutely vetted, an argument that we think is so self-evident a kindergartner could understand it not being accepted. It's a fluid environment, and it's not exactly predictable" (Interview Subject 6). On the other hand, others say that the only reason to put forward codes is when they will be increased, and "you don't put anything forth that you're . . . you don't think it's going to not pass. So everything that we . . . let's say that we have a code that we've been asked to review for the RUC, because they think the work values have changed, and they want us to be sure what . . . what the work values are. We never go before the RUC thinking that we're going to lose" (Interview Subject 9). Another participant saw the process as having moved toward greater objectivity and seemed optimistic regarding the validity of the process:

> While the RUC is still mysterious, there is a better job done nowadays in facilitation in trying to explain how the values become relative. There are codes that I could point to in the past, and people came up with convoluted explanations to explain why the values are where they are. And it's like a hat below, and three helpings of green pea soup, and standing upon your head until your ears are turning red.
>
> Nowadays it's, this code has work and, a work and intensity which, which is equivalent to this other code. So it's more . . . I mean, the RUC is not a scientific process. But it's much more . . . this valuation, this anchoring, in the process now, in the RUC survey, where you not only anchor your code to what your survey says, 25th [or] 50th percentile, median or whatever, but you anchor it to the MPC codes, Multi-Specialty Points of Comparison. And, you do a building block methodology. So it's a building inspector's methodology. (Interview Subject 3)

Others characterize the decision-making process as a bargaining process. Presenters and committee members often "split the difference." Committee members say that some presenters may use the possibility of anchoring bias to their advantage. Some societies come to the presentation "with outrageous asks" that people in the audience and around the table "just kind of take a deep breath and relax and get a smile on their face, because they're going to enjoy it because it's so ridiculous." Such a strategy, however, could be potentially successful because rather than consider that the presenter always gets "hammered down," "if you come in asking for three times what you should get, and you fight tooth and nail, and you walk out with 1.25 of what you should get instead of what you should get, you've arguably done your society's and your society's numbers a service" (Interview Subject 4).

Studies of how people make decisions may help us understand why the committee may not reflect real-world comparisons. Evidence is drawn from cognitive psychology and other studies of decision making and compared with the empirical information.

Psychology of Numbers

When making decisions using numbers, people are influenced by the nature of the measurement units and the relative and absolute numbers. Time is measured in minutes, as it was by Hsiao. Hsiao's method of work estimation, however, compared services using magnitude estimation. The committee uses a variety of methods, but its work assessments are based on relative value units—and counted in unit increments—rather than orders of magnitude. Hsiao and colleagues envisaged service value as changing in magnitude such that the multipliers could be calculated; this meant that an office visit or a simple surgical procedure could be used to determine relative value units across specialties. To do this, Hsiao used scales that asked respondents to rate the difficulty on a scale of zero to 100. Magnitude estimation tries to assess the total amount of work relative to the physician work for similar services across the physician fee schedule (Hsiao and Langenbrunner 1988). This method does not depend on explicitly valuing the components of that work but only asks respondents to say how much a service is worth relative to the comparison being made.

As said, the surveys allow a survey respondent to choose the reference service and then ask respondents to assess a specific work value measured in absolute relative value units, rather than orders of magnitude (McCall, Cromwell, and Braun 2006). Although societies are encouraged to pick from other specialties, the basket of services is more likely to reflect same-specialty services.

A related issue is the evaluation by specialty societies and the committee that establishes cut points in the survey data around percentiles. As one interviewee pointed out, the percentiles are a way of introducing a degree of supposed precision to the process that may not have a scientific rationale, but is used to more easily present the data: "It's an accident of the design of the instrument. We come to think of whatever it is, ninety percent of the sample size being within two standard deviations of the mean. But there's absolutely no evidence that the responses to the surveys that we get are normally distributed, none whatsoever. I think we talk about percentiles because we can. We've got software that calculates it automatically in a nanosecond. So we talk about this without really understanding what its significance is, in relation to this survey's, non-normally distributed survey" (Interview Subject 10).

Ad Hoc Use of Survey Data

The surveys of physicians sent out by specialty societies are said by participants to be the most important ingredient of a proposal. Participants say members like to see bigger samples (even if the selection process was not necessarily random) and a degree of consistency in the survey responses.

Large standard deviations or variance raise questions, as do outliers. Interviewees suggest that failure to accept recommendations usually reflects an unusually low sample size, a wide range in the work or time estimates, and/or a lack of what members believe is a "good" reference code.

Societies often have a view of what the right value is, and the survey results do not always conform to that. Committee participants admit that data from surveys can be strategically used in an ad hoc manner or even rejected completely if the survey results suggest the service takes less time or is less intense than its current valuation. Sometimes the society will spend considerable portions of the presentation explaining how the respondents did not understand the survey and may report that survey respondents had not accurately reported the work values. A specialty society might say physicians they had surveyed had underestimated times. When a society is asked why there are no data in the post-service time fields, the society might respond that the physicians filling out the survey do not understand the notion of post-service times.

There is a possibility that the Update Committee is willing to let such inconsistencies go. However, CMS is not always willing to overlook such problems. On occasion CMS has rejected recommendations, and noted in the *Federal Register* they did so because the recommendations did not match the survey data or there were inconsistencies between the committee's own data (based on specialty society data) or contradictions between the evidence and CMS claims data. For example, CMS said that on one occasion the committee recommended increases, even though survey respondents said the work for a service had not increased, or respondents reported times that were lower than those recommended by the committee (Centers for Medicare & Medicaid Services 2011). Defenders of the update process contend that this kind of discrepancy is generally nipped in the bud during the deliberation or called out when the survey does not fit with the data, but the fact that there are documented differences between real world and specialty society estimates suggests this may not happen as often as members believe it happens.

As said earlier, these kinds of problems are not limited to the update process: selective interpretation or rationalization occurs in many settings where people are using smaller samples to draw conclusions. When using small samples, conclusions can be rationalized: "He rarely attributes a deviation of results from expectations to sampling variability, because he finds a 'causal explanation' for any discrepancy" (Tversky and Kahneman 1982, 29).

Problems go beyond the selective interpretation of data, however, because the data can also be dismissed and jettisoned. When a specialty society does not like its own data, it may form an "expert panel" to develop alternative estimates that are used to override the survey data, although it has to provide both to the committee. If there are inconsistencies in the survey, "the expert panel can then say, ah, this was looked at by our expert panel, and they decided that five minutes was the appropriate amount of time" (Interview Subject 5). Some say that "specialty societies disagreeing with their own survey data convene 'expert panels' to pump up their RVU requests" (Anonymous observer notes, 2008). As one interviewee said, one society with resources would routinely fly people in and form expert panels: "They would fly in people. You do a survey, and then you can revise the survey by an expert panel. They wouldn't hesitate to fly people, to fly 20 doctors in, 20 [specialty] in. You know damn well they flew in and they were put up at . . . you know damn well it cost them a fortune to do that" (Interview Subject 5).

Single-specialty expert panels may be particularly troublesome, given what we know about the flaws in developing clinical guidelines. Research on guideline development suggests there are problems with "variable and opaque development methods, their often conflicted and limited panel composition, and their lack of significant external review by stakeholders throughout the development process," which means the trustworthiness of guidelines is limited (Shaneyfelt 2012, 1633).

In the past, the committee has avoided using real data—even when alternate sources are available. Many relevant data points are available to members in the "RUC Database" that members have in front of them during the meetings. Committee members can view aggregated data for each code from Medicare claims data such as patient characteristics (age, sex, comorbidities). Specialty societies do not usually systematically reference this information or outside information in the presentations. The only exception is the site of service information—where the service is usually provided and by whom (specialty); these categories come up in the discussions frequently. The issue of changing patient characteristics often comes up in the justification for higher RVUs in five-year reviews, but the data are not usually presented. The work has increased, groups argue, because procedures have become more difficult, and there are frequently references in the meetings to how patients are more difficult—this despite the fact that "the society has to provide compelling evidence if they're going to ask for an increase in a code" (Interview Subject 18).

On occasion, societies do bring data to the meeting showing increases in patient age or the incidence of diabetes in the patients they see (Shah et al. 2014). However, in the past, in some cases, CMS itself has discouraged use of alternative data sources because "there is the risk that applying the data randomly could distort the relativity between services" (Centers for Medicare & Medicaid Services 2006, 69729). It is true that these concerns might be justified, because there are instances where interviewees claimed that societies had successfully justified inflated values by using external data sources. Sometimes societies try to use data from systems such as the Veteran Affairs (VA) health care system. One interviewee recalled how one society created databases using VA data:

> *Interviewee:* Excuse me, everything takes three times as long at the VA Hospital. So I know that their operations weren't two and a half hours. I watched the god-damned things. I spent three days watching, okay? But I wasn't allowed to challenge it, because it was a database. This is where they put their money.
>
> *Interviewer:* Presumably not that many of them work in the VA anyway, right?
>
> *Interviewee:* Every big city has a VA hospital. Every academic department runs a VA hospital.
>
> *Interviewer:* But the bread and butter of their practices, would it be a big percentage of their earnings, the VA?
>
> *Interviewee:* No. But who cares about that, okay? If you get data that helps your case. (Interview Subject 5)

Availability Bias

Due to the availability bias, "events, quantities, or relationships that are more easily brought to mind are more apt to be judged as likely." "Familiarity, saliency and imaginability strongly enhance the retrievability of an event, even though the event itself may be rare" (Cleaves 1987, 159). Indeed, researchers who assembled a group of specialty society members to determine the work associated with a procedure found that physicians struggled to "average" their work such that it would reflect the services they provide. Instead, it was clear that when physicians estimated the work associated with procedures, "they tended to think of the last occasion where they performed the procedure" (Wynn et al. 2015, 161). In general, the effect of this bias seems to be upward rather than downward. Researchers noted that in a survey almost two-thirds of the choices physicians made were higher relative work RVUs, regardless of the source of the estimate.

The surveys sent to specialty society members do not ask respondents about the "the most recent" time they performed a task but are more general. One benefit of such wording is that by using specific parameters on which event is selected, such as asking what someone ate for breakfast today instead of generally, we will get a better understanding of what is typical. When physicians think about their work, they may be more likely to recall a particularly difficult or unusual case. For example, when psychiatrists evaluate their patients for suicidability, they tend to measure all patients against their suicidal patients of the past. This is because suicidal patients are likely to be more memorable and easier to recall than depressive patients who did not attempt suicide (Tversky and Kahneman 1973). Experts and groups seem to be particularly prone to recalling and giving more weight to vivid or memorable experiences (Cleaves 1987).

Anecdotal Evidence or Personal Experience

There is also a tendency for members to draw on anecdotal evidence. This is particularly a problem with commonly performed procedures as opposed to rarely performed ones: "Everybody's had a colonoscopy. And so everybody can compare what they perceive the work is for colonoscopy, compared to what they do . . . is what I do more complex or less complex to that procedure?" (Interview Subject 3). Participants say that society recommendations must generally fit with members' own "internal verification." However, one interviewee said that this meant people were better prepared, since all the voting members of the committee would have researched the procedure or service before the meeting:

> B°°°°°°°t detectors are on high. They're on alert . . . everybody on that panel has gone to their local institution, their hospital, their academic medical center, their clinic, and they've asked questions "do you guys really do this once a day or once a year?" . . . and they will do this, they will go to OR [operating room] logs, and they'll say, you know, "How much time do you book for this procedure?" And if someone says . . . "We believe that this procedure's going to take an hour and a half," and the OR logs show that this procedure gets booked every 20 minutes, it's like, as I said, your BS detector's

on high . . . if they sense . . . that they're being snowed, then it's not a pretty sight. (Interview Subject 3)

Likewise, another interviewee recalled going to the OR, and "after watching a bunch of things, I stopped and I said, 'How many RVUs do I get paid for the hardest thing that I do?' I did a little calculation and I decided that the surgical fee schedule was way undervalued." In another case, committee members were convinced that a procedure was mostly done under anesthesia "because a couple of the people on the RUC who were at academic facilities knew that the [procedure name redacted] in that academic facility did it under general anesthesia." Or, "when the issue of whether one or two lasers was used, some of these panelists went onto say, 'Well, in our facility, our folks, they're only using one laser.' And of course, you know, the amount of time to wheel another laser in, set it up, tune it up, and utilize it would significantly affect at least the time value of the work" (Interview Subject 6).

Members say that they and their colleagues inspect operating room logs and do their own research before meetings, although with many services on the meeting agenda, it would be difficult to collect even anecdotal data on all of the codes coming up at every meeting. The question also arises as to whether this approach is beneficial or effective. If committee members are influencing the committee recommendations by comparing them with norms at their own practices or hospitals, the research comparing operating logs against committee time recommendations suggests that those anecdotal estimates are not used or, if they are, that they overstate times. Committee members may be less effective than they believe in reducing exaggerated time estimates made by specialty societies, given that differences in work valuations are so different from "real-world" times.

Group Effects and Groupthink

Groups can be hampered by groupthink mentalities that reduce the effectiveness of decision making. Group work reflects individual psychology, and the composition of those in the group has a large impact, since group work is a synergistic collection of individual thinking. Groupthink has four structural features that make it more likely. First, there is more groupthink if there is (1) insulation, such as "if it relies primarily on its own members for counsel and information"; (2) a lack of tradition of impartial leadership;

(3) a lack of norms requiring methodological procedures; and an (4) homogeneity of members' backgrounds and ideologies, which leads to people "potentially shutting out other voices and perspectives" (Schafer and Crichlow 2010, 65). Certain beliefs may create the conditions for groupthink, such as when groups have an illusion of invulnerability and think that they have more control than they do and "make mistakes, take risks, and engage in sloppy analysis" (Schafer and Crichlow 2010, 66).

Just as expertise does not protect people from anchoring, expertise does not guard against groupthink. Experts are usually more confident of their abilities: "The expert is much less likely to say: 'I don't know,' which can lead to disastrous consequences in subsequent decisions" (Cleaves 1987, 157). In many cases, such as stock traders who believe they can do better than others in the market, "experts" are not significantly better than nonexperts at assessing probabilities of future outcomes and are prone to developing an illusion of skill whereby the expert becomes unrealistically overconfident (Tetlock 2005).

There can be a tendency for people to go along with the group, even when they disagree with the recommendation in deference to political reality or fait accompli: "When there's some surgical code coming through that is way overvalued, and there's just no discussion around the table about how to bring it down, I recognize it's going through. And the AMA may say, 'Well, 23 out of 26 people voting supported the value'" (Interview Subject 4).

Quantitatively demonstrating groupthink or group effects is difficult. However, most interviewees feel that the process has its own psychology and norms that are somewhat predictable, and therefore someone practiced in the art of the committee's work would successfully navigate the process. But to be successful, specialty societies need to understand the group mentality and the process. They have consultants and staff who have been working with the RBRVS for decades: "We rely heavily on the knowledge of our consultants. They're very experienced in these matters" (Interview Subject 10). One said you need a good "Sherpa." Sherpas are often savvy specialty society staff, with "their masters in RUC-ology. They know how the process works, and because they know how the process works, they know what you can and what you can't get away with." They usually have titles such as senior director or vice president of reimbursement. Such people become valuable and help societies prepare for presentations, making suggestions such as, "'I know what the number shows, but I think we're going to be . . . I don't think we're going to be able to sustain that . . .' 'I think that one really needs to be adjusted this way or that way'" (Interview Subject 3).

Such experts are seen at the meetings apparently guiding or closely coordinating with committee members, according to interviewees, and the current format of the meetings stands in contrast to those when the Update Committee first began:

> Because it was collegial, more doing our best, I think it was sort of a biased process but given the biased process, people were sort of friendly. And yes, there were some . . . I wouldn't emphasize the fights, I think mostly it was people working stuff out and came up with the wrong outcomes in a relatively collegial way. By 10 years later, it was clearly big business. Consultants really analyzing everything, and I'm assuming, telling their members how to vote. I'm assuming that's what was going on but I don't know that, I don't have any direct knowledge [of that]. There's no question there is a belief that the societies that are well funded have a real advantage. (Interview Subject 25)

The complexity of the committee creates a kind of longevity by virtue of the need to invest time and resources in the effort to function effectively. The incentives to remain in the process seem strong, for panelists, staff, and specialty society representatives. That longevity and consistency may facilitate shared views among those involved, but as said, this is difficult to prove.

Groupthink may be particularly common when specialties form expert panels of the sort mentioned earlier. Single-specialty panels have been shown to be very insular in their thinking, with one study of guideline development showing that "panel membership is a main determinant of the trustworthiness of guidelines. Most panels are composed of single-specialty clinicians sharing similar values and biases" (Shaneyfelt 2012, 1633). "Members of a clinical specialty are likely to recommend interventions for which their specialty serves a role" (Shaneyfelt 2012, 1633).

One specialty society staff consultant said that at times, the group seems to move together in terms of its rigor (or not) and scrutiny of specialty societies: "It just seems like sometimes there's sort of an afternoon where . . . where everybody's getting beat up on, and then . . . and then it sort of mellows. And then the mood . . . it changes." Often, these effects are a result of randomness and unrelated contextual effects. There are different tempos and moods throughout the meeting days. The consultant to specialty societies said that based on many meetings attended, "it depends on where we are. If they like the hotel, if they had a good night's sleep, if they really enjoyed the restaurant they went out to and had a good bottle of wine. . . . That's how the mood goes, you know. But I think that's just human nature." Likewise, personal dislike can play a role in the process too, such as one specialist who was from a very lucrative specialty where physicians "make millions of dollars a year," "but it's like they don't like him, because like they think of him as an arrogant personality. So I think finally they . . . the [society] finally figured to keep him less vocal. But it's kind of like for years, we go through . . . and oh, my God, every time he opened his mouth, he'd get shot down [laughs]" (Interview Subject 19).

Conclusion

The way fee schedules are updated influences the relativity of medical prices. If there are perceived problems with the update process, the long-term integrity of the fee schedule is called into question. Overstated times for surgical and other procedures, as well as the fact that work values rise persistently upward, have led to questions about the objectivity and evidence base underlying decisions.

If the committee were an expert panel, members with voting seats would have a degree of independence. Committee members' roles in societies' reimbursement and advocacy programs and their leadership positions suggest they are active participants in their societies and see themselves as representing their organizations. Furthermore, when asked in interviews, where anonymity is protected and people are free to talk, many participants spoke frankly regarding deals and coalitions that contradict the notion of an expert panel. On balance, while facts and data play a role, specialty society interests and economic factors seem to characterize particularly high-stakes reviews. More than one interviewee described how, when nonsurgical societies pushed for increases in the relative value units for E&M visits around 2007, alliances developed along specialty lines to block the change.

For the most part, participants say that the committee relies heavily on the specialty society survey data in its evaluation of society-recommended work relative value units. A significant problem is that the method of surveys of physicians is not sufficiently strong given the use to which this information is put. Societies have some discretion regarding the comparison codes they select, and these may unduly influence the work estimation process. The sampling procedure and the response rates make the estimates of work questionable. The survey relies heavily on estimating how much time things take but may be so long that people either do not complete it or may work too rapidly through it. People are also likely to base their estimates of work depending on the anchors they have available to them, as a way to minimize cognitive effort. Specialty societies try to educate members and solicit volunteers and standing panels of physicians who can complete the surveys, sometimes including the coding and reimbursement committee members. The specialty-administered surveys may have the effect of priming the responses given their prominent role in advancing payment increases for their members as one of their key advocacy areas.

When societies make recommendations, voting members evaluate the evidence presented. Societies believe that the process has a degree of rigor and that the committee challenges their proposals. However, the committee's process of decision making may not compensate for the quality of information available and may rely on anecdotal or other evidence that confirms members' views. Less consideration is given to established reputable survey data or other more representative sources of information. Members have a tendency to accept societies' ad hoc justifications for anomalies or problems with the survey data.

The committee's approach to evidence has long been questioned. A 1994 report by the Office of Inspector General inside the Department of Health and Human Services, quoted the Physician Payment Review Commission as saying that "the rating of work is inherently subjective" and that "decision rules and criteria should be established to ensure consistency of work values to safeguard the equity of the Fee Schedule" (Office of Inspector General 1994b, 15). Serious concerns about the committee's methods receded until 2006, when the Medicare Payment Advisory Commission recommended that CMS review its use of the committee. At the time of writing, policy makers continue to be concerned that the committee's valuations cannot be validated in real-world settings, particularly in the area of time estimation, which is an important influence on the work value of a service. The relativity of services has also been called into question because certain lucrative procedures appear to be easily and quickly provided relative to some services that people believe are more intense and lengthier. The committee defends its process as objective and says its recommendations to CMS are based on survey data and scientific expertise. Yet a number of weaknesses in the estimation of work, when combined, may cumulatively explain time discrepancies and other problems that have been documented.

The need for societies to consider the so-called fixed pie of Medicare funding was supposed to moderate unreasonable fee increases. Given that those budgetary constraints appear to be ineffective, we have to consider whether the committee's process provides the best estimates of work. Close ties between members and specialty organizations, societies administering their own surveys, problems with survey design, and ever-increasing units diminish confidence in the overall process.

That said, committee members are dedicated and committed to providing their labor to do this job, and they see their work being a benefit to society. There is no doubt that the process does draw upon the significant expertise of the members and their knowledge of physician work. However, when the actual functioning of the committee is closely examined and the facts weighed and evaluated according to recognized evidentiary standards, even a highly qualified panel of experts may be unable to develop accurate physician values using these data and working under the structure set up as it is today.

SIX

Complexity, Agency Capture, and the Game of Codes

IN DEMOCRATIC POLITICAL systems, public policies reflect the voices and preferences of many political actors. For many years, the House of Medicine worked to shape payment policy. The House of Medicine's political leverage on issues such as capitation and national health insurance depended on outside lobbying and legislative politics. Often, victories involved making dire predictions about the slippery slope toward socialism and (famously) enlisting Ronald Reagan's help on a long-playing record lambasting government-run health care.

With the arrival of Medicare and a national fee schedule, the attention of the House of Medicine shifted to the federal level. Delegation to the bureaucracy to calculate relative value units under federal rulemaking increased the relevance of the regulatory process to the House of Medicine from the moment the RBRVS was established. The shift to the rulemaking process was a profound development, by means of which the House of Medicine became part of what political scientists call "sub-governments" (Heclo 1978).

Such sharing of responsibilities risks a diminution of accountability, at least partly because the issues in question are not of high concern to voters. Specialized subjects discourage public involvement and reduce the attention of legislators (Peterson 1993). Ideological slogans recede and technical knowledge and know-how become the currency. The specialized content of rulemaking is its key characteristic, and regulatory actions in government are marked by policy complexity. Complex policy issues pose factual questions that are unable to be answered by laypeople. They require specific expertise and training (Gormley 1986) and mastery of problem-solving processes (Lee, Rainey, and Chun 2010).

In the rulemaking process, information is valuable and necessary for both regulators and those trying to exert influence. Complexity makes information scarce and acquiring it burdensome, costly, or both. The "acquisition, filtering, manipulation and analysis of information becomes more difficult" partly due to the cognitive and temporal constraints on our ability to process information (i.e., bounded rationality) but also because of the opaqueness or nonavailability of information (Awrey 2012, 244). Complexity is a defining characteristic of the RBRVS, which confers informational advantages on the House of Medicine relative to other actors in the health policy process, especially patients and generalist policy makers.

Complexity

Complexity of information breaks down the usual assumptions about free and functional markets. Substantial evidence proves that complexity is, if not a problem, at least a characteristic of markets that producers use in a variety of ways to gain competitive advantages. When regulating financial markets, one factor regulators take into account is how difficult or costly it is to acquire information, because regulators recognize this is a key part of leveling the playing field (Awrey 2012). Economists, linguists, and researchers in the financial and accounting sectors have explained how dealing with complexity entails high informational search costs. Therefore, for the beneficiaries of regulatory policies, barriers that discourage casual involvement are desirable.

Oversight of the committee and RBRVS process is difficult for one big reason: policy impacts are not always easy to measure. CMS has made an effort to consistently report its annual decisions in response to committee recommendations, as noted earlier, but the agency sometimes aggregates changes in ways that make it hard to disentangle different components.[1]

Estimating changes in the codes and work values for the same services over time is difficult, and deletions and edits make it more so. When changes are made by CMS, baseline units are not reported alongside the new values to show the changes in the values as a result of the review process. CMS keeps no centralized database of deletions and code value changes. The AMA has its own internal tracking system, but the public version it provides for sale allows comparison of only one code at a time.

The complexity of the Update Committee and the RBRVS is an example of how the high cost of information can benefit market actors seeking to gain policy advantage or to obscure accountability. Because well-organized interests of regulated industries are advantaged compared to the diffuse interests of consumers (Wilson 1980; Yackee and Yackee 2008), the complexity of the RBRVS means that those who understand it have significant informational capital that they build over time and leverage for further success in achieving higher work valuations. Under conditions of complexity, knowledge and expertise beget more knowledge and expertise. The House of Medicine was an early proponent of and participant in the Hsiao study and occupied what was described earlier as a front-row seat—physicians were well positioned and already amassing informational capital before the RBRVS was implemented.

Legislatures, financial institutions, and interest groups are all prone to make issues more complex on occasion. When information and its sources are deliberately obscured or become difficult to understand, the costs of searching rise, and accountability declines. For example, studies of firm responses to executive compensation and financial regulation show how readability can be manipulated. Firms exceeding the regulatory benchmarks for executive compensation tend to have less readable financial reports. When there is a larger gap between what we would expect a firm to pay its executives (as indicated by its size or profitability) and the actual compensation given, firms may try to obfuscate the true level of executive compensation (Laksmana, Tietz, and Yang 2012). Firms that have bad news to share also tend to have lower levels of report readability (Li 2008). Firms generally want some degree of obfuscation, but firms benefit differentially in different price brackets. "The more difficult the industry, the more uninformed consumers there will be and the more market share the high-price firms will receive. Industry confusion is the way high-price firms gain market share" (Carlin 2009, 3).

In other cases, policies may emanate from a confusing process, that is, one designed to confound people as to what was decided and how. Legislative rules and procedures can make it difficult for voters to understand whether a legislator actually supported or opposed a policy (Sinclair 2012). Therefore, complexity biases participation toward those with resources; in nursing home reimbursement, one study found that only well-resourced groups could navigate the "complex maze of rules and regulations" that shape reimbursement levels (Miller et al. 2009). That study shows that resource differences among policy actors are exacerbated by complexity. Therefore, complexity potentially reduces the number of people who might consider participating in the policy process. Only individuals with considerable patience and an expectation that there will be a reward associated with that persistence will invest the upfront time to master the policy content.

The Harvard researchers who designed the RBRVS assumed that government would carefully manage updates to the system. Indeed, under the right conditions, regulators have considerable information, but agency staff working in highly complex areas are almost always outnumbered and outresourced by the industry they regulate. The complexity of administering the RBRVS is not unlike the challenges faced by regulators in the financial industry. One reason new products such as mortgage-default swaps traded by financial institutions were so difficult to regulate before the financial crisis in 2008 was that people could not understand them.[2] The RBRVS created immediate difficulties for the agency administering Medicare, which was under pressure to both address the problems in the fee schedule and provide a new set of payment levels quickly, in time for implementation by 1993. This pressure gave the House of Medicine an opportunity to step in, and HCFA handed the task of valuing physician services to the Update Committee. The committee's update process and rulemaking around fees are technically complex and invoke difficult terminologies and rules. These complexities create opportunities for the House of Medicine to devise and maintain favorable payment policies.

The Complexity of Medicare Payment Policy

The scale and intricacy of the fee schedule mean that annual changes to the fee schedule published in the *Federal Register* require hundreds of pages of explanation. Others who are outside the process argue that the power of the AMA over the process comes from a lack of understanding of what happens in payment policy: "The idea that these guys think that they are . . . that they have the right to decide 150 billion dollars of federal spending in a closed room, financed and organized and staffed by the AMA, in my opinion, is a disgrace. And the only reason it goes on is because nobody understands it" (Interview Subject 22).

TABLE 6.1 Characteristics of Medicare Final Rules and Readability Levels, 2009–2012

	2009	2010	2011	2012
Medicare Final Rule Text				
Acronyms	246	296	332	89
Comments received	266	90	952	1,279
Words	11,966	4,431	8,118	10,443
Pages	451	692	449	483
Sample Pages				
Reading level	Difficult	Difficult	Very confusing	Very confusing
Flesch score	37.1	31.9	23.6	25.8
Words per sentence	15.7	11.8	18.5	18.6

Source: Author's own analysis.

Notes: Selected from Final Rules. Specific dates are November 25, 2009, November 29, 2010, November 28, 2011, and November 16, 2012. Acronyms were sourced from the Table of Contents for each rule. Words in sample texts were 3,309, 2,797, 2,105, and 3,453, in order of year. Three pages were randomly selected from the random-number generator (except for pages comprising tables, in which case a new number was generated). Calculated based on the Flesch Reading Ease Formula (http://www.readabilityformulas.com).

Both the voluminous quantity of information and its elevated reading level reduce its accessibility to the general public as well as those unable or unwilling to invest the time and burden required to understand it. Table 6.1 indicates the length of recent rules and the associated comments. The length of rules reflects the number of Medicare codes and the technical discussions associated with CMS decisions, as well as responses to the committee and commenters on their code recommendations.

One measure of complexity is readability of the material, which was calculated using samples from four Final Rules published by CMS on November 25, 2009, November 29, 2010, November 28, 2011, and November 16, 2012. From each of these rules, three randomly selected pages were chosen using a random-number generator. If the random number was a page that included only a table, a new number was generated until a page composed substantially of text was located. Text readability was measured using the Flesch Reading Ease Formula (used by the Department of Defense and many organizations), which is reported in bands that correspond to difficulty.[3] This demonstrates that rules reported by CMS are inherently difficult to read. The results are shown in Table 6.1. The readability level was 37.1 in 2009, 31.9 in 2010, 23.6 in 2011, and 25.8 in 2012. The levels are equivalent to "difficult" for 2009 and 2010 and "very confusing" for 2011 and 2012. The length of sentences, which tends to predict the readability scores, shows an increase from 15.7 in 2009 to 18.6 in 2012, although there is no reason to assume this represents a trend upward.

Search costs increase when information is missing or difficult to locate. The rulemaking process is a morass of detail and depends on extensive knowledge of the fee schedule. For its five-year (now annual) reviews, the committee's unique role ensured a back-and-forth between it and CMS, creating a multistaged process different from the routine notice and comment process. Until recently, the committee and CMS's approach to conducting the mandated reviews was convoluted, taking almost two years, during which codes were sometimes withdrawn in mid-process.

The Complexity of the Update Process and Participants' Specialized Knowledge

Requesting a change in relative value units is ill-advised for anyone without a firm mastery of the process and its rules. The specificity of the committee's language and jargon, which includes unique terms known only by insiders, limits the accessibility of information. Linguists studying the legal process have shown that creating new names—"relexicalization"—increases complexity—for example, when a noun-like compound is created that obscures the meaning (Little 1998).

Informants say that a complex terminology and language are required to engage in rulemaking and committee meetings. In casual conversation, participants liken the mastery of the process to learning ancient Greek and portray the world of committee meetings as a subculture with folkways and practices that have to be learned, rather like, as one participant said, a game of *Dungeons and Dragons*. Almost everyone connected with the process mentions its steep learning curve and the need for considerable time to get up to speed to participate. An interviewee described how "it takes three years to learn the process. It really does . . . this is a real job that you're going to have for life because you're really . . . once you get it, you get hooked in the whole concept" (Interview Subject 19). As the interviewee suggests, participants also gain a sense of satisfaction in mastering the material.

Navigating the committee's process is difficult for newcomers and outsiders. There are always new people entering the Advisory Committee, who usually apprentice before taking on active roles, and changes in the committee membership, but the level of stability on the main committee is relatively high. Interviewees say that a "core of people, the guys that I work with have been there and they've been doing this right from the beginning. They've been to . . . probably 50 of these meetings" (Interview Subject 1). At four meetings, the author observed that some events were translated or explained by veteran panelists. A seeming victory for one organization might work to the disadvantage of another, with indiscernible effects (to an outsider) that cannot be parsed. What is required, then, is

> the knowledge of how this whole system works, understanding that is critical, understanding the interplay between, time, position, work, intensity. So that's . . . part of it—a knowledge thing on the part of the physician who's a presenter. And also part of it is staff. I mean . . . there's no book. There's no "RUC for Dummies." We have a staff member who's been observing this process now for three years. And he finally thinks, quote, "I think I get it." You have to sit, you have to sit there. You have to listen to the discussions. You have to watch the arguments. You have to follow the rationale behind the argument. You have to read what CMS publishes with the proposed and a final rule. And you . . . and you really have to study it until you really understand. There's like, moving parts in four dimensions. If you're coming in from the outside, and you haven't done this beforehand, it's like being put in the middle of Greece, and you don't know how to speak the language. So part of the problem is you have to learn how to speak the language. And then the other part of it is, you have to understand how to be meaningful in the language. So it's not enough that you know how to read Greek, you have to be able to put together a sentence in a meaningful manner. You want to be able to say something to the effect of, "Thank you very much, where is the bathroom?" not "The bathroom is in my head." You can go to Berlitz, and you can learn how to say "The bathroom is in my head," and people will look at you strange. "But I can speak Greek." No, you don't understand Greek. And that's the problem with the RUC. (Interview Subject 3)

A casual observer would not necessarily understand if or when a society is stonewalling or slow-walking the review process (to postpone a potential code reduction, for example) or trying to accelerate the process for a lucrative new technology. Or there may be contradictions that are difficult to understand. For example, if the committee is driven by a need to divide a fixed pie, a service being considered for children might appear to the un-initiated to be destined to pass through easily given the very small propor-tion of children eligible for Medicare. Yet according to one interviewee, this is much more complicated than it might first appear, due to the alliances on the Update Committee and how services are referenced to one another. Cognitive services for children do not always do well, due to the concern that high valuations would later be used by primary care societies to extrapo-late to adult cognitively based services. Meanwhile, "a procedurally ori-ented pediatric service would be subject to less scrutiny because there would be other procedures that could conceivably be linked to it and bootstrapped to a higher value" (Interview Subject 4).

Strategies can have unintended consequences, and so decisions have to be made with a view to the possible downstream consequences. Societies have to balance their desire to seek "artificially and improperly inflated values" (Interview Subject 4). If societies aim too high, "this code goes down and there's five others out there linked to it, [then] those other five become fair game. And then each one of those needs to be evaluated, and if those go down or in a family, then that whole family goes down, as well as other things that are linked to them" (Interview Subject 4).

Success in the update process requires ongoing experience because the process changes over time:

> And that's the problem with the RUC. The RUC is not static. . . . The RUC is dynamic. And just because something was that way five years ago, or 15 years ago, doesn't mean it's that way today. And so you have to continually be cog-nizant of the fact that the process continues to evolve, and that the rationale evolves. And that what might have been good in 1999 isn't going to fly in 2011. CMS's rationale evolves over time. All these things move, and that's the problem for some people. As I said, you have to be able to speak the language, you have to understand their language, you have to be cognizant of the fact that it changes, it's fluid, it's dynamic. And when you aren't coming from that environment, it can be very daunting for people. Because now you're sitting in front of a panel of almost 30 very smart people. Don't feel so bad, because most people will tell you, it easily takes three to five years of watching this before you actually understand it. (Interview Subject 3)

This dynamic quality of the committee and CMS increases the need to have inside knowledge and to closely follow the process. It also raises the search costs. Moreover, lobbying by the House of Medicine in Congress can result in further complexity in the Medicare law by complicating the raft of rules around the updates and budget neutrality. There are exceptions for certain types of services: for example, the ACA exempted some types of imaging services from the budget neutrality adjustment.

Complexity and Specialty Societies' Game of Codes

Committee supporters believe that the need for sophisticated clinical judgment justifies leaving the updating of the RBRVS to the House of Medicine, and they also argue that the process is rigorous. The premise that the committee may be perceived as a tough, sophisticated customer suggests that voting members are so savvy that specialty societies will not be able to hoodwink them. Yet specialty society representatives admit that they find strategies and workarounds that put them at an advantage. Supposedly, the desire by the people around the table and the specialty societies to maintain budget neutrality acts as a brake on unrestrained behavior, but as the discussion shows, this obstacle seems to operate more weakly, if at all.

Moreover, the committee is composed of highly embedded specialty society members, so the ability of voting members to police specialty societies is prima facie problematic. The specialty representatives on the panel know where the proverbial bodies are buried for their codes, but they are not allowed to review their own specialties out of concern for conflict of interest. The specialty society representative on the Update Committee is likely the most informed regarding the intricacies of the services in that area—and how the coding system can be used to its advantage, not to mention recent changes in technology that might be unknown to those outside the specialty.

It may be particularly difficult for those outside the specialty to understand why some codes are not being reviewed. Among several strategies that can be used to circumvent the budget neutrality restraint, one of the most important (discussed below) is maintaining the status quo value.

Salami Slicing and Unbundling

One strategy discussed by specialty societies is using the coding process to redefine medical services. The coding process, well integrated with the work of the committee, is an underappreciated potential source of health care price inflation.

The AMA has a separate committee for coding, called the CPT committee. Before the RBRVS was created, the coding system was not so closely tied to reimbursement. At that time, "the descriptor was quite general" and procedures "could vary considerably in time and complexity" (Bean 2002, 1). Asked about budget neutrality, interviewees discussed how procedural specialties were at a distinct advantage due to the possibility of dividing codes. They described how, over the past 15 years, societies had used a strategy of reintroducing CPT codes that then come to the committee for valuation. "So if you have . . . a code for knee arthroscopy, there's two of them . . . and then all of a sudden you've got six. Those two are broken into six" (Interview Subject 18).

Outside of the process, people may not realize that codes are designed with the level of work in mind. Discussions inside specialty societies suggest that the definition of the code is influenced by the level of work associated with it. In one meeting, a specialty society member specifically mentions the need to have several codes to cover different levels of work:

> Dr. Friedman spoke to this request to convert existing Category III codes for internal fixation of rib fracture to Category I status. After discussion and review of the literature, advisors support this request with modification. The group felt that three codes for reporting these procedures was more appropriate: 2181X1 Open treatment of rib fracture with internal fixation, any approach (e.g. open or thoracoscopic), unilateral; 1–3 2181X2; 4–6; 2181X3 7 or more. Dr. Blasier led the discussion on new codes for growing rods and VEPTR (vertical expandable prosthetic titanium rib). Dr. Blasier once again queried the committee on whether it would be beneficial to bring forward a code change request. Dr. Haynes felt that the need for new CPT codes to describe this procedure would be supported by existing literature but also stated that drafting vignettes would be challenging. He emphasized that the vignette should be for the most common scenario and patient. However, it was also suggested that it may be beneficial to have two codes representing different degrees of work with two patient vignettes to accommodate for more complex cases. It was also stated that these codes would include fusion. After discussion, the group agreed that Dr. Blasier should proceed with the creation of a code change proposal with the assistance of Dr. Haynes. (American Academy of Orthopedic Surgeons 2013, 28)

New codes can be legitimately new; they may also constitute elaborate segmentation or "salami slicing" into more finely disaggregated codes. Indeed, people who have studied new CPT codes speculate that most of the new codes are "probably just relabeled or reclassified old procedures, rather than true innovations" (Lichtenberg 2006). Such a strategy is reasonably well documented and has been a concern since the 1950s, when physicians developed relative value–based fee schedules. The way codes are defined is vitally important, and one that is carefully addressed when there are opportunities or threats to the status quo:

> I had worked on the [specialty] codes for five years or six years, ever since we kind of smelled that they were going to come up. And that's what the [society name] RUC team strength was, is that we were a bunch of paranoid individuals, and we also looked far ahead in the future. And I had been working with [name], who is the [society name] RUC representative. And we were coming up with all kinds of things, ways to divide the codes and. . . . We were going to actually use the [redacted] system of dividing them up on by systems. We worked hard on it. The powers that be at the [society] decided they wanted to see if they could get the codes pushed through as is. And once we were presented with that reality, I worked very hard with [name] who was the [society] advisor. And we came up with plans, and by God, we did it. We pushed them through. Should they have been pushed through? Well, they're almost impossible to break apart. (Interview Subject 5)

As the quote indicates, the effort to influence codes is worth it in some cases. Countervailing pressures on specialty societies include limited time and resources and reputational costs. One interviewee said that the specialty society she or he was most familiar with strongly discouraged unnecessary introduction of codes, mainly because it is time intensive and burdensome. However, if one code is going to be introduced, the marginal cost of adding more codes would presumably be low, especially since many codes are evaluated as "families" given their similarity.

A potentially more rewarding strategy involves unbundling closely related services. This adding and disaggregating of new codes so that a service has more components is called "component coding." A case in point is complex spinal surgery.[4] The specialty society creates add-on codes, which can increase the reimbursement of the service. Specialty societies benefit by increasing their reimbursement, without needing to prove additional work or changing the work value through the committee. "As additional components are added to the procedure, they are explicitly itemized and included as an additional charge, because the base global fee is fixed by regulation. Although physicians cannot alter global fees within the MFS [Medicare Fee

TABLE 6.2 Total Number of Services in the Medicare Fee Schedule and Mean Work Relative Value Units, 2000–2013

Year	Mean work relative value unit	Number of services
2000	7.76	7,749
2001	8.05	8,021
2002	8.05	8,021
2003	8.09	8,147
2004	8.08	8,235
2005	8.05	8,336
2006	8.05	8,409
2007	8.93	8,316
2008	8.94	8,396
2009	8.93	8,459
2010	9.03	8,545
2011	9.01	8,597
2012	9.09	8,584
2013	9.15	8,572
Percent change	18.00	10.6

Source: Author's compilation of work relative value units from CMS relative value unit files, downloaded from www.cms.gov.

Schedule], they can increase the value by itemizing new components of the procedure as add-on codes" (Bean 2002, 3).

Many codes are deleted in the CPT process and then replaced by similar codes (and with more derivations). Table 6.2 shows an increase in the number of codes in the fee schedule with associated relative value units, from 7,749 in 2000 to 8,572 in 2013. Data on the number of services deleted are not available, but the growth in Table 6.2 suggests deletions are compensated by new codes. The number of codes appears to be limited mainly by the resources available to review and make recommendations on them and by Medicare's coverage determinations. New codes could potentially conceal increases in fees.

Overlooking Technological Changes That Alter Work

Choosing to overlook technological changes that reduce the time it takes to provide a service is another strategy to maintain fees, although this is not exclusive to the committee and has been used for decades. For example, in

1969, a new procedure to investigate potential colon cancer and polyp removal (colonoscopy with polypectomy), which was pioneered in Massachusetts, could be done on an outpatient basis, without general anesthesia and in one hour. Insurers were prone to pay it at a lower rate than its surgical equivalent because it took less time. Then physicians in Massachusetts found a way around the reduced payment rate: by using the traditional procedure code, for which insurers would pay as for a surgical service. In the four years before a new code existed, from 1969 to 1973, this became a lucrative procedure for Massachusetts physicians (Law and Ensminger 1986, 36).

Societies have to weigh the risk that new timesaving technologies might have the effect of reducing current reimbursement. Fortunately for them, they have some degree of control over new codes for new technology. Only societies can sponsor new code applications to the AMA CPT committee, through which any proposal to create a new code must filter. Potentially, this process gives specialty societies the ability to protect their existing codes. Therefore, specialty societies carefully consider the implications of any new technology for their existing reimbursement levels: "Say you make a new device that will decompress the spine, but will do it percutaneously and take one-third of the time of a standard open decompression. In addition it has very little associated risk. But you're billing it as if it were the more expensive, work-intensive, risky procedure." "In the short term, that may be very good for the device company. . . . But in the long term, it puts all decompression procedures on the insurer's radar. The decompression CPT code gets on the radar for CMS and the whole family of CPT codes gets revalued and often downvalued" (Eisner 2009, 18). An interviewee described another similar scenario:

> So if you have a society that has what we call is a "bread and butter" procedure, something that's frequently done by your members . . . why on earth would you want to bring forward a new CPT code for a new procedure. . . . Let's say that you can do a new procedure, and you can do it in a third less time. But by bringing this new procedure forward, in other words by getting a CPT code for this new procedure, you're now faced with the dilemma as a society. Do you want to bring this new code forward, which could then trigger the CMS or the RUC to saying, well, your base code really needs to be looked at. It hasn't been valued since 1995, and hasn't it changed in the past 15 years' time? Or could CPT . . . or CMS or someone else say, "Well, you know what? We liked your new procedure . . . we don't really want to

create a scenario . . . that people who do that procedure should get paid as much as we're getting paid for our currently overinflated surgical procedure. So, if you want to bring a new procedure through, you can do it, but understand that . . ."—they won't tell you this in public—but "understand that you run a risk, that if you do that, your new procedure, because it saves time," . . . the RUC is all about time intensity; the RUC is not about value. So if you're saving time because it takes less time to do the procedure, you're going to get less money for doing your new procedure. (Interview Subject 3)

Sometimes the existing work value (based on a traditional surgical removal) becomes inaccurate when there is new technology, but there is no incentive to change it. Using the old code artificially inflates the prices of the services, because the efficiencies are not being passed on. If, on the other hand, the society could make a case that a service is more intense, even if it is quicker, then the society would be better off requesting a new code. If the intensity of the procedure were the same, a quicker procedure than the existing technique would normally be paid at a lower rate.

Overlooking Analogous or Related New Technologies

Sometimes a new technology could justify creating a new code if the society considers it in its interest and it can be shown to be distinct from other services. But a problem arises when the technology is different but analogous or closely related to an existing one. Similarities make the committee more likely to compare the service to other "bread and butter" codes that have existing generous valuations. If a new code clearly fits into an existing group of codes, the similarity of the code to others may trigger a review of the other codes in close proximity. Sometimes this can be achieved by simply leaving a code in a transitional stage in the CPT process rather than requesting a new code from CPT, which would then be eligible for a work value from the committee. Donovan (2012) said this was the strategy used by the American Society for Neuro-Interventional Radiology economics team members, which avoided committee review of some commonly performed codes by not advancing a code called CT perfusion of the head through the CPT process.[5]

Had the society requested a new code and it had been evaluated by the Committee, the society would need to request a "formal survey and reevaluation of the basic head CT codes . . . these codes had never been through the 'modern' RUC survey process; their values were incorporated into the RBRVS from the radiology RVS. Had the society asked for RUC to provide work values for the CT perfusion code, they may have put the valuation of the most commonly performed CT examination in the Medicare population at risk." (Donovan 2012, 429)

Therefore, societies may choose not to propose a new code. Another example from the Society of Nuclear Medicine illustrates the dilemma, in this case for a technology without a track record. The society initially considered creating new codes for a proposed single-photon emission computed tomography (SPECT). One reason not to go forward was that this innovative technology without much published research on its effectiveness and not yet in wide use might not get a code in the CPT. But a more likely reason is that the whole code family might be reviewed in the course of developing a new code. The society worried that it would attract attention that could jeopardize other similar codes in that family: "SPECT/CT CPT is likely to pull into play all or many of the SPECT codes, putting current RVU for SPECT in jeopardy. With the work of the ongoing rolling five year review workgroup of the AMA RUC we suspect that SPECT will come forward during one of those screens in the next two years. Committee agreed to monitor the literature before moving forward" (Society of Nuclear Medicine 2010d).

Calculations such as these all involve a similar choice—namely, whether to seek a new code or keep the status quo and simply use existing ones. The latter choice means protecting the reimbursement of similar codes, which, as the following section shows, is especially important for high-volume codes.

Keeping the Status Quo for the Bread and Butter Codes

Some interest groups spend more time maintaining the status quo than advocating for policy change. They are content with most of the policies in place because they benefit from them (Baumgartner et al. 2009). Interest groups also hope to keep arrangements that favor them out of the limelight to avoid uncomfortable questions. For example, in what is called a "global period" approach used by Medicare and adopted by private payers, the total payment includes all the postoperative visits in the surgical and other procedure payments within a time period such as 10 or 90 days. The work for this service could include the procedure and five office visits, say within a 90-day period. No documentation that the service was actually provided is required in order for the service to receive full reimbursement—the payment is the same regardless of whether the patient ever saw the physician for all five visits. In contrast, for services without a bundling of surgical and office visits, all office visits have to be documented. A surgical society representative on the committee spoke about this policy as best kept below the radar, because the societies thought they were doing well under it: "Let's don't play that game, let's stay out of that arena, because we are doing fairly well" (Mabry et al. 2005, 940).[6] CMS proposed investigating postoperative visits, but Congress prevented CMS from reviewing the global periods in the 2015 Medicare Access and CHIP Reauthorization Act.

Just as political scientists like to focus on major bills and legislative policy changes, observers of the process are prone to focus on how much the codes change, because that is what the process is supposed to be about. But the most significant win for specialties is arguably when their higher reward codes are not reviewed. Societies try to keep the status quo and do not ask questions about services they want to preserve. Their strategies can be subtle (or invisible) and would be missed without extensive knowledge of the process.

There is a bias toward review of existing codes that are undervalued. The codes that are reviewed by the committee represent a selection of codes that societies want to have reviewed, for the most part. Historically, CMS was required to consider the appropriateness of the work value of existing services only every five years. Five-year reviews were generally an opportunity for societies to advocate for increases in services they considered undervalued; as a result, fees were rarely reduced. Instead of CMS initiating a detailed study of the work values in the fee schedule, codes were usually nominated by societies themselves and overwhelmingly saw increases, with very few decreases. After the committee was criticized in a 2006 Medicare Payment Advisory Commission report, it initiated its own workgroup jointly with CMS to review "potentially misvalued codes."

Specialty society members told the author that they try to protect the value of "bread and butter" services—defined as "something that's frequently done by your members"—and the term came up repeatedly in interviews. As one participant said, more generously paid codes should be protected, and societies have to create a bulwark against threats to their favored codes. An "unwritten duty of the RUC advisory teams from ASNR [American Society for Neuro-Interventional Radiology], ACR [American

College of Radiology], and SIR [Society for Interventional Radiology] through the years has been to ensure as much as possible that 'historically valued' procedures such as these stayed out of the limelight; for instance, by not using them as validation for other codes, and by declining to bring them forward to the RUC in an attempt to increase their valuation, a process that can backfire" (Donovan 2012, 429).

As the quote suggests, the two main ways this protection is achieved are by not using codes as comparison codes and by not asking for increases. In this way too, the budget neutrality adjustment fails to act as a restraint on the committee: it only applies to codes that are reviewed and that change the status quo and not to those that are not reviewed.

One interviewee discussed a service that a society had tried unsuccessfully to keep from being reviewed. As it turned out, the review created a win for the specialty, because the procedures were more differentiated: "And everybody knows that everyone's playing this game. But we just left [laparoscopic procedure] under the radar, and for the first time in several years, just this five-year review, [laparoscopic procedure] and [investigational procedure] came through review and we got a substantial increase in [investigational procedure], whereas [laparoscopic procedure] remained the same" (Interview Subject 1).

Societies may not be able to play this game indefinitely, however. Section 3134 of the ACA requires CMS to identify and adjust "misvalued services," including ones associated with fastest utilization growth, new technology, multiple code billing for a single service, or services that have not been reviewed since the RBRVS was implemented (also known as "Harvard" codes). The ACA put the committee under pressure to tighten up the review process, so societies are likely more risk averse. The Protecting Access to Medicare Act of 2014 extended some of these requirements, but to date, there has not yet been independent review of this effort and its outcomes.

One example of how societies will defend the value of existing codes is given in an example from the Society for Cardiovascular Angiography and Interventions (SCAI), which reported that its members, along with American College of Cardiology members, presented values and times for diagnostic cardiac catheterization procedures to the RUC with data dating to 1992. According to SCAI's representative to the RUC, Dr. Cliff Kavinsky, "We focused on how patients who undergo these services have become increasingly complex over the years and we offered an in-depth examination of the relativity of recommended values for diagnostic caths compared to other services," and "Ultimately we were able to show the members of the RUC that cardiac catheterization procedures were already fairly valued and did not deserve reductions in reimbursement" (Society for Cardiovascular Angiography and Interventions 2011, 2). Here, the society appears to defend existing values. The society also said that it faced a new challenge due to CMS reviews of coronary stenting codes. Dr. James B. Blankenship, a member of the Update Committee and chair of the SCAI Advocacy Committee, said that

> the advocacy challenge will be bigger than the one addressed this spring on diagnostic cardiac catheterization: Unlike the diagnostic cardiac cath codes, the current coronary stent codes were valued through the existing RUC process and the valuations, which reflect 120 minutes of intra-service "skin-to-skin" time, will be harder to defend. SCAI and ACC are approaching the challenge at the level of new code development—meaning the best way to effectively capture the value of more complex coronary stent services that have evolved in the past 15 years is to create new codes that reflect the increased time and intensity of many current interventional procedures. We envision a large family of codes to describe coronary stent services. What that means for members is a complex but vitally important RUC survey process. (Society for Cardiovascular Angiography and Interventions 2011, 2)

Using Sacrificial Lamb Codes

While information obtained by the author suggests that specialty societies not infrequently try to keep services off the review roster, sometimes it cannot be avoided. Then, to improve their image, societies may enable that process for specific codes, so they can say that they are willing to reduce relative value units. On the surface, this looks admirable, but the payoff it provides is to protect the codes they consider more important by conceding on less important codes—ones that do not matter. One interviewee said his or her society was facing a low-ball valuation of work that was a "bread and butter" code. To head off that possibility, the society "went around making adjustments and concessions on the lower volume procedures, so you get a reputation for being honest and fair and all that sort of stuff. But in the background, we are really protecting our bread and butter procedures, very strongly" (Interview Subject 1). A similar observation appeared in a specialty society newsletter in 2009: "There are times that we have to lose some of the low-hanging fruit in order to maintain credibility for the big things. We are just trying to protect the things that are the bread and butter of our surgeons and other members" (Eisner 2009, 18).

The Fox-Henhouse Problem and Agency Capture

The complexity of the update process and payment policy reduces the possibility of oversight of both the process and the RBRVS itself. Understanding the impact or even the nature of the policies in place makes it difficult to monitor the policies and especially challenging to understand impact. Two important components of oversight are discussed: the fact that budget neutrality opacity and workaround tactics by specialty societies imply that government has not been able to effectively constrain the activities of specialty societies. Second, the complexity of the process encourages CMS to depend heavily on the committee, leaving it potentially captured by the organization it needs to closely monitor.

The probability of capture under conditions of complexity occurs for a variety of reasons. First, in keeping with theories of interest group provision of information, interest groups have more to offer bureaucrats on complex issues than on simpler ones (Shapiro 2008). When agencies are dependent on information, they will tolerate policies that the firm supports (McCarty 2014). Second, agencies often lack the capacity (staff, resources) to have equivalent levels of information as interest groups. In some complex industries (and some areas of medicine are such), the wage premium makes it hard to hire people to work as regulators (McCarty 2014). Agencies can try to address a lack of capacity by using advisory committees (Moffitt 2010), but this may not address informational asymmetries. A third possible reason why capture occurs originates in the potential for cultural capture. Cultural capture occurs when shared social and cultural networks, cognitive biases, or worldviews shape the decisions of agency staff in favor of the organizations they are regulating (Kwak 2014).

Capture requires evidence that one group has had a clear influence on policy and has been advantaged over others (Carpenter, 2014)—it is not sufficient to observe "policy outcomes that appear to favor well-organized and wealthy interests" (Yackee 2014, 300). For example, in the case of the RUC, the AMA defends its role and argues that agreement between the committee and CMS is evidence of the agency's confidence in the recommendations and the validity of the process.

Capture is only present if the advantages extended to one group have a negative impact on policy; it is only negative if it leads to suboptimal policies (Carpenter 2014). If capture leads to better policy, it might be desirable (Carpenter 2014). Fee increases are largely driven by the Update Committee's changes to the relative value units. Price changes are therefore one area where the Update Committee has had a demonstrably important—and negative—role: fee increases directly account for a significant proportion of increases in Medicare expenditure (Maxwell, Zuckerman, and Berenson 2007). Over time, relative value units are increasing, not staying the same, and only a minority (10 percent) of codes are reduced by CMS (Laugesen, Wada, and Chen 2012). Policy experts say that the fee schedule "defies gravity" (Ginsburg and Berenson 2007), and in the 1990s, the mean RVU increased 17 percent between 1993 and 1998 (Laugesen and Rice 2003).

Theories of regulatory capture and complexity suggest that more complex decisions, which are characterized by less programmability, are more likely to be captured because regulators are more uncertain and rely on information provided by the House of Medicine. Empirically, one test of this theory is to differentiate services reviewed by CMS by levels of complexity and compare CMS's receptivity of the Update Committee recommendations. Using data from Update Committee recommendations and CMS decisions, we might expect CMS to be more dependent on information from the committee for new codes, because they are likely to be more complex given they are technologically novel or may introduce new techniques or changes in medical practice. CMS makes smaller changes to committee recommendations, on average, for new codes (–0.7 percent) than for existing codes (–2.0 percent). When CMS considers the Update Committee's recommendations on new codes, its final decisions are closer to the original committee recommendation than they are for existing codes.

Another indicator of the influence of complexity is the agency treatment of different kinds of medical services. Among the range of services reviewed by the committee and CMS, E&M services would likely be the most easily understood by nonclinicians, since the clinical terminology is simpler given that the descriptions refer to physician office visits and hospital consultations/observations. However, the results of this comparison are less conclusive than the analysis of new and existing codes. The mean change in RVUs to committee recommendations for E&M visits is –1.2 percent. Although CMS also has changed the values of pathology and laboratory services ($n = 46$), E&M services have been changed at a much lower level (–1.2 percent) than

TABLE 6.3 CMS Decisions on Relative Value Unit Recommendations Made by the Relative Value Update Committee, 1994–2010

CMS response to committee recommendation	Number	Percentage of the total
No change to work value	2,419	87.4
Increased work value	51	2.0
Decreased work value	298	10.8
Total	2,768	100

Source: Author's calculations.

every other kind of service. Both the treatment of new/existing codes and the approach to less medically complex services support the hypothesis that agencies tend to act with less certainty (and therefore may be more receptive to interest group information) in areas where they have less information.

CMS usually accepts and reduces few of the committee's recommendations (Table 6.3). Among 2,700 recommendations to the CMS between 1994 and 2010, CMS accepted 87 percent. Understanding why CMS follows recommendations is important for understanding how the committee influences the process.

Payment experts tend to believe that CMS has not received enough support to do its job, and policy experts believe that the distortions in the fee schedule can be attributed to that lack of oversight:

> And although the RUC makes recommendations and it is up to CMS to make final determinations, there is a certain amount of politics involved that constrains CMS. Moreover, CMS has never been adequately funded to collect the kinds of cost data that one ideally would want to have in order to truly support accurate assignment of RVUs. So, in a sense, a lot of this is sort of faith-based fee setting, or self-interested fee setting as the case might be, so that all has contributed to the distortions that we see in the Medicare fee schedule. (Interview Subject 11)

The complexity of the payment system and the update process increases CMS's reliance, reduces external scrutiny, and likely exacerbates the fact that CMS does not have the resources to either replicate the process or closely monitor every code revision: the agency's lack of financial resources means it cannot "do anything other than rely on the RUC" (Interview Subject 25). When the author asked whether CMS could replace the job of specialty societies and survey physicians, one interviewee said, "They could, but then how would they get them to support? And I know what a difficult job we have in arm-twisting people to participate. I couldn't imagine how CMS would ever get anything reasonable. And they'd have to do it for the entire fee schedule. See, right now, part of the reason they . . . they take over 90 percent of the recommendations is because they don't have enough [inaudible] to do all that work themselves. RUC and all the societies are free labor for them" (Interview Subject 4). Furthermore, in the past there has also been resistance inside the agency to challenging or changing the status quo. An interviewee with inside knowledge of CMS said that the career staffers at CMS avoid rocking the boat, because "If we sort of say 'we don't trust the RUC's judgment,' what the hell are we going to do?" The interviewee then went on to say that career staff at CMS and the AMA were "outwitting" those individuals questioning the committee's role (Interview Subject 25). Another interviewee who worked in government was surprised to be told that the decisions made by the committee would be implemented as recommended.

> I was informed that . . . what the payment rates were going to be "Well, the RUC's decided," and I said, "You got to be out of your mind. The RUC is an advisory group to me." "Oh, well, no, that's not the way it works." [Then] I said, "B°°°°°°° that is the way it works?" [laughter] I said, "I don't have to pay attention to the RUC." "Well, they've been doing this for years." And I said, "Well, I don't really care." So, but the problem is CMS didn't have the staff to replace the RUC. Who wants to pick a fight with the AMA? (Interview Subject 22)

As another interviewee said, all the incentives were structured toward CMS cooperating rather than fighting with the Update Committee. The agency's

> incentive is to go along with it, because if they don't go along with it, then they have got to do a lot of roll-up-your sleeves equity sweat. They have to go provide a rationale and a notice of proposed rule making and why they rejected the RUC argument. They have to do a lot of legwork to go through the fee schedule and find other codes that are similarly valued with an

appropriate resource to maintain the resource-based system in accord with the legal mandate. They have to then go and come up with a rationale for whatever numbers they put into the fee schedule as interim, and then they have to deal with the onslaught of all the complaints and responses during the public comment period. So that's a boat load of work. They're going to be very judicious about what they disagree with. (Interview Subject 4)

Yet given the complexity of the process, oversight of both CMS and the Update Committee is difficult, because it requires extensive knowledge of how it works. A key source of oversight is the Medicare Payment Advisory Commission, which advises Congress on Medicare. The organization is small, however, and has limited resources to heavily focus on the RBRVS. As one interviewee described it, "MedPAC covers all of Medicare," so staffers and board members have to consider many topics, including home health, nursing homes, inpatient hospital payments, and outpatient payments (Interview Subject 11). In Medicare Payment Advisory Commission reports, "what you'll see is Part B payments might be one or two chapters out of nine or ten chapters. So the bulk of the time is not spent on either of those. When you had a physician payment review commission, that is what it did. So it was much more focused on what was going on with physician payments" (Interview Subject 11). Others agreed, saying that the Medicare Payment Advisory Commission has no power, and they were cognizant of how physician groups were sometimes inclined to retaliate against agencies through Congress, as had happened with the former Agency for Health Care Policy Research, which was unpopular with spine surgeons:

They don't have any power . . . they just make recommendations. . . . But, you know, I think if you're at MedPAC and you're an advisory board, you don't necessarily want to pick a fight with somebody and somebody like them, you know . . . wipe you out . . . the point is, if you pick a fight with the wrong doc group, you can disappear overnight. So if you're MedPAC, do you really want to go have a war with the AMA or something that most people don't understand? You know, it could cause you a lot of problems. (Interview Subject 22)

In recent years, CMS received some additional funding to study the measurement of physician work and intensity, and the agency was able to contract with the Urban Institute and the RAND Corporation to provide CMS with technical assistance that would allow it to develop new ways of assessing physician work. At the time of writing, the impact of these efforts is not clear, but it is an encouraging sign that CMS has a larger budget and support from some legislators to develop its own capacities to more effectively scrutinize work.

Frequent access to decision makers is one determinant of agency support for interest group positions (Hansen 1991; Nicholson-Crotty and Nicholson-Crotty 2004). Both the level and frequency of access to CMS decision makers are arguably very high at the meetings, given the length of the meetings (approximately three days for 8 to 10 hours per day). At all Update Committee meetings, two CMS representatives have a seat "at the table." They are not involved in the deliberations directly, and CMS staffers do not often participate in the committee discussions often. Evidently, they are there to provide technical advice or to clarify CMS policy. However, there are frequent opportunities for committee members and CMS staff to interact outside the formal meeting process too, given smaller shared lunches limited to the 30 committee members, AMA staff, and CMS representatives, as well as associated events. Social ties between the committee and CMS are therefore fostered in a process that occurs far from Washington, DC, and puts committee members and CMS staff in close proximity.

Limited evidence indicates that CMS and AMA staff collaborate in shared presentations explaining the committee process and the content of proposed rules (American Medical Association 2012). Meeting records further disclose that CMS staff have participated in conference calls of committee working groups formed by the AMA on select issues, such as the Chronic Care Coordination Workgroup (American Medical Association 2011b). Likewise, CMS staff may find the meetings valuable because they can more clearly explain the decisions of the committee to their colleagues. The author was at a meeting where the CMS representative commented that the committee's recommendation and rationale would need to be essentially defended by CMS to their colleagues.

Indeed, the committee is a community whose members gain a body of knowledge far beyond the comprehension of outsiders. Participants in these meetings say that the shared knowledge is one aspect of the bonds and friendships generated. Committee participants told the author that they draw camaraderie from their common language and lament that no one outside the process understands what they do or how significant it is. At committee meetings and in this community, some gain power and prestige. A shared sense of mission might be explained by the bonding that comes about from mastery of the language, the rules, and the peculiar world of the RBRVS system.

Conclusion

Complex policies, which usually fall within the domain of experts, confer a number of advantages on the organizations participating. As discussed above, the complexity of payment policy and the specialized language and rules of the committee process itself create high informational search costs. The complexity of the process, the RBRVS, and the opacity of medical codes allow specialty societies to use a host of strategies such as disaggregating codes, maintaining the high-value "bread and butter" codes, and holding back code changes to prevent codes from being valued. These strategies and the seemingly anemic impact of budget neutrality adjustments may explain increases in relative value units and a proliferation of codes in the fee schedule.

The complexity of the RBRVS and the process also likely explains why the decisions of the committee and CMS so seldom diverge. The committee does not "control" CMS, but recommendations have a significant impact on their decisions. The committee is clearly the most important influence on CMS decisions, which closely track committee recommendations. This closeness may warrant application of the label "regulatory capture," which scholars define as "the control of agency policy decision-making by a subpopulation of individuals or organizations" and as the omnipresence of a single set of interests (Yackee 2014, 300). On issues of high complexity, regulators are likely to acquiesce and lend their support to proposals from industry (Gormley 1986; McCarty 2014). Another indicator of capture is the committee's exclusive role outside conventional rulemaking structure and processes. The committee coordinates and internalizes a process that might normally be entrusted to public rulemaking and does its work unburdened by the requirements of that process. It is a private committee not subject to Federal Advisory Committee Act (1972) rules regarding transparency. There is great diversity in how agencies engage in rulemaking, but the committee appears to have played an unusual role in the process. The committee's unusual role emerges from the complexity of the process that in turn has created conditions that may increase cultural commonalities between the agency and the regulated entities arising from acculturation.

The influence of the committee depends partly on the willingness of CMS to accept its recommendations. Whether CMS is cognizant of strategies used by specialty societies is not clear. Like all agencies, CMS faces competing pressures and resource constraints. Resource constraints are a significant problem for CMS, reducing the ability of government to create alternative processes or heavily scrutinize the recommendations of the committee. Congress's nonpartisan advisor on Medicare payments, the Medicare Payment Advisory Commission, is considered an effective counter to CMS and the committee when it is able to give the fee schedule attention, but it also suffers from resource constraints. Yet its potential impact is significant. The Medicare Payment Advisory Commission's concern about the closeness of CMS to the committee in 2006, as well as its recommendation that the agency should establish its own "standing panel of experts" (Medicare Payment Advisory Commission 2006b), was one of the most important factors contributing to ACA provisions and other changes that have been directed toward holding the committee process more accountable. These new policy efforts suggest that if sufficient attention can be directed toward payment policy problems and provided long-term resources are available, the complexity of the process may be countered successfully.

SEVEN

Conclusion

THIS BOOK HAS explored how one big payer—Medicare—determines prices for physician services. Prices for physician services ultimately reflect the relationship between physician groups and government, as well as the private sector. In this respect, the House of Medicine in the United States is similar to other countries, and historically, physicians in the United States have had similar goals to their colleagues elsewhere. Whenever national health insurance was proposed, the dominant concern of organized medicine was remuneration and ongoing control over payment issues. Inevitably, trade-offs are made, and political institutional structures in some countries provide physicians with more or less leverage (Immergut 1992). In many countries, passing national health insurance requires meeting physicians' demands, suggesting that at least historically, the power of the House of Medicine is not exclusive to the United States. Famously, to ensure the United Kingdom had a National Health Service, Aneurin Bevan took a realpolitik strategy when getting the hospital specialists on board. As he put it, he "stuffed their mouths with gold." Yet at the same time, there are distinctive characteristics of the way physician-government relations have played out in the United States, and early gains in power were exacerbated.

This book explores the terrain of physician payment policy and the political interests that shape the prices paid for physician services in the United States, particularly how the House of Medicine influences the relative values used to calculate payment for Medicare services. By exploring how relative prices of physician services in the United States are established, we gain insight on why some physician services are more expensive in the United States than in other countries. By going inside the "black box" of how we value Medicare services, we also understand how changes to relative value units ripple across the health care system. With unprecedented access to the participants and the committee itself, we now have a more in-depth understanding of this committee and are better able to understand why some—but not all—Medicare payments have became distorted over time. Fee levels have remained high for physicians engaged in providing procedural and surgical services. The previous chapters connect the dots across a wide array of primary sources in order to inform policy makers and researchers, as well as physicians and health professionals, why what Congress intended in 1989—to better compensate primary care doctors—has failed.

As one observer described it, "Two committees within the AMA have been instrumental not only in developing but most importantly in maintaining, updating, and defending the current system," and both the Update Committee and the CPT committees have great potential to influence the course of health policy (Beyer and Mohideen 2008, 187). In its defense, supporters of the Update Committee argue that relative values represent a zero-sum game that imposes discipline on a part of the participants. Yet, this does not necessarily square with the fact that, as Beyer and Mohideen note, the House of Medicine's influence over fees has successfully maintained many historical pricing differences.

The RBRVS was set up in the hope that public officials would assess the cost associated with providing physician services, and that officials would serve the public interest, but the House of Medicine successfully advances its own interests. That dynamic is the essence of what economists and political scientists describe as policy capture. To assert a policy is captured, however, one must also meet a burden of proof and a degree of intentionality:

Full diagnoses of capture need (a) to posit a defensible model of public interest, (b) to show action and intent by the regulated industry, (c) to demonstrate that ultimate policy is shifted away from the public interest and towards industry interest. If a capture analysis (whatever its conclusions) is lacking in one or more of these demonstrations, then the analyst must accordingly be circumspect about what she or he has shown. To demonstrate all three of these conditions—preferably by a combination of quantitative and qualitative evidence in which various types of evidence corroborate one another—amounts to a "gold standard" of proof. (Carpenter 2014, 63)

With these attributes of capture in mind, there are three conclusions we can draw from the previous chapters. First, while prices for some services have been high for many decades, the Update Committee has effectively *upheld* the historical influence of the House of Medicine over medical prices. Second, the capture of payment policy suggests that the decline in the political influence of physician organizations never happened to the extent that was predicted. In fact, we should understand the House of Medicine's influence as less expansive in its focus, but more potent, because government now is more influential in the health care marketplace. With its goals more sharply defined, the House has consolidated and concentrated its influence through the Update Committee, through societies' comments on regulations, and via legislative processes. Due to the private sector's use of the RBRVS, these efforts pay dividends beyond the public sector. Third, the Update Committee has successfully dominated the regulatory process in particular, by claiming an aura of science of payment policy under the cover of complex subject matter and a seemingly technocratic process.

The Persistence of Policy Capture

Prices for physician services and other health care services, such as hospital services and pharmaceuticals, are considered a primary, though not the only, cause of higher health care costs in the United States (Anderson et al. 2003; Laugesen and Glied 2011). This raises the question of whether, if prices for some services have long been viewed as too high, the current pricing structure is persistent and immutable, a feature of the US political economy of health care rather than the Update Committee. Indeed, it is true that many services reflect longstanding favorable prices. Yet the question is not simply whether prices of individual services are increasing, but whether they change in response to the changing resources required. The fact that for many services there is persistent price stickiness reflects the political—not resource-based—context of payment policy and the beneficial effects of the Update Committee process. Participants, both those societies making recommendations and the Update Committee, have *maintained* longstanding advantages secured decades earlier. The House has not only recommended relative values that are not reflective of the time it takes to provide a service, but has also being willing to overlook new technologies that decrease the time associated with providing a service. Under increased pressure to be more accountable, the Update Committee has asked societies to re-evaluate services. However, it is unclear as to whether this approach will produce more appropriate prices.

The role of the House in private standard setting via the coding system is one way House interests are advanced, because by defining services societies define payment. New technology and methods of diagnosing and treating disease can create pathways to higher relative values, especially compared to services such as primary care, which can be devalued "passively" over time in relative terms (Zuckerman et al. 2015, D-8). In contrast, office visits used by primary care physicians are lumped together under a label of "evaluation and management" CPT codes (Kumetz and Goodson 2013) that do not accurately capture the work involved. For a service such as removing a benign lesion, there are 18 distinct coding categories, each one varying by body part and by size of lesion, and 18 different payment rates (Cox et al. 2007).

The Update Committee is an outgrowth of decades of House influence over health policy. Previous chapters trace the longstanding use of relative value scale fee schedules starting in the 1950s. Since then, physician-developed fee schedules have been in almost continuous use, and fee schedules maintained by the California Medical Association and other physician organizations continued once Medicare was established. Medicare's fees were a mix of charge-based and CRVS fees, because in the absence of charge profiles for all physicians, insurers also relied on physician-created fee schedules. Even after physician organizations could no longer update their fee schedules after antitrust investigations made them untenable, payers continued to use modified relative value fee schedules. The period between the elimination of relative value fee schedules due to antitrust concerns and the involvement of the committee in the updating process happened to be brief.

In addition to direct pricing levers, the House has fundamentally shaped the private marketplace of health care, sometimes through seemingly indirect policy levers that have had far-reaching consequences. Indeed, one could say that a majority of the other public policy efforts of the House, from limiting medical school enrollment and licensing medical schools to restricting competition from other providers, have artificially increased (even if some of these unintentionally influence prices) the price of medical care.

Repeated success in thwarting efforts to enact government-sponsored health insurance reinforced the market power of physicians in determining prices. The AMA discouraged its own members and others who sought capitation or prepaid group practice arrangements (Stevens 1971). By discouraging some forms of health care financing and supporting others, the House was able to restrict early financing alternatives that would have put downward pressure on fees. Some of the roads blocked off by the House of Medicine might have better met the needs of employers and workers, thus suggesting the public interest was permanently compromised. The policy success of the House of Medicine forever shifted the trajectory of the US health care system toward artificially inflating prices.

The Arc of Decline

Paul Starr's book *The Social Transformation of American Medicine* traced the ascent and decline of the House of Medicine. In the book, Starr argued that the best days of organized medicine were behind them (Starr 1982). That assertion became the received wisdom regarding the role of the medical profession in policy and society more generally, with the exception of some scholars who questioned whether medicine had truly suffered a loss of public confidence (Stevens and Rosner 1983). Some predicted that in 30 years, historians might question the conclusion of Starr's book (Stevens and Rosner 1983). Stevens argued that the AMA would become more powerful, not less, and that its scope would also become less broad and it would become primarily a negotiating body with government (1971, 532). That conclusion fits with the findings of the book.

The evidence presented in previous chapters may challenge common assumptions about professional power and the role of physicians in formulating payment policy. Starr's elaboration of the deep roots of professional power remain intact, but subsequent events raise questions about the rise and decline thesis. Across a range of policy areas from licensure to education, professional scope of practice, and reimbursement rules that limit other professions' payments, specialty organizations in particular remain powerful political actors, as Stevens (2001) asserted. In addition, so too does the AMA, in the form that Stevens predicted it would. As the chapters show, the House of Medicine has a front-row seat in the process of determining important policies related to health care delivery and financing.

One example of the power of the House stands out precisely because it rewrote history in a way that conformed more to Starr's interpretation. That is the story of the RBRVS and the role of the House in payment policy, which contradicts the idea of a decline in influence. The House has worked hard to win the hearts and minds of the public and policy makers alike and wields "soft power" in health policy. That soft power is indicative of the legitimacy and credibility medical sociologists have documented. Physicians are held in high regard, and the House benefits from the deep respect people have for physicians. The retention of power thus reflects less tangible but important sources of power based on physicians' roles as healers.

The soft power of the House of Medicine explains some of its policy successes. The House has shaped the narrative of the RBRVS such that it claims that the Update Committee is a panel of experts leveraging medical science and objective analysis. These frames and narratives are important, because the framing of policy problems and solutions influences the way policy elites design and conceive of policies (Stone, 2002). As Hsiao himself said, the care they took to develop objective measures of physician work was deliberately designed to deflect politics. Subsequently, the House appropriated the mantle of objectivity advanced by Hsiao. Likewise, the history of the involvement of the House in the development of the RBRVS was mostly forgotten. Gradually, the story of the politics behind the RBRVS creation receded into the background, and was subsumed by a revisionist narrative that downplayed the role of the House in its creation. As discussed earlier, in the years before the RBRVS was created, the House of Medicine saw a threat to the status quo and began its efforts to preserve fee-for-service medicine. The House was united by a coalition intent on both preservation and improvement that joined surgical, procedural, and nonprocedural specialties. It is notable, after all, that the House of Medicine successfully persuaded Congress to fund a study on relative values.

If science was appropriated by the Update Committee, another prominent use of soft power was the rhetoric of fiscal responsibility, which would supposedly occur through a mix of professionalism and expenditure caps. A core premise of the RBRVS was that budget caps for physician expenditure and a budget neutrality provision would ensure restraint. These mechanisms allowed the idea of an RBRVS to be a feasible option, because everyone believed that fee increases would be constrained. In doing so, government had seemingly gained leverage over pricing, and it almost appeared to be breaking the longstanding trend of having a limited number of policy levers with which to influence Medicare fees. As payment reform legislation worked its way through Congress in 1989, however, legislators' anxiousness to get a deal meant it conceded to the House of Medicine's request that it remove hard expenditure caps. The caps were modified to expenditure "targets."

At that time, policy elites supported these changes based on their belief of countervailing mechanisms. Policy makers believed that the structure of payment reform was solid, but they may not have anticipated how core pieces of it would be removed that would threaten the overarching objectives. The House, on the other hand, was engaged in a game much like "Jenga," a game where the goal is to try and remove as many pieces of a towering structure as possible without toppling the tower. The surgical removal of policies disadvantageous to the House helped it without compromising its goal of preserving existing reimbursement levels. These extractions were partly allowed because there was optimism that we were entering a new era of evidence-based practice and expenditure discipline. Policy makers, perhaps somewhat naïvely, trusted the commitments made by the House of Medicine that physicians would act responsibly to reduce expenditure growth through practice guidelines, and that evidence-based medicine would work hand-in-hand with these efforts toward fiscal responsibility. In short, the future would be different. Unfortunately, after the law was passed and the reality of evidence-based medicine emerged, prior commitments made by the House were meaningless because the House was unable to ensure compliance by all members. One specialty society (representing spine surgeons) successfully lobbied to have the wings of the responsible agency clipped, due to the potential for cuts in their income (Gray, Gusmano, and Collins 2003).

Policy makers believed that the interlocking mechanisms and policies of payment reform would change the behavior of individual physicians. Physicians would, it was predicted, adapt their practices out of fear of what would happen when expenditure exceeded targets. The target determined the size of updates through a formula later renamed the sustainable growth rate (SGR). The SGR was eventually abolished, partly because the House was unable to keep expenditure within the growth rate, and therefore faced ever-increasing potential cuts every year; policy makers themselves realized that physicians had no reason to change their practice given that cuts were was applied to all equally, regardless of individual physicians' utilization profiles (Laugesen 2009; Oberlander and Laugesen 2015). Policy makers hoped that over time, physicians would organize themselves into specialty-specific and/or geographically disaggregated expenditure groupings that would bring the incentives to bear more directly on smaller aggregations than a national target, but this never happened.

The power of threats and objections made by the House shows the soft power of the House. When the House feels the sting of losses, either real or threatened, legislators are inclined to think that the cost of putting cuts into practice is politically too painful in the short term. The House enjoys prestige and legitimacy in the legislative process and it is prepared and able to raise an alarm, substantively and politically in Congress, if things do not go their way. The House of Medicine is readily mobilized to lobby Congress for increases and scare seniors based on unproven or even erroneous rhetoric of "cutting Medicare." Exceptions do occur—for example, in the Affordable Care Act Congress required CMS to identify overvalued procedures—and the abolition of the SGR did not happen quickly. In general, however, Congress has a history of finding it difficult to say no to the House of Medicine, and it is possible to shift the costs of Medicare to other actors. Shifting the costs to other actors is sometimes easier because other actors can be less attentive, and they may not even perceive, for example, that higher Medicare premiums are a reflection of trade-offs. Voters are certainly unlikely to directly connect higher private insurance premiums to congressional or regulatory lack of action on misvalued services. These incentives favor keeping the status quo. No one wants to pick a fight with the House, especially the AMA. Congress finds it easier to say no to other groups or cut other programs than reduce funding for physician fees. One example is the 1997 Balanced Budget Act, where nursing homes (among others) experienced cuts while physicians were largely unscathed. Congress also funds losses through cuts to other programs. In one effort to eliminate the SGR (which required paying for the difference in fees), legislators went as far as to propose funding fee increases by raiding the budget of the Overseas Contingency Operations Fund. That fund is set aside to fund national security–related overseas operations and the war in Afghanistan (Viebeck 2014).

Regulatory Capture

The RBRVS was created with the expectation that public officials could make decisions that serve the public interest. In theory, Medicare uses administered prices. Traditionally, however, an "administered price" is one that is determined independently and connotes bureaucratic neutrality. Growth in RVUs due to price increases (Maxwell, Zuckerman, and Berenson

2007), and review of the actual process for pricing of health services here, provide evidence that the committee has successfully increased relative value units to the advantage of the House of Medicine. Medicare prices are "administered" more in name only.

The House of Medicine established the Update Committee, and its role developed in a vacuum of human resources in the Health Care Financing Administration, during an interregnum of agency leadership. Left largely on its own to develop its own policies and practices over two decades, the Update Committee designed a process that set demonstratively varied evidentiary requirements, which, based on the overall facts in this book, have likely contributed to the problems identified by other researchers with the RBRVS, such as inaccurate time measurements. The membership and structure of the decision-making process mean that the Update Committee cannot discern or address the conflicts of interest inherent in the overall process. As shown, a key part of the committee's influence also arises from its link to the CPT process.

The complexity of the RBRVS acts as a veil that obscures the process by which societies achieve favorable reimbursement. Thus, capture of the RBRVS is partly a function of the subject matter, which is very complex and seemingly technocratic. Given that the RBRVS was perceived as an initially technical solution, it is striking how it stretched so far from its roots. One lesson from this analysis is that "technical" solutions like the RBRVS sometimes provide more opportunity for gaming, precisely because they give policy makers the illusion of control.

While Congress wanted to better compensate primary care doctors, professional might stymied these intentions. At first, the unraveling of what seemed like Congress's masterstroke in reforming professional reimbursement in 1989 is startling given its rapidity. On the other hand, the porous rulemaking process in the United States renders the belief that government has control as deeply problematic, because rulemaking is specifically designed to open up policymaking to stakeholders with financial or other policy interests. Regulation, according to the way Congress stipulated the parameters of rulemaking under the Administrative Procedure Act (1946), must be created in a way that allows interests to have their say. The law was designed to reduce the ability of agency officials to make policy insulated from interest groups. This again shows the influence of political institutional structures on policy, and the divergence of the United States in comparison to other countries. Interest groups participating in the rulemaking process have a natural interest in participating because they directly benefit from the decisions, compared to diffuse interests (such as Medicare enrollees), and the benefits the House accrues make investment in the process worthwhile. Considering the views of stakeholders (even if one does not actually change policies) puts constraints on agency staff that reduce their autonomy. External pressure for greater transparency and increases in funding for CMS to evaluate misvalued codes are positive steps. CMS may choose to listen to a more diverse set of voices or change the way the committee interacts with CMS, but even if it was no longer part of the formal review process (which it currently is), a private organization cannot be removed from the policy process. Even early in the history of the fee schedule, the rulemaking process functioned as designed and offered many access points for the House of Medicine. HCFA suffered escalating criticism of the fee schedules it proposed. More than 95,000 comments made by the House of Medicine during the rulemaking process contributed to significant pushback. Therefore, maintaining a scientifically neutral process is challenging given the participatory requirements of the regulatory process and a continual source of tension that can make it difficult for agency officials to do their job. Thus interest group participation in rulemaking gives voice to organized interests. As Chapter 3 showed, for example, the rulemaking process (and the committee) adjusted the fees, such that by 1996, fees were different from those projected.

The adaptation of policies has quietly continued, even in the face of reforms directed at moving our health care system towards value-based payment. In recent payment reforms, a similar dynamic is apparent, whereby changes in the rulemaking stages have weakened policies in favor of providers. For example, of 65 measures originally developed for accountable care organizations, only 33 were eventually adopted, and CMS removed claims-based quality measures (Centers for Medicare & Medicaid Services n.d.; Laugesen 2015). Policies such as two-sided risk sharing are diluted or scaled back through small changes and formula adjustments (Laugesen 2015; Oberlander and Laugesen 2015). Furthermore, with control over not only reimbursement but also coding, current efforts to steer the health care system toward rewarding teams and providers for chronic care management and medical home may face deeper challenges than are apparent.

Policy capture is likely to shift to different venues as policy evolves, and there are some signs that specialty societies are likely to focus increasingly on quality metrics that are just as complex as the RBRVS. Some specialty organizations are closely monitoring, and hoping to influence, the measurement of quality in the same way that they have been involved in the update process. Noting that Congress and CMS were proposing linking reimbursement to quality, one specialty society proposed that it take an active role in guideline development, appropriateness criteria, and practice guidelines, to reduce inappropriate utilization. In doing so, it planned to work with other imaging organizations and "become a member of the National Quality Forum (NQF), learn how they operate and properly network, and nominate members to get involved in work groups"; work with other societies to develop new guidelines "that will be beneficial to all involved"; and develop evidence-based guidelines that can be used in the pay-for-performance area regulated by Congress and CMS (Society of Nuclear Medicine 2010a, 4). This is counter to the idea that policy is made using technical criteria and shows the constant adaptation of strategy in response to policy changes.

A truly technical policy requires expertise, rather than representation of an organizational view, as suggested in the expert/advocate distinction. The committee considers its members as disinterested and impartial experts. Yet they are closely integrated into their specialty societies, which challenges that assumption. They may consider themselves objective and as "equal-opportunity torturers" (of those appearing before the committee) as one interviewee put it, but the tendency to increase rather than decrease codes suggests otherwise. The conflicts of interest and tendency of the committee members to coordinate and vote in blocs also challenge the idea that the committee is simply an expert panel. In contrast, federal advisory committees (which the committee is not) choose individuals based on their expertise or knowledge, which may include advocacy experience, but they are not usually filling a designated spot. Such committees do not routinely make decisions that are less favorable to the industry being regulated, and may do the opposite (Moffitt 2014).

As said, agency officials and Congress have allowed this partly because, at least at the beginning, they perceived the Update Committee as a scientific process. The legitimacy of the Update Committee reflects the pedigree of the RBRVS, created as it was inside the walls of one of the world's most prestigious universities. Researchers created a transparent method of assessing physician work under that imprimatur. The originators of the Update Committee may have held this ideal in their head when it was established. Yet without the oversight or coordination of a disinterested arbitrator like Hsiao and his team, the approach was doomed to fail. Many people associated with the Update Committee staunchly defend its approach as honoring the study's legacy; however, the impartiality of the Update Committee is constantly put to the test. The Harvard study therefore gave the Update Committee a veneer of science and authority, a favorable association that also purported to be responsibly operating under strict conditions of budget neutrality. Unintentionally, the Hsiao study was a segue for a physician-driven process. The fact that study methods were transparent and scientifically valid, based as they were on samples from national lists of physicians, not specialty society members, was not questioned. There may have been the expectation, or simply a hopeful assumption, that the House would work hard to preserve these best practices in the implementation of the fee schedule. As discussed earlier, the problems and flaws of the specialty society surveys are increasingly apparent. A recent government report from the Government Accountability Office (GAO) (United States Government Accountability Office 2015) has particularly highlighted flaws in the methods used in committee surveys. Possible cognitive distortions that occur in the process raise questions about how effective the committee is for determining physician work.

Technical processes create informational asymmetries that favor those with the ability to master the technical knowledge required. Societies groom their representatives by appointing them as advisors for years before they are nominated for service on the Update Committee. The RBRVS and the Update Committee itself created complexity that the specialty society members can use to gain advantages. Mastery of the process and the RBRVS is absolutely necessary in order to advance specialty society interests. Without significant and direct resource gains, other organizations would be unlikely to invest their personal and professional time mastering the burdensome process. The complexity of the RBRVS and the way the committee itself operates have created an asymmetric game of resources, given the small staff of regulatory agencies relative to interested parties. The specialized nature of payment policy provides cover for increasing relative value units (or avoiding review). In theory, gaming is prevented by the fact that the committee and its constituent members must "divvy up" the pie and work under constant pressures of a constrained and budget-neutral environment. However, the reality of budget neutrality is not necessarily so straightforward, and the complexity of the committee and the RBRVS obscures the supposed effect of budget neutrality, particularly because strategies such as not reviewing codes or changing codes with very few specialists (which yield gains for small groups of physicians) reveal why budget neutrality is less relevant than it is perceived. Overall, the complexity of the RBRVS reduces the ability of government to counteract and address the incentives that specialty societies have to play the "game of codes." For two decades, CMS has closely followed the recommendations of the committee, partly due to the complexity of the process and also because of the demands that complexity imposes on an agency lacking resources in proportion with its responsibilities.

Fixing Medical Prices

Under administered prices, prices should reflect underlying resource costs and change over time so they are not artificially inflated due to productivity gains. Fixing price disparities requires multiple solutions. More information about pricing is one solution often proposed, although we cannot assume more price information will compress prices or that consumers will force prices down. Research suggests that transparency does not necessarily compress price differences or result in more consistency (Tu and Lauer 2009). Prices do not necessarily converge; meanwhile, more information increases the costs for consumers (Maestas, Schroeder, and Goldman 2009). Many patients seem to find shopping for health care as they would for other goods very challenging (Frank and Lamiraud 2009; Hanoch and Rice 2006; Hanoch et al. 2009; Rice 2001). After all, Medicare pricing information is more transparent than for other payers, but that has not reduced prices.

Increasingly, to its credit, the committee appears to be trying to address some of the criticisms leveled at the update process, such as introducing rules like those requiring disclosures of conflicts of interest. It has increased the size of its minimum threshold for survey responses to 50 responses. Some people argue that such changes also need to be paired with efforts to make the process more public, with a hope that more information would hold the House of Medicine more accountable. The Update Committee has been making more information about its process available to the public. Unfortunately, while more information may be desirable, it does not guarantee substantial payoffs in terms of improved outcomes. For example, in the area of campaign finance, more information about donors and donations has increased our knowledge of who is funding campaigns, but greater transparency has not diminished the role of private financing of political campaigns or resulted in public policies that routinely go against donor interests. Unfortunately, the complexity of the process will likely diminish, or limit, the effects of any efforts towards transparency. Resolving pricing issues requires addressing informational asymmetries as much as possible.

Indeed, the committee's ability to powerfully influence Medicare payments reflects a lack of countervailing power. The agency that preceded CMS, HCFA, came into being in 1977, but overall, other than the MEI and overvalued service reductions, there was a degree of passivity over the delivery system of Medicare since local carriers handled claims. In the early 1980s, HCFA began to invest more in research, and it had an active research program that investigated key issues such as changes in utilization and responses to price changes. But across the entire program, HCFA and then CMS had not aggressively used its role as a purchaser (Vladeck and Rice 2009).

Greater investment is needed in organizations charged with stewardship over Medicare if Congress wants to reign in Medicare spending and address pricing. Even though they disagree on the solutions, both parties in Congress are concerned about the spiraling costs of Medicare. Legislators may not realize the need for greater stewardship. MedPAC's role should also be boosted, especially if it is to increase its scrutiny of overvalued codes. MedPAC was one of the first to raise the alarm regarding the reliance of CMS on the committee, and it provides Congress with its own source of advice on Medicare. Unlike other congressional agencies, it focuses exclusively on one area of government only. However, it is a small agency that has to monitor many different areas of Medicare.

In short, CMS requires more staff and resources. There are more than 100 specialty societies on the Advisory Committee yet fewer than 10 staff in the CMS unit reviewing updates (United States Government Accountability Office 2015). In the past few years, Congress has given CMS more resources to review overvalued codes. The Protecting Access to Medicare Act of 2014 and the MACRA (2015) provided new powers to CMS in relation to changing misvalued codes and collecting data. Physicians will be paid to provide billing data, which would be used for revising practice expenses. The law expanded the number of codes that would potentially be evaluated, creating a new target for relative value adjustments, with a savings target of 0.5 percent of expenditure every year between 2017 and 2020; in theory (although like cuts under the SGR, they may or may not materialize), cuts can be made if the savings fall short of the target. These are promising directions; the key will be evaluating the actual impact and effectiveness of the reviews carried out, including how savings are offset or cancelled out. For example, the Update Committee has, whether inadvertently or for other reasons, described misvalued code reviews successful even though these claims have not been subject to detailed scrutiny. Indeed, the committee's claims of significant savings may appear to be very promising, but closer examination reveals their estimates include codes *deleted* from the fee schedule. This approach may overestimate cost savings, since physicians billing Medicare may be able to use a different code similar in value or the Update Committee may subsequently develop a related code. Again, to evaluate the success of any policy like this, careful scrutiny is needed of how savings and cuts are counted and whether true impacts are being assessed by CMS. Attention to the growth and change in CPT codes is also vital.

There are also moves afoot to introduce more objective measures of physician work. CMS has commissioned studies on how best to evaluate physician work (Wynn et al. 2015; Zuckerman et al. 2015) but as yet it is not clear how or whether work review processes will change. These are encouraging developments, however, and suggest that CMS is exploring how it might better evaluate the RBRVS using independent sources of data. Perhaps a key question is how much not reviewing updates costs the Medicare program. If a case can be made that spending money on accurate pricing of services provides clear cost-savings, perhaps the argument for greater investment would be persuasive to lawmakers. Other changes could also be made, such as giving more scrutiny to survey recommendations, particularly the potential to cherry-pick from the results. Since 1992 there has been a substantial improvement in the availability of data on the kinds of patients physicians see, and electronic medical records presumably give us more information about the time and resources used in delivering services. The only caveat to this is that some databases are coordinated by specialty societies, and therefore this would defeat the purpose of using more independent sources.

If the Update Committee is to continue to have an important role in advising Medicare on relative values, it will likely make changes to the process. After all, having input into the RBRVS is critical for ensuring the fee schedule continues to be adopted by private payers and that payers do not move to develop alternative payment methods. It is unlikely that an organization such as the AMA would be unable to independently develop and publish its own distinct relative value guide if it were not used by CMS, given what happened in the 1970s. Therefore the key question is what is in the interests of the House of Medicine. As a private organization, the committee itself is not subject to policy directives. The only organization that can change the committee's process is the committee itself, through a formal two-thirds majority vote to change the rules of the organization. The internal processes and rules are determined by voting members.

Changing representation is often raised as the solution to problems in the committee. With more primary care physicians, it is argued, the committee would be more balanced in its decision making. Yet this fails to address the underlying assumptions relating to physician work and what is "complex" versus not "complex" that are only partly controlled by the Update Committee. Primary care representation also does not address the structure of the coding system (Kumetz and Goodson 2013). The problem is not only who sits around the table: it is the structure of the RBRVS itself. The definition and conceptualization of physician work are outdated for primary care, since it relies on a small number of codes. The current system evolved from a specialty services billing model in the 1950s that is inappropriate for primary care reimbursement. New approaches to defining primary care work are needed.

Thus the coding of medical services and the exponential growth in the number of billing codes contribute to the fact that primary care earnings have been lagging. As we saw, the game of codes at the committee provides many strategies simply by virtue of thousands of opportunities to game the payment system. A key question is whether we really need as many codes as we do. Should we cap the changes allowed by the AMA or limit the number of changes that can be made to the CPT and committee codes? Physicians generally argue that they need changes to account for variations in medical practice and technology. Yet it is unclear how much changes in coding are driven by such revisions—some have argued that true change is not necessarily common (Lichtenberg 2006).

CMS could also decide to change the fee schedule less often or reduce the number of reimbursable codes. CMS also could work more closely with private insurers (insurers participate in the code revision process coordinated by the AMA) and discuss the administrative effects and trade-offs to using new CPT and RVUs every year. These and other policy changes addressed at reducing the complexity of the fee schedule would also encourage greater accountability. Clarity, transparency, and accountability may be increased with a more simplified coding system.

Finally, more attention needs to be directed toward the impact of the coding and update process on other professions. Payment rules are not only important for physicians: nursing organizations, physician assistants, and allied health professionals participate in this process. Other health professionals participating have been given only one seat at the Update Committee and the committee of professionals is not autonomous of the Update Committee.

The Future Politics of Prices

Up until around 2005 or 2006, the Update Committee largely "flew under the radar," and many policy makers and others did not pay much attention to its activities. The Medicare Payment Advisory Commission drew attention to the Update Committee in 2006, when it expressed skepticism of the update processes. Since then, criticism of the committee and the RBRVS has been growing.

A focus on physician services in this book should not lead to a conclusion that it is the only area of health care where pricing policies might be reformed. Fixing the way we determine prices is essential for improving the US health care system as a whole. Closer attention to prices and how prices are set could yield benefits to our health care system and point to ways we can increase its efficiency and quality. Pricing anomalies across many areas of health care, from substantial price variation in inpatient care services in the same geographic area to predatory pharmaceutical pricing, are both examples of fertile questions for future research. Scholars, policy makers, physicians, patients, and others who are interested in developing a health care system that is more efficient and higher in quality should be more mindful of prices and how they are established. Regardless of the type of service or provider, this requires a combination of understanding macro policy levers, and it also requires close study of micro-level policies and organizations that have a seemingly small footprint, such as the Update Committee. Understanding the details of policies and holding actors accountable is necessary if we are to resolve thorny and persistent policy issues the Unites States faces in improving the efficiency, affordability, and quality of health care. With regard to the price of medical services, the hope is that highly technical issues associated with service codes and payment rates are now more visible and that people ask more questions about why health care costs what it does.

Based on earlier chapters, it is clear that there are some characteristics of physician pricing that make efforts at reforming physician fees vulnerable or more difficult to do. First, the fees charged by physicians reflect the ability of the House of Medicine to secure many wins early in the development of the health system—at a time when restrictive practices were often overlooked and "learned professions" were not subject to antitrust law—has given it substantial advantages. Therefore, a set of policies other than prices specifically maintain or perpetuate pricing power, such as limits on residencies. Physicians' professional credibility and the respect afforded to physicians have served to reinforce its political goals in a way that organizations such as pharmaceutical manufacturers or insurers lack.

To make progress requires looking past two kinds of rhetoric, the first being overly hopeful predictions regarding health care reforms. Current payment reforms continue to seek a more coordinated primary care through primary care medical homes, addressing specialty-primary reimbursement differences, accountable care organizations, better chronic disease management, and value-based purchasing. The optimism is high, but so is the amnesia regarding the fact that well-designed payment innovations and disruptions were stifled in the past. In short, policy makers and even researchers tend to overplay new policy solutions. The optimism placed in the RBRVS serves as an important lesson. Understanding the politics of physician payment and the way that the RBRVS changed under the influence of the committee is therefore important for informing future solutions. The book suggests that to understand how best to encourage more coordinated and better-compensated primary care and the steps necessary to build a more sustainable Medicare program, we need to be considerably more mindful of the opportunities that complex technical policies provide for gaming.

Prices matter, and yet partly due to the political challenges of "appropriate" valuations of services, it is easier to avoid the question. This may be why developing the most appropriate prices for physician services (which can mean reducing absolute prices) is not said to be the primary goal of the ACA. The ACA did not directly try to reduce the absolute price of health care. The decision to not address absolute prices is understandable, given the toxicity of the political process (and after) that shaped its enactment. Targeting misvalued services is one policy lever mentioned in the law, but the overall prices of physician services were not targeted for reductions. The

ACA also increased payments for primary care services to encourage better front-line management of chronic conditions and to prevent costlier episodes of care. The ACA therefore aims to "bend the health care cost curve"; the goal was to change health care so much that the unusually deterministic and linear trend line of expenditure would point downward. In theory, a moderate curve or arc would appear once efficiencies were realized.

In other parts of the program, penalties for readmissions addressed prices in hospitals, and Medicare's Part D pharmaceutical program extracted some savings from changes in that program. Much of what was desired was to maintain the current level of expenditure and hopefully change the rate of growth. Prices and quantities would be addressed by changing payment mechanisms in the service of potentially reshaping the delivery system and making it perform at a higher level of efficiency. By creating new initiatives centered on improving delivery and quality, people believed that quantity could be reduced as well. The law provided Medicare funds to experiment with alternative payment models that could potentially replace fee-for-service reimbursement.

A single arrow but also arguably one of the sharpest arrows in reformers' quivers on this issue was the Independent Payment Advisory Board (IPAB). It was to be a truly independent organization, which could counter the medical-industrial complex more effectively than Congress. Not surprisingly, many industries and groups viewed an independent organization charged with reducing cost growth and expenditure as a threat to their livelihood, and it became the target of overwhelming lobbying efforts to Congress to resist its implementation.

For prices to change, rhetoric needs to be countered, including the habitually Cassandra-like backlash from the House in response to proposed changes. Instead, we should carefully understand the distribution of costs on the public and providers, rather than assume that threats of physicians closing practices, for example, will necessarily materialize. Such objections to government policy changes may seem straightforward, but as shown in previous chapters, payment policy is a complex web of rules and incentives. Therefore, it is prudent to carefully examine claims made regarding proposed or implemented government policies. For example, it is true that the new requirements for physicians to document quality and report information could put particular pressure on smaller practices. However, new laws that do so were partly put in place as a workaround to maintain the status quo. To avoid the politics of physician payment policy, policy makers trade off the expected fallout from one policy compared to another. Efforts such as quality reporting are therefore preferred to wiping the slate clean.

The failure to implement the IPAB and address the high cost of health care (not just its growth) leaves a gaping hole in the ACA. Again, recognizing the political obstacles to achieving what the law did, that compromise is understandable. Prices of health care must be fixed, because ultimately access to health care will decline—unless wages or incomes increase for the majority of Americans. The problem is the lack of incentives for any one actor or leader to do so, because the costs of doing so, as we have seen, are immediate and create political risks. Failure to address those problems will mean that as premiums adjust to meet high prices every year, fewer people will be able to afford coverage, and fewer employers can offer coverage, leading to both increases in the uninsured and lowered use of services at the cost to our health. To the extent that fixing payment is an economic issue as much as a political issue, the prices Americans pay for health care will ultimately need to be in proportion to their resources.

Notes

1. Introduction: The House of Medicine and Medical Prices

1. Recently, California adopted Medicare's system for its workers' compensation program—following a long list of states already using Medicare's prices as a baseline for its fees.

2. Although the Council of Medical Specialty Societies is an organization that brings organizations together, the AMA appears to have been successful, perhaps due to its financial resources or its leadership of advocacy campaigns (such as those organized to repeal the sustainable growth rate).

3. Starr describes a corporate transformation of medicine occurring on five different levels: (1) a change in ownership and control from nonprofit to for profit, (2) the shift from freestanding institutions to horizontally integrated national institutions, (3) poly-corporate and conglomerate enterprises, (4) vertical integration, and (5) industry concentration.

4. The power to define how services were named and coded is not trivial. The AMA created and copyrighted a system of billing codes in 1966. Inadvertently, because services covered by insurance were those that physicians needed billing codes for, the way we classify physician work was honed early on for billing complex procedures but not primary care. Some argue this has disadvantaged primary care physicians due to a smaller number of billing codes (Kumetz and Goodson 2013).

5. The Health Care Financing Administration later became CMS.

6. CPT © 2015 by the American Medical Association. All rights reserved. CPT is a registered trademark of the American Medical Association.

7. This book complies with requirements of an agreement between the author and the AMA regarding nondisclosure.

2. The Enduring Influence of the House of Medicine over Prices

1. Indeed, the history of US health policy reveals how events such as World War II, party alignments between North and South, the decision to put health insurers under state jurisdiction, and the prioritization of income-related assistance over national health insurance in the 1930s had longer-term consequences.

2. Few countries shifted wholly to capitation as a reimbursement method—fee-for-service retained a foothold in many social insurance systems such as France and Germany (in many countries, specialists were, however, often absorbed into salary-based practice as employees of hospitals).

3. Interestingly, whereas today's fee schedule does not take into account patient characteristics other than physical health, the CRVS accounted for such variations. Fees differed depending on the disposition of the patient: for "simple lacerations," the fees varied according to the "cooperative ability of the patient."

4. Many scholars who have researched the history of Medicare and the legislative enactment of Medicare are a rich source of information (see, e.g., Holloway et al. 1993, Marmor 2000, and Oberlander 2003). Therefore, the details of Medicare's passage are truncated, suffice for a few key points.

5. I thank Ted Marmor for clarifying this point to me.

6. By 1974, the Medicare Economic Index put limits on how much each physician could increase his or her fees.

7. A senator from Washington, Henry "Scoop" M. Jackson, who served as chairman of the Permanent Subcommittee on Investigations, initiated the inquiry. The committee's jurisdiction then, as now, includes fraud and the use of resources by government. Jackson asked his staff to investigate the use of the CRVS by a Blue Shield plan and Medicare claims processor (created by the CMA), called the California Physicians' Service. The California Physicians' Service processed the most federally funded claims in the country through its health plans for federal employees and as a processor for Medicare. He was also interested in understanding the relationship between the California Physicians' Service and the CMA (US Senate Permanent Subcommittee 1979). Jackson had staff detailed from the (then) General Accounting Office in San Francisco. Two of those staff (according to the report) analyzed a large number of documents and interviewed people in California.

8. The report showed a close relationship between CMA and the California Physicians' Service—since its founding in 1939, the CMA House of Delegates had selected the California Physicians' Service Board of Trustees. This close relationship reinforces the discussion earlier about the role of the medical profession in shaping reimbursement policies in the private and public sectors for decades.

9. The CRVS lost support of payers in 1974. Payer perceptions are key in maintaining fee schedules. The integrity of a relative value scale depends significantly on the process by which it is developed and the credibility of the decision-making process. There must be trust in the price-setting process—payers are not likely to use a pricing system that is perceived as untrustworthy or not reflecting accurate values.

10. When Medicare carriers in California switched from the 1964 edition to the expanded 1969 version, terminology changes increased fees by 5 percent for office visits and 7 to 8 percent for hospital visits (n442).

3. The Science of Work and Payment Reform

1. As Chapter 2 shows, the California fee schedule partly framed the approach to the RBRVS, based as it was on physician work derived from relative differences in the intensity of work, time, and skill.

2. Thanks to Rick Mayes for bringing this page to my attention.

3. Capitation was ruled out by the Office of Technology Assessment, because there were not enough HMOs operating to absorb Medicare enrollees, who might not be eager to enroll in HMOs anyway.

4. The Consolidated Omnibus Budget Reconciliation Act (OBRA) 1986 set the completion date of July 1, 1987, but the completion date for the project was changed to July 1, 1989.

5. This method to establish consensus among groups is often used to develop clinical guidelines, whereby people modify their answers on questionnaires after discussion in a group, and subsequent modifications are made until the group develops a common score. Panelists' scores remain anonymous throughout the process.

6. The original report mentioned 407 services.

7. In the resource model that was actually implemented, the Physician Payment Review Commission decided to omit specialty training from the model because it saw adding this as double counting, since the skill derived from training would be reflected in the physician ratings of work (Ginsburg 1989, 767), and malpractice insurance premium costs were separated from practice expenses as a stand-alone relative value unit.

8. The reasons that the AMA agreed to this are unclear, but perhaps it believed either specialty societies would have to do this or that it would work to undermine such efforts later.

9. The Medicare Volume Performance Standard (VPS) estimated likely Medicare expenditure, which influenced the conversion factor update. The calculations had to adjust for differences among fiscal (October 1–September 30),

April 1 to March 31, and calendar years, leading to additional complexities in the formulas. After the Balanced Budget Reconciliation Act of 1999, the basis of the adjustment factor calculation was changed from an April 1 to March 31 year to a calendar year.

10. Some specialty societies opposed the idea that the AMA alone would represent them (Iglehart 1989).

4. How Doctors Get Paid

1. Medicare provides these RVUs as a service to private payers and other public payers.

2. The variations in premiums across specialties are averaged and used to calculate professional liability insurance RVUs for each service. Where there is more than one specialty providing the service, the relative value unit for a service reflects premiums of the main specialties providing the service. In the final payment, however, these differences disappear, since like the other RVUs, the total RVU is the same for a primary care physician, a pulmonologist, or a general surgeon.

3. In 2005, the Update Committee grandfathered those member societies that did not have American Board of Medical Specialties recognition. The American Board of Medical Specialties is an organization composed of 24 boards that certify specialists as having met the requirements in that specialty; decisions are made jointly by the American Board of Medical Specialties and the American Medical Association Council on Medical Education and the Liaison Committee for Specialty Boards (American Board of Medical Specialties 2014).

4. In terms of its budget line, there is no separate official number reported by the AMA in its budget, but the organization falls under the budget category of "Advocacy and Federal Relations."

5. Many (but not all) of the professions represented on the Health Care Professionals Advisory Committee have distinct billing codes and can bill Medicare independently and also for services that physicians also bill for. Others use primarily physician codes, and therefore when the Update Committee is reviewing relative value unit changes or new codes that are pertinent to Health Care Professionals Advisory Committee members, they present alongside medical societies. For example, review of psychotherapy codes would involve social workers, psychologists, and psychiatrists.

6. For example, one society requested a change of the wording of a code for laminectomy "with drainage of intramedullary cyst/syrinx; to peritoneal space, should be changed to add the words 'or pleural space' to make the

code consistent with other cerebral spinal fluid shunt codes currently listed in CPT. The CPT Editorial Panel considered this an editorial change and does not expect the code to require revaluing by the AMA's RUC panel" (Hassenbusch 2002).

7. As mentioned earlier, at that time, medical societies were permitted to develop fee schedules.

8. Codes are usually brought before the Update Committee only once during the yearlong cycle of review; if there is a problem with the service description, the survey used by the society, or other issues, they are usually asked to return at a future meeting. Depending on the problem, a society may or may not succeed in getting the code included in the upcoming fee schedule.

9. This quotation shows no subject number to protect the identity of the interviewee.

5. Conflicts of Interest and Problems of Evidence

1. Favorable payments arising from committee decisions accrue to members and nonmembers alike; therefore, like all membership groups, societies offer exclusive benefits to attract and retain members. One membership benefit is the advice and information that members receive from their society coding departments. They also provide assistance to members who are having trouble getting paid or confused about coding. Participation in the committee allows societies to efficiently and easily harvest as much information as possible about coding and policy changes in a relatively short space of time. Their participation allows them to keep their members abreast of important coding and reimbursement changes and to provide accurate advice to their members.

2. For example, the Coding and Reimbursement Committee of the American Association of Neurological Surgery/Congress on Neurological Surgeons, which, while independent, "works closely with" the Washington Committee, and budget decisions are also made in consultation with the Washington Committee (Bean 2000).

3. "SNM is looked to as a lead organization for new code applications, revaluing of codes, and general coding guidance. To be a full-fledged player in reimbursement politics will require an even more intensive effort. Legislation, rules and regulations on reimbursement issues happen at a non-stop pace and are ever-changing. Coalitions are a vital part of any effort on these issues. At the same time personal relationships with Members of Congress and committee staff can be an important part of fighting these issues. Taking the time and effort to coordinate SNM's reimbursement policy work with

other government relations work and to assess what strategic relationships are needed and the best way to position SNM as a leader on molecular imaging reimbursement policy will pay dividends in the end and help to make SNM a strong, recognizable authority on these issues" (Society of Nuclear Medicine 2010a, 3).

4. The survey provides information on time and work intensity based on vignettes and comparisons with other services. Respondents are asked to rate the intensity for each component of the surveyed code against a "reference" code that they select. They are given a choice of responding 1–5 (with 1 = low, 3 = medium, and 5 = high) and instructed to base evaluations on "the universe of codes your specialty performs."

5. In April 2012, there was a voice vote to approve a case where the society put together a list of people "trained and using" a piece of equipment in the specialty because they said it was not a widespread procedure accepted by the committee, while at other times, the societies survey people who do not do the procedure.

6. "Hsiao: Then you may say, 'I'm only willing to do one, or only one half hysterectomy.' Then that's the relative amount of work surgeons judge between appendectomy and hysterectomy. We also tried the trade-off method. Interviewee: And that did not work? Hsiao: That did not work. Logically it sounded very appealing, but what we found was that physicians actually had the price of the relative procedures in their minds when they make their trade-off. The answers they gave us were very highly correlated with the prices that were being charged" (Hsiao 1995, 393).

7. In this particular case, the training did not happen, because the AMA staff member responsible left the job and the society said that the issue was being followed up.

6. Complexity, Agency Capture, and the Game of Codes

1. For misvalued services, in 2008, for example, CMS reported the relative value units it and the committee had reviewed. But the information about the misvalued codes is stated in total number terms, and information is buried in long tracts of text. In the 2012 Final Rule, the agency did not break out expected changes across different relative value units but instead combined all the work, including malpractice relative value units, and the impact of changes due to potentially misvalued codes.

2. In the financial and health care worlds, complexity is obviously not intentional, but even if it is not by design, it creates problems for regulators.

3. See http://www.readabilityformulas.com.

4. "Nowhere has this tendency to unbundle, or itemize, been more evident than in complex spinal surgery, in which a spinal decompression and fusion may have six or more codes" (Donovan 2012, 429).

5. Category III codes are "temporary" codes and are not valued by the committee. Category III codes do not have work values by CMS. New technologies have to go through a new code application to reach category I status, which makes them eligible for review of work relative value units, although third-party payers may reimburse providers for category III services (Donovan 2012).

6. "The one thing we don't have to worry about that the E&M standalones have to worry, we don't have to demonstrate . . . in every record the intensity of documentation for the E&M level of service that we provide in the hospital and in the office that the primary care or standalone E&M code users have to do. That may be onerous, and because it may be a tradeoff, we decide, let's don't play that game, let's stay out of that arena, because we are doing fairly well" (Mabry et al. 2005, 940).

References

Accreditation Council for Graduate Medical Education. 2016. "ACGME Fact Sheet." Accessed February 14, 2016. http://www.acgme.org/acgmeweb /Portals/0/PDFs/ACGMEfactsheet.pdf.

Allen, Bibb. 2006. "Presentation: How Radiologists Influence Reimbursement: The Relative Value Update Committee Valuing Our Professional Work; November 27, 2006, Radiological Society of North America." http://www .acr.org/~/media/ACR/Documents/PDF/Economics/Medicare/RBV/RSNA _2006_Presentation_How_Radiologists_Influence_Reimbursement.PDF.

The AMA/RUC Physician Work Survey. n.d. Accessed May 24, 2016. http://asts .org/docs/default-source/survey-documents/47135_survey.doc?sfvrsn=2.

American Academy of Dermatology. 2010. "Agenda for American Academy of Dermatology and Association, Board of Directors Meetings, November 13 2010, The Four Seasons Hotel, Philadelphia, PA." http://www.aad.org/File Library/Global navigation/About the AAD/Board of Directors/Nov--13-2010 -agenda-and-AAD-AADA-background-materials.pdf.

American Academy of Dermatology. 2011. "American Academy of Dermatology Board of Directors Meetings, February 5, 2011." Accessed March 30, 2014. http://.aad.org/File%20Library/Global%20navigation/About%20the%20AAD /Board%20of%20Directors/Feb--5-2011-agenda-with-AAD-and-AADA -background-materials.pdf.

American Academy of Orthopedic Surgeons. 2013. "AAOS Coding Coverage & Reimbursement Committee: Agenda, Minutes and Background Materials, November 22–November 23, 2013." Accessed March 12, 2014. http:// teamwork.aaos.org/ccr/Shared Documents/CCRC November Agenda Book.pdf.

American Academy of Orthopedic Surgeons. 2014. "AAOS Coding Coverage & Reimbursement Committee." Accessed April 16, 2014. http://www.aaos.org /member/coding/AAOS_Coding_Coverage.asp.

American Board of Medical Specialties. 2010. *ABMS Guide to Medical Specialties*. Chicago: American Board of Medical Specialties.

American College of Obstetricians and Gynecologists. 2014. "Executive Staff." Accessed October 20, 2014. http://www.acog.org/About-ACOG/Executive -Staff.

American College of Radiology. 2001. "ACR Works toward New Codes and Reimbursement for IMRT." Reprinted from *ASTROnews,* November/ December. Accessed May 13, 2016. http://www.acr.org/Advocacy/Economics -Health-Policy/Managed-Care-and-Private-Payer/Common-Coverage-Issues -with-Private-Payors/Intensity-Modulated-Radiation-Therapy/ACR-Works -Toward-New-Codes-and-Reimbursement-for-IMRT.

American College of Radiology. 2012. "American College of Radiology 2012 Annual Meeting and Chapter Leadership Conference (AMCLC), Sunday, April 22–Tuesday, April 25, 2012, Hilton Washington Hotel, Washington, DC." Accessed March 20, 2014. http://amclc.acr.org/LinkClick.aspx?fileticket=m401 -Yh525A%3D&tabid=103.

American College of Radiology. 2014. "Ezequiel "Zeke" Silva III, MD [CV]." Accessed October 20, 2014. http://www.acr.org/~/media/ACR/Documents /PDF/Membership/Governance/CSC/Silva.pdf.

American College of Radiology. 2016. "Relative Value Update Committee." Accessed January 6, 2016. http://www.acr.org/Advocacy/Economics-Health -Policy/Medicare-Payment-Systems/Developing-RBVs/Relative-Value -Update-Committee.

American Medical Association. 1993. *Medicare RBRVS: The Physicians' Guide 1993.* Chicago: American Medical Association.

American Medical Association. 1996. *Medicare RBRVS: The Physicians' Guide 1996.* Chicago: American Medical Association.

American Medical Association. 1999. *Improving the Medicare Sustainable Growth Rate System: Statement of Richard F. Corlin of the American Medical Association.* Washington, DC: Subcommittee on Health and Environment, House Commerce Committee: United States Congress.

American Medical Association. 2005. "Reports of the Board of Trustees to the House of Delegates, Nos. 1–19." Accessed March 23, 2014. http://www .amaassn.org/resources/doc/hod/i05botdoc.doc.

American Medical Association. 2008. "Reports of the Board of Trustees, Annual Meeting of the House of Delegates, Nos. 1–37." Accessed March 18, 2014. http://www.ama-assn.org/resources/doc/hod/a08botreports .pdf.

American Medical Association. 2010a. "AMA/Specialty Society RVS Update Process Annotated List of Actions." Accessed March 20, 2014. http://www.ama-assn.org/resources/doc/rbrvs/chronologyactions.pdf.

American Medical Association. 2010b. "American Medical Association/ Specialty Society Relative Value Scale Update Committee ('RUC') Conflict of Interest Policy." Accessed March 20, 2014. http://www.ama-assn.org/resources/doc/rbrvs/chronologyactions.pdf.

American Medical Association. 2011a. *Annual Report*. Chicago: American Medical Association.

American Medical Association. 2011b. "Chronic Care Coordination Workgroup (C3W) CPT Editorial Panel and AMA/Specialty Society RVS Update Committee Strategy Workgroup, Wednesday, October 5, 2011." Accessed September 20, 2013. http://www.ama-assn.org/resources/doc/rbrvs/c3w-minutes-10-5-11.pdf.

American Medical Association. 2012. "The Beltway and CPT: From Road Way to Code Way—Lessons from the Proposed Rule (PowerPoint Presentation at the American Medical Association's 2012 Current Procedural Terminology Meeting, October 12)." Accessed September 20, 2013. http://www.ama-assn.org/ama/pub/physician-resources/solutions-managing-your-practice/coding-billing-insurance/cpt/cpt-editorial-panel-meeting/oct-2012-cpt-annual-meeting-presentations.

American Medical Association. 2013. "Reports of the Board of Trustees, House of Delegates Annual Meeting 2013." Accessed March 18, 2014. http://www.ama-assn.org/assets/meeting/2013a/a13-bot-reports.pdf.

American Medical Association. 2014. *AMA/Specialty Society Relative Value Update Committee (RUC) Final Vote Release—CPT 2014 for Meetings October 4–6, 2012; January 24–17, 2013; and April 25–28, 2013*. Chicago: American Medical Association. Computer file.

American Medical Association. 2016. *The RVS Update Committee*. Accessed June 7, 2016. http://www.ama-assn.org/ama/pub/physician-resources/solutions-managing-your-practice/coding-billing-insurance/medicare/the-resource-based-relative-value-scale/the-rvs-update-committee.page?

American Medical Association Board of Trustees. 1999. "Report of the Board of Trustees Report 17-A-99: Explanation of Public-Private Partnerships that Exist between Government and Our American Medical Association." Accessed December 5, 2003. http://www.ama-assn.org/meetings/public/annual99/reports/bot/botmac5/botrep17.mcw.

American Medical Association Board of Trustees. 2001. "Board of Trustees Report I-01: The RBRVS and the RUC—Ten Years Later." Accessed July 3, 2009. http://www.ama-assn.org/ama1/pub/upload/mm/380/ruc10yrslater_bot.pdf.

American Osteopathic Association. 2010. "Help Determine Proper Values for OMT Codes AOA Daily Report, October 18, 2010." Accessed June 28, 2013. http://blogs.do-online.org/dailyreport.php?blogid=4&archive=2010.

American Society for Gastrointestinal Endoscopy. 2016. "The RUC Survey Process." Accessed May 14, 2016. http://www.asge.org/practice/practice -management.aspx?id=16034.

American Society of Anesthesiologists. 2014. "Payment and Practice Management Memo. No. 7: The Rulemaking Process and the Medicare Fee Schedule." Accessed October 7, 2014. http://www.asahq.org/For-Members/Practice -Management/~/media/For Members/Practice Management/PPMM/The Rulemaking Process and the Medicare Fee Schedule January 2014.pdf.

American Society of Dermatology v. Shalala, 962 F.Supp. 141, 144 (D.D.C. 1996).

Anderson, Gerald F., Uwe E. Reinhardt, Peter S. Hussey, and Varduhi Petro-syan. 2003. "It's the Prices, Stupid: Why the United States Is So Different from Other Countries." *Health Affairs* 22 (3):89–105.

Anonymous. 2008. Update Committee Meeting Notes. Unpublished.

Auerbach, David I., and Arthur L. Kellermann. 2011. "A Decade of Health Care Cost Growth Has Wiped Out Real Income Gains for an Average US family." *Health Affairs* 30 (9):1630–1636.

Awrey, Dan. 2012. "Complexity, Innovation and the Regulation of Modern Financial Markets." *Harvard Business Law Review* 2:235–267.

Balla, Steven J. 1998. "Administrative Procedures and Political Control of the Bureaucracy." *American Political Science Review* 92 (3):663–673.

Balla, Steven J. 2000. "Political and Organizational Determinants of Bureau-cratic Responsiveness." *American Politics Research* 28 (2):163–193. © 1998 American Political Science Association. Reproduced by permission of Cambridge University Press.

Baradell, Janet, and Nancy Hanrahan. 2000. "CPT Coding and Medicare Reimbursement Issues." *Clinical Nurse Specialist* 14 (6):299–303.

Baumgardner, James R. 1992. "Medicare Physician-Payment Reform and the Resource-Based Relative Value Scale—A Re-Creation of Efficient Market Prices." *American Economic Review* 82 (4):1027–1030.

Baumgartner, Frank R., Jeffrey M. Berry, Marie Hojnacki, David C. Kimball, and Beth L. Leech. 2009. *Lobbying and Policy Change: Who Wins Who Loses, and Why.* Chicago: University of Chicago Press.

Baumgartner, Frank R., and Bryan D. Jones. 1993. *Agendas and Instability in American Politics.* Chicago: University of Chicago Press.

Bean, James R. 2000. "Coding Committee Serves as an Advocate." *Bulletin of the American Association of Neurological Surgeons* 9 (4):22–23. https://www.aans.org/bulletin/pdfs/winter00.pdf.

Bean, James R. 2002. "Valuing Neurosurgery Services: Part II. The Interdependence of Current Procedural Terminology and Federal Medicare Payment Policy." *Neurosurgical Focus* 12 (4):1–4. Quotations reprinted by permission of Rockwater, Inc., Journal of Neurosurgery Publishing Group (JNSPG) on behalf of the American Association of Neurological Surgeons (AANS).

Bell, Clark W. 1991. "Administration Was Wise Not to Tinker with RBRVS." *Modern Healthcare,* February 18.

Berenson, Robert A. 1989. "Physician Payment Reform: Congress's Turn." *Annals of Internal Medicine* 111 (5):351–353.

Bergersen, Lisa, Kimberlee Gauvreau, Sandra Fenwick, David Kirshner, Julie Harding, Patricia Hickey, John Mayer, and Audrey Marshall. 2013. "Capture of Complexity of Specialty Care in Pediatric Cardiology by Work RVU Measures." *Pediatrics* 131 (2):258–267.

Beyer, David C., and Najeeb Mohideen. 2008. "The Role of Physicians and Medical Organizations in the Development, Analysis, and Implementation of Health Care Policy." *Seminars in Radiation Oncology* 18 (3):186–193.

Blumberg, Mark S. 1984. "Medical Society Regulation of Fees in Boston 1780–1820." *Journal of the History of Medicine and Allied Sciences* 39 (3):303–338.

Blumenthal, David, and James A. Morone. 2009. *The Heart of Power: Health and Politics in the Oval Office.* Berkeley: University of California Press.

Bodenheimer, Thomas, Robert. A. Berenson, and Paul Rudolf. 2007. "The Primary Care-Specialty Income Gap: Why It Matters." *Annals of Internal Medicine* 146 (4):301–306.

Bodenheimer, Thomas, and Kevin Grumbach. 1994. "Paying for Health Care." *Journal of the American Medical Association* 272 (8):634–639.

Bonke, Jens. 2005. "Paid Work and Unpaid Work: Diary Information versus Questionnaire Information." *Social Indicators Research* 70:349–368.

Boyle, J. F. 1989. "Passing a Major RBRVS Milestone." *The Internist* 30 (1):34–36.

Braun, Peter, William C. Hsiao, Edmund R. Becker, and Margaret DeNicola. 1988. "Evaluation and Management Services in the Resource-Based Relative Value Scale." *Journal of the American Medical Association* 260 (16):2409–2417.

Braun, P., and Nancy McCall. 2011a. *Improving the Accuracy of Time in the Medicare Physician Fee Schedule: Feasibility of Using Extant Data and of Collecting Primary Data.* Washington DC: Medicare Payment Advisory Commission.

Braun, Peter, and Nancy McCall. 2011b. *Methodological Concerns with the Medicare RBRVS Payment System and Recommendations for Additional Study: A Report Prepared for MedPAC.* Washington, DC: Medicare Payment Advisory Commission.

Braun, Peter, Douwe B. Yntema, Daniel Dunn, Margaret DeNicola, Thomas Ketcham, Diana Verrilli, and William C. Hsiao. 1988. "Cross-Specialty Linkage of Resource-Based Relative Value Scales—Linking Specialties by Services and Procedures of Equal Work." *Journal of the American Medical Association* 260 (16):2390–2396.

Brill, Steven. 2013. "Why Medical Bills Are Killing Us." *Time*, April 4.

Brown, Lawrence D. 1992. "Political Evolution of Federal Health Care Regulation." *Health Affairs* 11 (4):17–37.

Brunt, Christopher S. 2011. "CPT Fee Differentials and Visit Upcoding under Medicare Part B." *Health Economics* 20 (7):831–841.

Buntin, Melinda J., Jose J. Escarcé, Dana Goldman, Hongjun Kan, Miriam J. Laugesen, and Paul Shekelle. 2004. "Increased Medicare Expenditures for Physicians' Services: What Are the Causes?" *Inquiry* 41 (1):83–94.

Burtless, Gary, and Sveta Milusheva. 2013. "Effects of Employer-Sponsored Health Insurance Costs on Social Security Taxable Wages." *Social Security Bulletin* 73 (1):83–108.

Campbell, Andrea Louise. 2003. *How Policies Make Citizens: Senior Political Activism and the American Welfare State*. Princeton, NJ: Princeton University Press.

Canby, William C., and Ernest Gellhorn. 1978. "Physician Advertising: The First Amendment and the Sherman Act." *Duke Law Journal* 1978 (2):543–585.

Carlin, Bruce I. 2009. "Strategic Price Complexity in Retail Financial Markets." *Journal of Financial Economics* 91 (3):278–287.

Carpenter, Daniel. 2014. "Detecting and Measuring Capture." In *Preventing Regulatory Capture: Special Interest Influence and How to Limit It*, edited by Daniel Carpenter and David Moss. New York: Cambridge University Press.

Centers for Medicare & Medicaid Services. n.d. *Proposed Rule versus Final Rule for Accountable Care Organizations (ACOs) in the Medicare Shared Savings Program*. Accessed May 14, 2016. http://cms.gov/Medicare/Medicare -Fee-for-Service-Payment/ACO/downloads/appendix-aco-table.pdf.

Centers for Medicare & Medicaid Services. 2006. "Medicare Program; Revisions to Payment Policies, Five-Year Review of Work Relative Value Units, Changes to the Practice Expense Methodology under the Physician Fee Schedule, and Other Changes to Payment under Part B; Revisions to the Payment Policies of Ambulance Services under the Fee Schedule for Ambulance Services; and Ambulance Inflation Factor Update for CY 2007. Final Rule with Comment Period." *Federal Register* 71 (231):69623–70251.

Centers for Medicare & Medicaid Services. 2010. "Medicare Program; Payment Policies Under the Physician Fee Schedule and Other Revisions to Part B for CY 2011: Final Rule." *Federal Register* 75 (228):73169–73860.

Centers for Medicare & Medicaid Services. 2011. "Medicare Program; Payment Policies Under the Physician Fee Schedule, Five-Year Review of

Work Relative Value Units, Clinical Laboratory Fee Schedule: Signature on Requisition, and Other Revisions to Part B for CY 2012, Final Rule With Comment Period." *Federal Register* 76:73025–73474.

Centers for Medicare & Medicaid Services. 2012. "Medicare Program; Revisions to Payment Policies under the Physician Fee Schedule, DME Face-to-Face Encounters, Elimination of the Requirement for Termination of Non-Random Prepayment Complex Medical Review and Other Revisions to Part B for CY 2013." *Federal Register* 77 (222):68891.

Centers for Medicare & Medicaid Services. 2013. *Medicare Physician Fee Schedule (Payment System Fact Sheet Series)*. Baltimore: CMS.

Cleaves, David A. 1987. "Cognitive Biases and Corrective Techniques: Proposals for Improving Elicitation Procedures for Knowledge-Based Systems." *International Journal of Man-Machine Studies* 27 (2):155–166.

Clemens, Jeffrey, and Joshua D. Gottlieb. 2013. *Bargaining in the Shadow of a Giant: Medicare's Influence on Private Payment Systems*. NBER Working Paper. Cambridge, MA: National Bureau of Economic Research.

Clemens, Jeffrey, Joshua D. Gottlieb, and Tímea Laura Molnár. 2015. *The Anatomy of Physician Payments: Contracting Subject to Complexity*. NBER Working Paper. Cambridge, MA: National Bureau of Economic Research.

Congress of Neurological Surgeons. 2009. "Summary of 2010 Medicare Physician Fee Schedule." Accessed October 16, 2014. https://cns.org/sites/default/files/legislative/2010MedicarePhysicianFeeScheduleSummary.pdf.

Cooper, Zack, Stuart V. Craig, Martin Gaynor, and John Van Reenen. 2015. *The Price Ain't Right? Hospital Prices and Health Spending on the Privately Insured*. NBER Working Paper. Cambridge, MA: National Bureau of Economic Research.

Costilo, L. Barry. 1981. "Competition Policy and the Medical Profession." *New England Journal of Medicine* 304 (18):1099–1102.

Cox, Donald, Jerry Cromwell, Nancy T. McCall, Sonja Hoover, Carol Urato, Genevieve Cromwell, and Peter Braun. 2007. *Assessment of the Potential Impact of Productivity Changes on Medicare RVUs*. Research Triangle, NC: Research Triangle International.

Cromwell, Jerry, Sonja Hoover, Nancy McCall, and Peter Braun. 2006. "Validating CPT Typical Times for Medicare Office Evaluation and Management (E/M) Services." *Medical Care Research and Review* 63 (2):236–255.

Cromwell, Jerry, Nancy McCall, Kathleen Dalton, and Peter Braun. 2010. "Missing Productivity Gains in the Medicare Physician Fee Schedule: Where Are They?" *Medical Care Research and Review* 67 (6):676.

Cromwell, Jerry, and Janet B. Mitchell. 1986. "Physician-Induced Demand for Surgery." *Journal of Health Economics* 5 (4):293–313.

Culbertson, Richard A., and Philip R. Lee. 1996. "Medicare and Physician Autonomy." *Health Care Financing Review* 18 (2):115.

Culpepper, Pepper D. 2010. *Quiet Politics and Business Power: Corporate Control in Europe and Japan.* New York: Cambridge University Press.

Delbanco, Thomas L., Katherine C. Meyers, and Elliot A. Segal. 1979. "Paying the Physician's Fee: Blue Shield and the Reasonable Charge." *New England Journal of Medicine* 301 (24):1314–1320.

Doherty, Robert B. 2002. "After 10 Years, Has RBRVS Helped Your Bottom Line?" *ACP-ASIM Observer,* January.

Donovan, William D. 2012. "The Resource-Based Relative Value Scale and Neuroradiology: ASNR's History at the RUC." *Neuroimaging Clinics of North America* 22 (3):421–436.

Duszak, Richard. 2006. "How Radiologists Influence Reimbursement: CPT Code Development and Accurate Coding Initiatives." Presentation. Accessed April 5, 2013. http:// acr.org/~/media/ACR/Documents/PDF/Economics/Coding/RSNA%202006%20CPT_Code_Development.PDF.

Eisenberg, Barry S. 1980. "Information Exchange among Competitors: The Issue of Relative Value Scales for Physicians' Services." *Journal of Law and Economics* 23 (2):441–460.

Eisner, Walter. 2009. "NASS: Interesting Times." *Orthopedics This Week* 5 (36):16–19.

Englich, Birte, Thomas Mussweiler, and Fritz Strack. 2006. "Playing Dice with Criminal Sentences: The Influence of Irrelevant Anchors on Experts' Judicial Decision Making." *Personality and Social Psychology Bulletin* 32 (2):188–200.

Enthoven, Alain C. 1988. *Theory and Practice of Managed Competition in Health Care Finance.* Vol. 9, *Professor Dr F. De Vries Lectures in Economics Theory, Institutions, Policy.* Amsterdam: North Holland.

Falk, I. S. 1973. "Medical Care in the USA: 1932–1972. Problems, Proposals and Programs from the Committee on the Costs of Medical Care to the Committee for National Health Insurance." *The Milbank Memorial Fund Quarterly, Health and Society* 51 (1):1–32.

Feldstein, Martin S. 1970. "The Rising Price of Physician's Services." *The Review of Economics and Statistics* 52 (2):121–133.

Filler, Blair C. 2007. "Coding Basics for Orthopaedic Surgeons." *Clinical Orthopaedics and Related Research* 457:105–113.

Fischer v. Berwick, No. 12-1713, 503 Federal Appendix 210 (4th Cir. Jan. 7, 2013).

Foreman, Julie. 1991. "AMA Responds to RBRVS with Grassroots Campaign." *Archives of Ophthalmology* 109 (9):1207.

Frank, Richard G., and Karine Lamiraud. 2009. "Choice, Price Competition and Complexity in Markets for Health Insurance." *Journal of Economic Behavior & Organization* 71 (2):550–562.

Furlong, Scott R., and Cornelius M. Kerwin. 2005. "Interest Group Participation in Rule Making: A Decade of Change." *Journal of Public Administration Research and Theory* 15 (3):353–370.

Furnham, Adrian, and Hua Chu Boo. 2011. "A Literature Review of the Anchoring Effect." *The Journal of Socio-Economics* 40 (1):35–42.

Gesensway, Deborah. 1995. "AMA Proposes 'One Voice' for Medicine." *ACP Internist,* December. Accessed August 7, 2016. http://www.acpinternist.org/archives/1995/12/amafed.htm.

Ginsburg, P. 2002. *CMS Oral History Project.* Edited by Richard Shuster. Baltimore: Centers for Medicare & Medicaid Services.

Ginsburg, Paul B. 1989. "Medicare Physician Payment Reform." *Saint Louis University Law Journal* 34:759–776.

Ginsburg, Paul B. 2010. "Wide Variation in Hospital and Physician Payment Rates Evidence of Provider Market Power." *Center for Studying Health System Change Research Brief* 16:1–11.

Ginsburg, Paul B. 2016. "Telephone Conversation with Author," February 8.

Ginsburg, Paul B., and Robert A. Berenson. 2007. "Revising Medicare's Physician Fee Schedule—Much Activity, Little Change." *New England Journal of Medicine* 356 (12):1201–1203.

Ginsburg, Paul B., and Philip R. Lee. 1989. "Defending US Physician Payment Reform." *Health Affairs* 8 (4):67–71.

Ginsburg, Paul B., Lauren B. LeRoy, and George T. Hammons. 1990. "Medicare Physician Payment Reform." *Health Affairs* 9 (1):178–188.

Goldfarb v. Virginia State Bar, 421 U.S. 773 (1975).

Goodson, John D. 2007. "Unintended Consequences of Resource-Based Relative Value Scale Reimbursement." *Journal of the American Medical Association* 298 (19):2308–2310.

Gormley, William T. 1986. "Regulatory Issue Networks in a Federal System." *Polity* 18 (4):595–620.

"Government Realigning Fees Doctors Get under Medicare." 1991. *New York Times,* November 16.

Grad, Frank P. 1978. "The Antitrust Laws and Professional Discipline in Medicine." *Duke Law Journal* 1978 (2):443–486.

Gray, Bradford H. 1992. "The Legislative Battle over Health Services Research." *Health Affairs* 11 (4):38–66.

Gray, Bradford H., Michael K. Gusmano, and Sara R. Collins. 2003. "AHCPR and the Changing Politics of Health Services Research." *Health Affairs* W3 (June 25):283–307.

Gray, Gwendolyn. 1991. *Federalism and Health Policy: The Development of Health Systems in Canada and Australia.* Toronto: University of Toronto Press.

Group Health v. King County Medical Society, 39 Wash. 2d 586, 237 Pac 2d 737 (1951).

Gruber, Jon, John Kim, and Dina Mayzlin. 1999. "Physician Fees and Procedure Intensity: The Case of Cesarean Delivery." *Journal of Health Economics* 18 (4):473–490.

Hacker, Jacob S. 2002. *The Divided Welfare State: The Battle over Public and Private Social Benefits in the United States.* New York: Cambridge University Press.

Hacker, Jacob S. 2004. "Privatizing Risk without Privatizing the Welfare State: The Hidden Politics of Social Policy Retrenchment in the United States." *American Political Science Review* 98 (2):243–260.

Hadley, Jack, and Robert A. Berenson. 1987. "Seeking the Just Price— Constructing Relative Value Scales and Fee Schedules." *Annals of Internal Medicine* 106 (3):461–466.

Hadley, Jack, David Juba, Robert A. Berenson, and Margaret Sulvetta. 1984. *Final Report on Alternative Methods of Developing a Relative Value Scale of Physicians' Services.* Edited by J. Hadley. Washington, DC: Urban Institute.

Hadley, Jack, Jeanne S. Mandelblatt, Jean M. Mitchell, Jane C. Weeks, Edward Guadagnoli, and Yi Ting Hwang. 2003. "Medicare Breast Surgery Fees and Treatment Received by Older Women with Localized Breast Cancer." *Health Services Research* 38 (2):553–573.

Hafferty, Frederic W. 1988. "Theories at the Crossroads: A Discussion of Evolving Views on Medicine as a Profession." *The Milbank Quarterly* 66 (S2):202–225.

Hammer, Peter J., and William M. Sage. 2002. "Antitrust, Health Care Quality, and the Courts." *Columbia Law Review* 102 (3):545–649.

Hanoch, Yaniv, and Thomas Rice. 2006. "Can Limiting Choice Increase Social Welfare? The Elderly and Health Insurance." *Milbank Quarterly* 84 (1):37–73.

Hanoch, Yaniv, Thomas Rice, Janet Cummings, and Stacey Wood. 2009. "How Much Choice Is Too Much? The Case of the Medicare Prescription Drug Benefit." *Health Services Research* 44 (4):1157–1168.

Hansen, John Mark. 1991. *Gaining Access: Congress and the Farm Lobby, 1919–1981.* Chicago: University of Chicago Press.

Hariri, Sanaz, Kevin J. Bozic, Carlos Lavernia, Ann Prestipino, and Harry E. Rubash. 2007. "Medicare Physician Reimbursement: Past, Present, and Future." *Journal of Bone & Joint Surgery* 89 (11):2536–2546.

Harris, T. Reginald. 1997. Statement of the American Medical Association to the Subcommittee on Health Data Needs, Standards and Security, National Committee on Vital Health Statistics, Department of Health and Human Services, Re: Physicians' Current Procedural Terminology (CPT),

Washington, DC. Accessed May 14, 2016. http://www.aapsonline.org:/medi care/amacpt.htm.

Hassenbusch, Samuel J. 2002. "Actively Seeking Remuneration: AANS/CNS Coding and Reimbursement Committee Works for Neurosurgeons." Accessed April 12, 2014. https://www.aans.org/Media/Article.aspx?ArticleId=9968.

Haug, Marie R. 1988. "A Re-Examination of the Hypothesis of Physician Deprofessionalization." *The Milbank Quarterly* 66 (S2):48–56.

Havighurst, Clark C., and Philip C. Kissam. 1979. "The Antitrust Implications of Relative Value Studies in Medicine." *Journal of Health Politics, Policy and Law* 4 (1):48–86.

Health Care Financing Administration. 1979. *Medical Procedural Terminology Systems: Development and Characteristics of Three Major Systems for Third Party Payment*. Baltimore: Health Care Financing Administration (Office of Research, Demonstrations, and Statistics).

Health Care Financing Administration. 1994. "Medicare Program; Refinements to Geographic Adjustment Factor Values and Other Policies under the Physician Fee Schedule; Proposed Rule." *Federal Register* 59 (121):15234.

Health Insurance Benefits Advisory Council. 1973. *A Report on the Results of the Study of Methods of Reimbursement for Physicians' Services under Medicare*. Washington, DC: Social Security Administration, Department of Health, Education and Welfare.

Heclo, Hugh. 1978. "Issue Networks and the Executive Establishment." In *The New American Political System*, edited by Samuel H. Beer et al. Washington, DC: American Enterprise Institute.

Helbing, Charles, Viola B. Latta, and Roger E. Keene. 1991. "Medicare Expenditures for Physician and Supplier Services, 1970–88." *Health Care Financing Review* 12 (3):109–120.

Hirsch, Joshua A., Ezequiel Silva III, Gregory N. Nicola, Robert M. Barr, Jacqueline A. Bello, Laxmaiah Manchikanti, and William D. Donovan. 2014. "The RUC: A Primer for Neurointerventionalists." *Journal of Neuro-Interventional Surgery* 6 (1):61–64.

Holahan, John. 1989. "Physician Payment Reform." *Saint Louis University Law Journal* 34:867–892.

Holloway, Donald C., Robert D. Hertenstein, George A. Goldberg, and Kelli A. Dugan. 1993. System and Method for Detecting Fraudulent Medical Claims via Examination of Service Codes. U.S. Patent 5,253,164.

Hsiao, William C. 1995. *CMS Oral History Project*. Edited by Richard Shuster. Baltimore: Centers for Medicare & Medicaid Services.

Hsiao, William. 2002. Interview by Rick Mayes. October 22. Unpublished transcript. Quotations reprinted by permission of Rick Mayes.

Hsiao, William C., Peter Braun, Edmund R. Becker, Nancy-Anne Causino, Nathan P. Couch, Margaret DeNicola, Daniel Dunn, Nancy L. Kelly, Thomas Ketcham, Arthur Sobol, Diana Verrilli, and Douwe B. Yntema. 1988. *A National Study of Resource-Based Relative Value Scales for Physician Services: Final Report.* Vol. 2. Boston: Department of Health Policy and Management, Harvard School of Public Health. Cambridge Health Economics Group, Inc. © 1988 William C. Hsiao, Peter Braun, Edmund Becker, Daniel Dunn, Nancy L. Kelly, Douwe B. Yntema.

Hsiao, William C., Peter Braun, Donald Dunn, and Edmund R. Becker. 1988. "Resource-Based Relative Values—An Overview." *Journal of the American Medical Association* 260 (16):2347–2353.

Hsiao, William C., Peter Braun, Donald L. Dunn, Edmund R. Becker, Douwe Yntema, Diana K. Verrilli, Eva Stamenovic, and Shiao-Ping Chen. 1992. "An Overview of the Development and Refinement of the Resource-Based Relative Value Scale—The Foundation for Reform of United-States Physician Payment." *Medical Care* 30 (11):NS1–NS12.

Hsiao, William C., and Jack Langenbrunner. 1988. *A National Study of Resource-Based Relative Value Scales for Physician Services: Final Report.* Vol. 1. Boston: Department of Health Policy and Management, Harvard School of Public Health.

Hsiao, William, and William Stason. 1979. "Towards Developing a Relative Value Scale for Medical and Surgical Services." *Health Care Financing Review* 1:23–28.

Hyman, David A. 2007. "Health Insurance: Market Failure or Government Failure." *Connecticut Insurance Law Journal* 14:307.

Iglehart, John K. 1988. "Payment of Physicians under Medicare." *New England Journal of Medicine* 318 (13):863–868.

Iglehart, John K. 1989. "The Recommendations of the Physician Payment Review Commission." *New England Journal of Medicine* 320 (17):1156–1160.

Iglehart, John K. 2002. "Medicare's Declining Payments to Physicians." *New England Journal of Medicine* 346 (24):1924–1930.

Immergut, Ellen M. 1992. *Health Politics: Interests and Institutions in Western Europe.* Cambridge, England: Cambridge University Press.

Jacobs, Jerry A. 1998. "Measuring Time at Work: Are Self-Reports Accurate?" *Monthly Labor Review* 121 (12): 42–53.

Jacobs, Lawrence R. 1993. *The Health of Nations.* Ithaca, NY: Cornell University Press.

Jacobson, Mireille, A. James O'Malley, Craig C. Earle, Juliana Pakes, Peter Gaccione, and Joseph P. Newhouse. 2006. "Does Reimbursement Influence Chemotherapy Treatment for Cancer Patients?" *Health Affairs* 25 (2): 437–443.

Jost, Timothy Stoltzfus. 2004. "Why Can't We Do What They Do? National Health Reform Abroad." *Journal of Law, Medicine & Ethics* 32 (3):433–441.

Kahan, James P., Sally C. Morton, Gerald Kominski, Hilary Farris, Arthur J. Donovan, and David L Bryant. 1992. *Issues in Developing a Resource-Based Relative Value Scale for Physician Work.* Santa Monica, CA: RAND Corporation.

Kahneman, Daniel, and Amos Tversky, eds. 2000. *Choices, Values, and Frames.* New York: Cambridge University Press.

Kallstrom, D. Ward. 1978. "Health Care Cost Control by Third Party Payors: Fee Schedules and the Sherman Act." *Duke Law Journal* 1978 (2):645–697.

Kerber, Kevin A., Marc Raphaelson, Gregory L. Barkley, and James F. Burke. 2014. "Is Physician Work in Procedure and Test Codes More Highly Valued Than That in Evaluation and Management Codes?" *Annals of Surgery* 262 (2):267–272.

Kessel, Reuben A. 1958. "Price Discrimination in Medicine." *Journal of Law and Economics* 1:20–53.

Kessler, Rodger. 2008. "Integration of Care Is about Money Too: The Health and Behavior Codes as an Element of a New Financial Paradigm." *Families, Systems, & Health* 26 (2):207.

King, Mitchell S., Martin S. Lipsky, and Lisa Sharp. 2002. "Expert Agreement in Current Procedural Terminology Evaluation and Management Coding." *Archives of Internal Medicine* 162 (3):316–320.

Klarman, Herbert E. 1969. "Approaches to Moderating the Increases in Medical Care Costs." *Medical Care* 1969:175–190.

Krause, Elliott A. 1999. *Death of the Guilds: Professions, States, and the Advance of Capitalism, 1930 to the Present.* New Haven, CT: Yale University Press.

Krupinski, Elizabeth A., Lea MacKinnon, Karl Hasselbach, and Mihra Taljanovic. 2015. "Evaluating RVUs as a Measure of Workload for Use in Assessing Fatigue." In *SPIE Medical Imaging,* International Society for Optics and Photonics 94161A-94161A. Accessed May 24, 2016. http://spie.org/Publications/Proceedings/Paper/10.1117/12.2082913.

Kumetz, Erik A., and John D. Goodson. 2013. "The Undervaluation of Evaluation and Management (E/M) Professional Services: The Lasting Impact of CPT Code Deficiencies on Physician Payment." *Chest* 144 (3):740–745.

Kwak, James. 2014. "Complexity, Capacity, and Capture." In *Preventing Regulatory Capture: Special Interest Influence and How to Limit It,* edited by Daniel Carpenter and David Moss. New York: Cambridge University Press.

Laksmana, Indrarini, Wendy Tietz, and Ya-Wen Yang. 2012. "Compensation Discussion and Analysis (CD&A): Readability and Management Obfuscation." *Journal of Accounting and Public Policy* 31 (2):185–203.

Lasker, Roz D., and M. Susan Marquis. 1999. "The Intensity of Physicians' Work in Patient Visits—Implications for the Coding of Patient Evaluation and Management Services." *New England Journal of Medicine* 341 (5):337–341.

Laugesen, Miriam J. 2009. "Siren Song: Physicians, Congress, and Medicare Fees." *Journal of Health Politics Policy and Law* 34 (2):157–179.

Laugesen, Miriam J. 2015. "Payment Policy Disruption and Policy Drift." *Journal of Health Politics Policy and Law* 40 (4):839–846.

Laugesen, Miriam J., and Robin Gauld. 2012. *Democratic Governance and Health*. Dunedin: Otago University Press.

Laugesen, Miriam J., and Sherry A. Glied. 2011. "Higher Fees Paid to US Physicians Drive Higher Spending for Physician Services Compared to Other Countries." *Health Affairs* 30 (9):1647–1656.

Laugesen, Miriam J., and Thomas Rice. 2003. "Is the Doctor in? The Evolving Role of Organized Medicine in Health Policy." *Journal of Health Politics Policy and Law* 28 (2–3):289–316.

Laugesen, Miriam J., Roy Wada, and Eric M. Chen. 2012. "In Setting Doctors' Medicare Fees, CMS Almost Always Accepts the Relative Value Update Panel's Advice on Work Values." *Health Affairs* 31 (5):965–972.

Lavernia, Carlos J., and Brian Parsley. 2006. "Medicare Reimbursement: An Orthopedic Primer." *Journal of Arthroplasty* 21 (6, Suppl. 2):6–9.

Law, Sylvia A., and Barry Ensminger. 1986. "Negotiating Physicians' Fees: Individual Patients or Society?" *New York University Law Review* 61 (1):1–87.

Lee, Jung Wook, Hal G. Rainey, and Young Han Chun. 2010. "Goal Ambiguity, Work Complexity, and Work Routineness in Federal Agencies." *American Review of Public Administration* 40 (3):284–308.

Lee, Philip R. 1990. "Physician Payment Reform—An Idea Whose Time Has Come." *Western Journal of Medicine* 152 (3):277–284.

Lee, Philip R., and Paul B. Ginsburg. 1988. "Physician Payment Reform—An Idea Whose Time Has Come." *Journal of the American Medical Association* 260 (16):2441–2443.

Lee, Philip R., and Paul B. Ginsburg. 1991. "The Trials of Medicare Physician Payment Reform." *Journal of the American Medical Association* 266 (11):1562–1565.

Lee, Philip R., Paul B. Ginsburg, Lauren B. Leroy, and Glenn T. Hammons. 1989. "The Physician-Payment-Review-Commission Report to Congress." *Journal of the American Medical Association* 261 (16):2382–2385.

Leroy, Lauren B. 2016. "Telephone Conversation with Author," February 11.

Levin, Sander, Henry A. Waxman, Jim McDermott, and Frank Pallone Jr. 2014. Letter to Honorable Marilyn Tavenner, Administrator Centers for Medicare

& Medicaid Services, April 8, United States Congress, House Energy and Commerce Committee.

Levitsky, Sidney. 1996. "Reimbursement for Cardiac Procedures: Past, Present, and Future." *Annals of Thoracic Surgery* 62 (5):S14–S17.

Levy, Barbara 2012. AMA/Specialty Society RVS Update Committee (RUC) Presentation at the CPT and RBRVS Annual Symposium, November 14, 2012. Chicago: American Medical Association.

Levy, Jesse M., Michael Borowitz, Samuel McNeill, William J. London, and Gregory Savord. 1992. "Understanding the Medicare Fee Schedule and Its Impact on Physicians under the Final Rule." *Medical Care* 30 (11), Supplement: The Resource-Based Relative Value Scale: Its Further Development and Reform of Physician Payment: NS80–NS94. © 1992 Lippincott Williams & Wilkins. Reproduced by permission of Wolters Kluwer Health, Inc.

Li, Feng. 2008. "Annual Report Readability, Current Earnings, and Earnings Persistence." *Journal of Accounting and Economics* 45 (2):221–247.

Lichtenberg, Frank R. 2006. *The Impact of New Laboratory Procedures and Other Medical Innovations on the Health of Americans, 1990–2003: Evidence from Longitudinal, Disease-Level Data*. Cambridge, MA: National Bureau of Economic Research.

Light, Donald. 1993. "Countervailing Power: The Changing Character of the Medical Profession in the United States." In *The Changing Medical Profession: An International Perspective*, edited by Frederic W. Hafferty and John B. McKinlay. New York: Oxford University Press.

Little, Danny C., Shawn D. St Peter, Casey M. Calkins, Sohail R. Shah, J. Patrick Murphy, John M. Gatti, George K. Gittes, Ron J. Sharp, Walter S. Andrews, and George W. Holcomb. 2006. "Relative Value Units Correlate with Pediatric Surgeons' Operating Time: When Perceived Myth Becomes Reality." *Journal of Pediatric Surgery* 41 (1):234–238.

Little, Laura E. 1998. "Hiding with Words: Obfuscation, Avoidance, and Federal Jurisdiction Opinions." *UCLA Law Review* 46 (1):75–160. http://ssrn.com:/abstract=149075.

Mabry, Charles D., Barton C. McCann, Jean A. Harris, Janet Martin, John O. Gage, Josef E. Fischer, Frank G. Opelka, Robert Zwolak, Karen Borman, and John T. Preskitt Sr. 2005. "The Use of Intraservice Work per Unit of Time (IWPUT) and the Building Block Method (BBM) for the Calculation of Surgical Work." *Annals of Surgery* 241 (6):929–940.

Maestas, Nicole, Mathis Schroeder, and Dana Goldman. 2009. *Price Variation in Markets with Homogeneous Goods: The Case of Medigap*. Cambridge, MA: National Bureau of Economic Research.

Marmor, Theodore R. 2000. *The Politics of Medicare*. 2nd ed. New York: A. de Gruyter.

Maxwell, Stephanie, Stephen Zuckerman, and Robert A. Berenson. 2007. "Use of Physicians' Services under Medicare's Resource-Based Payments." *New England Journal of Medicine* 356 (18):1853–1861.

Mayes, Rick, and Robert A. Berenson. 2006. *Medicare Prospective Payment and the Shaping of U.S. Health Care.* Baltimore: Johns Hopkins University Press.

McCall, Nancy, Jerry Cromwell, and Peter Braun. 2006. "Validation of Physician Survey Estimates of Surgical Time Using Operating Room Logs." *Medical Care Research and Review* 63 (6):764–777.

McCall, Nancy T., Jerry Cromwell, Ed Drozd, Sonja Hoover, and P. Braun. 2001. *Validation of Physician Time Data: Final Report.* Waltham, MA: Health Economics Research, Inc.

McCarty, Nolan. 2014. "Complexity, Capacity, and Capture." In *Preventing Regulatory Capture: Special Interest Influence and How to Limit It,* edited by Daniel Carpenter and David A Moss. New York: Cambridge University Press.

McKinlay, John B., and Joan Arches. 1985. "Towards the Proletarianization of Physicians." *International Journal of Health Services* 15 (2):161–195.

McMenamin, Peter. 1981. "Future Research and Policy Directions in Physician Reimbursement." *Health Care Financing Review* 2 (4):61–75.

Mechanic, David. 1991. "Sources of Countervailing Power in Medicine." *Journal of Health Politics, Policy and Law* 16 (3):485–498.

Medicare Payment Advisory Commission. 2006a. *Report to the Congress Effects of Medicare Payment Changes on Oncology Services.* Washington, DC: Medicare Payment Advisory Commission. http://www.columbia.edu/cgi-bin/cul/resolve?clio6142808.

Medicare Payment Advisory Commission. 2006b. *Report to the Congress, Medicare Payment Policy.* Washington, DC: Medicare Payment Advisory Commission.

Medicare Payment Advisory Commission. 2011. *Report to the Congress: Medicare Payment Policy.* Washington, DC: Medicare Payment Advisory Commission.

Memorandum to John Heinz from GLA. 1989. Finance Subcommittee Hearing on Physician Payment. 1989. John Heinz Archives.

Mettler, Suzanne. 2002. "Bringing the State Back in to Civic Engagement: Policy Feedback Effects of the G.I. Bill for World War II Veterans." *American Political Science Review* 96 (2):351–365.

Mettler, Suzanne. 2011. *The Submerged State: How Invisible Government Policies Undermine American Democracy.* Chicago: University of Chicago Press.

Miller, Edward Alan, Vincent Mor, David C. Grabowski, and Pedro L. Gozalo. 2009. "The Devil's in the Details: Trading Policy Goals for Complexity in

Medicaid Nursing Home Reimbursement." *Journal of Health Politics, Policy and Law* 34 (1):93–135.

Miller, George E. 1991. "RBRVS report: Activities of the Ad Hoc Committee for Physicians' Reimbursement." *The Annals of Thoracic Surgery* 52 (2):397–402.

Moffit, Robert Emmet. 1992. "Back to the Future: Medicare's Resurrection of the Labor Theory of Value." *Regulation* 15:54.

Moffitt, Susan L. 2010. "Promoting Agency Reputation through Public Advice: Advisory Committee Use in the FDA." *Journal of Politics* 72 (3):880–893.

Moffitt, Susan L. 2014. *Making Public Policy: Participatory Bureaucracy in American Democracy.* New York: Cambridge University Press.

Monk, Bradley J., and Robert A Burger. 2001. "Reimbursement for Surgical Procedures in Gynecologic Oncology." *Current Opinion in Oncology* 13 (5):390–393.

Moorefield, James M., Douglas W. Macewan, and Jonathan H. Sunshine. 1993. "The Radiology Relative Value Scale—Its Development and Implications." *Radiology* 187 (2):317–326.

Morgan, Kimberly J., and Andrea Louise Campbell. 2011. *The Delegated Welfare State: Medicare, Markets, and the Governance of Social Policy.* New York: Oxford University Press.

Morone, James A. 1990. *The Democratic Wish: Popular Participation and the Limits of American Government.* New York: Basic Books.

Morone, James A. 1993. "The Health Care Bureaucracy: Small Changes, Big Consequences." *Journal of Health Politics, Policy and Law* 18 (3):723–739.

Mussweiler, Thomas. 2001. "Sentencing under Uncertainty: Anchoring Effects in the Courtroom." *Journal of Applied Social Psychology* 31 (7):1535–1551.

Mussweiler, Thomas, and Fritz Strack. 2000. "Numeric Judgments under Uncertainty: The Role of Knowledge in Anchoring." *Journal of Experimental Social Psychology* 36 (5):495–518.

Newhouse, Joseph P. 2002. *Pricing the Priceless: A Health Care Conundrum, The Walras-Pareto Lectures.* Cambridge, MA: MIT Press.

Nguyen, Khang T., Michael S. Gart, John T. Smetona, Apas Aggarwal, Karl Y. Bilimoria, and John Y. S. Kim. 2012. "The Relationship between Relative Value Units and Outcomes: A Multivariate Analysis of Plastic Surgery Procedures." *Eplasty* 12 (e60):500–510.

Nicholson-Crotty, Sean, and Jill Nicholson-Crotty. 2004. "Interest Group Influence on Managerial Priorities in Public Organizations." *Journal of Public Administration Research and Theory* 14 (4):571–583.

Norredam, Marie, and Dag Album. 2007. "Review Article: Prestige and Its Significance for Medical Specialties and Diseases." *Scandinavian Journal of Public Health* 35 (6):655–661.

Oberlander, Jonathan. 2003. *The Political Life of Medicare, American Politics and Political Economy.* Chicago: University of Chicago Press.

Oberlander, Jonathan, and M. J. Laugesen. 2015. "Leap of Faith—Medicare's New Physician Payment System." *New England Journal of Medicine* 373 (13):1185–1187.

Obinger, Herbert, Stephan Leibfried, and Francis Geoffrey Castles. 2005. *Federalism and the Welfare State: New World and European Experiences.* Cambridge, UK: Cambridge University Press.

Office of Inspector General. 1994a. *Coding of Physician Services.* Washington, DC: Department of Health and Human Services.

Office of Inspector General. 1994b. *A Compendium of Reports and Literature on the Coding of Physician Services.* Washington, DC: Department of Health and Human Services.

Oliver, T. R., P. R.Lee, and H. L. Lipton. 2004. "A Political History of Medicare and Prescription Drug Coverage." *Milbank Quarterly* 82 (2):283–354.

Oliver, Thomas R. 1993. "Analysis, Advice, and Congressional Leadership—The Physician Payment Review Commission and the Politics of Medicare." *Journal of Health Politics Policy and Law* 18 (1):113–174.

Olson, Mancur. 1965. *The Logic of Collective Action; Public Goods and the Theory of Groups, Harvard Economic Studies.* Cambridge, MA: Harvard University Press.

Parks, Patricia. 1997. "The RUC—Its Past, Present, and Future. Interview by Patricia Parks." *Bulletin of the American College of Surgeons* 82 (5):13–16.

Patashnik, Eric M. 2014. *Reforms at Risk: What Happens After Major Policy Changes Are Enacted.* Princeton, NJ: Princeton University Press.

Payment for Physicians' Services. 2013. 42 US Code § 1395w–4.

Pediatric Orthopaedic Society of North America. 2012. "Minutes of the Board of Directors Meeting, February 8, 2012, Marriott Marquis, San Francisco, California." Accessed March 18, 2014. http://www.pwrnewmedia.com/2012/posna/newsletter/september2012/downloads/2012/64minutes8February12SanFran.pdf.

Peterson, Mark A. 1993. "Political Influence in the 1990s: From Iron Triangles to Policy Networks." *Journal of Health Politics Policy and Law* 18 (2):395–438.

Peterson, Mark A. 2001. "From Trust to Political Power: Interest Groups, Public Choice, and Health Care." *Journal of Health Politics Policy and Law* 26 (5):1145–1163.

Pfizenmayer, Rickard F. 1982. "Antitrust-Law and Collective Physician Negotiations with 3rd Parties—The Relative Value Guide Object Lesson." *Journal of Health Politics Policy and Law* 7 (1):128–162.

Physician Payment Review Commission. 1987. *Report to Congress.* Washington, DC: Physician Payment Review Commission.

Physician Payment Review Commission. 1989. *Report to Congress.* Washington, DC: Physician Payment Review Commission.

Physician Payment Review Commission. 1991. *The Role of Specialty Societies and Physicians in the Commission's 1991 Evaluation of Relative Work Values.* Washington, DC: Physician Payment Review Commission.

Physician Payment Review Commission. 1995. *Report to Congress.* Washington, DC: Physician Payment Review Commission.

Pierson, Paul. 1993. "When Effect Becomes Cause: Policy Feedback and Political Change." *World Politics* 45 (4):595–628.

Pressman, Jeffrey L., and Aaron B. Wildavsky. 1984. *Implementation: How Great Expectations in Washington Are Dashed in Oakland.* Berkeley: University of California Press.

Quadagno, Jill S. 2004. "Physician Sovereignty and the Purchasers' Revolt." *Journal of Health Politics, Policy and Law* 29 (4):815–834.

Quirk, Paul J. 2010. "The Trouble with Experts." *Critical Review* 22 (4):449–465.

Rayack, Elton. 1968. "Restrictive Practices of Organized Medicine." *Antitrust Bulletin* 13:659–720.

Redelmeier, Donald A., and Daniel Kahneman. 1996. "Patients' Memories of Painful Medical Treatments: Real-Time and Retrospective Evaluations of Two Minimally Invasive Procedures." *Pain* 66 (1):3–8.

Redelmeier, Donald A., Joel Katz, and Daniel Kahneman. 2003. "Memories of Colonoscopy: A Randomized Trial." *Pain* 104 (1):187–194.

Reinhardt, Uwe E. 2006. "The Pricing of U.S. Hospital Services: Chaos behind a Veil of Secrecy." *Health Affairs* 25 (1):57–69.

Rice, Thomas. 2001. "Should Consumer Choice Be Encouraged in Health Care?" In *The Social Economics of Health Care,* edited by John B Davis, 9–39. London and New York: Routledge.

Rice, Thomas H. 1983. "The Impact of Changing Medicare Reimbursement Rates on Physician-Induced Demand." *Medical Care* 21 (8):803–815.

Robinson, John P., and Geoffrey Godbey. 1997. *Time for Life: The Surprising Ways Americans Use Their Time.* University Park: Penn State Press.

Robinson, John P., and Ann Bostrom. 1994. "The Overestimated Workweek? What Time Diary Measures Suggest." *Monthly Labor Review* 117 (8):11–23.

Robinson, John P., Alain Chenu, and Anthony S. Alvarez. 2002. "Measuring the Complexity of Hours at Work: The Weekly Work Grid." *Monthly Labor Review* 125:44.

Roe, Benson B. 1981. "Sounding Boards. The UCR Boondoggle: A Death Knell for Private Practice?" *New England Journal of Medicine* 305 (1):41–45.

Roe, Benson B. 1985. "Rational Remuneration." *New England Journal of Medicine* 313 (20):1286–1289.

Roemer, Milton I. 1961. "Hospital Utilization and the Supply of Physicians." *Journal of the American Medical Association* 178 (10):989–993.

Roemer, Milton Irwin. 1959. "Hospital Utilization under Insurance." *Hospitals* 33:36–37.

Roemer, Ruth. 1968. "Legal Systems Regulating Health Personnel: A Comparative Analysis." *The Milbank Memorial Fund Quarterly* 46 (4):431–471.

Rosen, George. 1977. "Contract or Lodge Practice and Its Influence on Medical Attitudes to Health Insurance." *American Journal of Public Health* 67 (4):374–378.

Rosenthal, Elisabeth. 1990. "Medicare Fee Plan Sent to Congress." *New York Times,* September 1, 1.

Rosenthal, Elisabeth. 2013–2014. "Paying Till It Hurts" (Series). *New York Times.* Accessed September 10, 2014. http://www.nytimes.com/interactive/2014/health/paying-till-it-hurts.html?_r=0.

Rosoff, Stephen M., and Matthew C. Leone. 1991. "The Public Prestige of Medical Specialties: Overviews and Undercurrents." *Social Science & Medicine* 32 (3):321–326.

Rothman, David J. 1997. *Beginnings Count: The Technological Imperative in American Health Care.* New York: Oxford University Press.

Rubin, Ross N., Mark J. Segal, and Sandra L. Sherman. 1989. "AMA and Medicare Physician Payment Reform." *Saint Louis University Law Journal* 34:893–916.

Sandy, Lewis G., Thomas Bodenheimer, L. Gregory Pawlson, and Barbara Starfield. 2009. "The Political Economy of US Primary Care." *Health Affairs* 28 (4):1136–1145.

Schafer, Mark, and Scott Crichlow. 2010. *Groupthink versus High-Quality Decision Making in International Relations.* New York: Columbia University Press.

Schieber, George J., Ira L. Burney, Judith B. Golden, and William A. Knaus. 1976. "Physician Fee Patterns under Medicare: A Descriptive Analysis." *New England Journal of Medicine* 294 (20):1089–1093.

Schlesinger, Mark. 2002. "A Loss of Faith: The Sources of Reduced Political Legitimacy for the American Medical Profession." *Milbank Quarterly* 80 (2):185–235.

Schoenman, Julie. A., Kevin J. Hayes, and C. Michael Cheng. 2001. "Medicare Physician Payment Changes: Impact on Physicians and Beneficiaries." *Health Affairs* 20 (2):263–273.

Schroeder, S. A., and J. A. Showstack. 1977. "The Dynamics of Medical Technology Use: Analysis and Policy Options." In *Medical Technology: The Culprit behind Health Care Costs (Proceedings of the 1977 Sun Valley Forum on National Health),* edited by Stuart H. Altman and Robert Blendon. Hyattsville, MD: US Department of Health, Education, and Welfare. Accessed June 22, 2016. https://catalog.hathitrust.org/Record /000736376.

Schwartz, Jerome L. 1965. "Early History of Prepaid Medical Care Plans." *Bulletin of the History of Medicine* 39 (5):450.

Schwartzbaum, Allan M., John H. McGrath, and Robert A. Rothman. 1973. "The Perception of Prestige Differences among Medical Subspecialties." *Social Science & Medicine (1967)* 7 (5):365–371.

Scully, Thomas A. 2002. Interview by Rick Mayes. October 24. Unpublished transcript.

Scully, Thomas A. 2012. *Written Testimony before the United States Senate Finance Committee "Medicare Physician Payments: Understanding the Past So We Can Envision the Future."* Washington, DC: Government Printing Office.

Shah, Dhruvil R., Richard J. Bold, Anthony D. Yang, Vijay P. Khatri, Steve R. Martinez, and Robert J. Canter. 2014. "Relative Value Units Poorly Correlate with Measures of Surgical Effort and Complexity." *Journal of Surgical Research* 190 (2):465–470.

Shaneyfelt, T. 2012. "In Guidelines We Cannot Trust: Comment on 'Failure of Clinical Practice Guidelines to Meet Institute of Medicine Standards.'" *Archives of Internal Medicine* 172 (21):1633–1634.

Shapiro, Stuart. 2008. "Does the Amount of Participation Matter? Public Comments, Agency Responses and the Time to Finalize a Regulation." *Policy Sciences* 41 (1):33–49.

Shortell, Stephen M. 1974. "Occupational Prestige Differences within the Medical and Allied Health Professions." *Social Science & Medicine (1967)* 8 (1):1–9.

Showstack, Jonathan A., Bart D. Blumberg, Judy Schwartz, and Steven A. Schroeder. 1979. "Fee-for-Service Physician Payment: Analysis of Current Methods and Their Development." *Inquiry* 16 (3):230–246.

Sinclair, Barbara. 2012. *Unorthodox Lawmaking: New Legislative Processes in the U.S. Congress.* 4th ed. Washington, DC: CQ Press.

Sinsky, Christine A., and David C. Dugdale. 2013. "Medicare Payment for Cognitive vs Procedural Care: Minding the Gap." *JAMA Internal Medicine* 173 (18):1733–1737.

Skowronek, Stephen. 1982. *Building a New American State: The Expansion of National Administrative Capacities, 1877–1920.* New York: Cambridge University Press.

Smith, David G. 1992. *Paying for Medicare: The Politics of Reform.* New York: A. de Gruyter.

Smith, David G., and Judith D. Moore. n.d. *CMS Oral History Project 2003–2006.* Baltimore: Centers for Medicare & Medicaid Services.

Smith, Sherry L., ed. 2012. *Medicare RBRVS: The Physicians' Guide 2012.* Chicago: American Medical Association.

Society for Cardiovascular Angiography and Interventions. 2011. "Advocacy Victory: RUC Agrees to Oppose Fee Cuts for Diagnostic Cardiac Cath." *SCAI News & Highlights,* May/June. Accessed Feb 9, 2016. http://scai.org/Assets/9815b688-8fe6-49d4-a00e-523a06b585de/634431439547870000/scai-nwsltr-may-june2011-pdf.

Society for Cardiovascular Angiography and Interventions. 2012. "2013 Coding Update: The House of Cardiology Prepares You for Sweeping Changes in Cardiology Coding Coming in 2013." Accessed February 21, 2016. http://webinars.scai.org/session.php?id=9695.

Society of American Gastrointestinal and Endoscopic Surgeons. 2011. "GSCRC and RUC Meetings Report: GSCRC Meeting Chicago, August 12–13, 2011." Accessed October 18, 2014. http://www.sages.org/documents/file/gscr-ruc-cpt-oct-2011/.

Society of Nuclear Medicine. 2003. Minutes of the Coding and Reimbursement Committee Meeting, June 20, 2003. Accessed March 15, 2014. http://snmmi.files.cms-plus.com/docs/Min-Chcp-Crc-0306.pdf.

Society of Nuclear Medicine. 2010a. Committee Report, SNM Board of Directors Coding and Reimbursement, January 2010. Accessed June 14, 2016. http://www.snm.org/docs/snm_committee/MWM10/Coding_Reimbursement_Committee.doc.

Society of Nuclear Medicine. 2010b. Committee Report to the SNM Board of Directors January 30 2010, SNM-ACNM Joint Government Relations Committee. Accessed May 14, 2016. http://snmmi.org/files/docs/snm_committee/MWM_2010_Minutes_Open.pdf.

Society of Nuclear Medicine. 2010c. Environmental Scan. Accessed March 15, 2014. http://snmmi.files.cms-plus.com/docs/Environmental_Scan_Background_4-14-2010_2.pdf.

Society of Nuclear Medicine. 2010d. "Minutes of the Society of Nuclear Medicine 2010 Annual Meeting, Friday, June 4, 2010, Grand America Hotel, Salt Lake City." Accessed April 11, 2014. http://interactive.snm.org/docs/snm_committee/CodingReimb_2010_AM_Minutes_v1_final.pdf.

Society of Vascular Surgeons. 2003. "Minutes of the Coding and Reimbursement Committee, June 20, 2003 Hilton Riverside Hotel, New Orleans." Accessed March 14, 2014. http://snmmi.files.cms-plus.com/docs/Min-Chcp-Crc-0306.pdf.

Society of Vascular Surgeons. 2013. "Society of Vascular Surgeons Board of Directors Meeting, January 5, Fort Lauderdale, Florida." Accessed April 4, 2014. http://vesurgery.org/docs/councilfiles/8SVSBODMee ting2013-01-07.pdf.

Somers, Herman Miles, and Anne Ramsay Somers. 1961. *Doctors, Patients, and Health Insurance; the Organization and Financing of Medical Care.* Washington, DC: Brookings Institution.

Starr, Paul. 1982. *The Social Transformation of American Medicine.* New York: Basic Books.

Steinmo, Sven, and Jon Watts. 1995. "It's the Institutions, Stupid! Why Comprehensive National Health Insurance Always Fails in America." *Journal of Health Politics, Policy and Law* 20 (2):329–371.

Stevens, Rosemary. 1971. *American Medicine and the Public Interest.* New Haven, CT: Yale University Press.

Stevens, Rosemary. 1999. *In Sickness and in Wealth: American Hospitals in the 20th Century.* Baltimore: Johns Hopkins University Press.

Stevens, Rosemary A. 2001. "Public Roles for the Medical Profession in the United States: Beyond Theories of Decline and Fall." *Milbank Quarterly* 79 (3):327–353.

Stevens, Rosemary, and David Rosner. 1983. "State-of-the-Art in Medical Historiography: Perspectives, The Social Transformation of American Medicine." *Journal of Health Politics, Policy and Law* 8 (3):607–616.

Stone, D. A., 2002. *Policy Paradox: The Art of Political Decision Making.* New York: Norton.

Stone, Deborah. 1977. "Professionalism and Accountability Controlling Health Services in the United States and West Germany." *Journal of Health Politics, Policy and Law* 2 (1):32–47.

Stone, Deborah A. 1993. "The Struggle for the Soul of Health Insurance." *Journal of Health Politics, Policy and Law* 18 (2):287–317.

Stone, Deborah A. 1997. "The Doctor as Businessman: The Changing Politics of a Cultural Icon." *Journal of Health Politics, Policy and Law* 22 (2):533–556.

Sweetland-Edwards, Haley 2013. "Special Deal: The Shadowy Cartel of Doctors That Controls Medicare." Accessed April 4, 2014. http://www.washingtonmonthly.com/magazine/july_august_2013/features/special_deal 045641.php?page=all.

Tetlock, Philip E. 2005. *Expert Political Judgment: How Good Is It? How Can We Know?* Princeton, NJ: Princeton University Press.

Thelen, Kathleen Ann. 2004. *How Institutions Evolve: The Political Economy of Skills in Germany, Britain, the United States, and Japan.* New York: Cambridge University Press.

Todd, James S. 1988. "At Last, a Rational Way to Pay for Physicians' Services." *Journal of the American Medical Association* 260 (16):2439–2441.

Tu, Ha T., and Johanna R. Lauer. 2009. "Impact of Health Care Price Transparency on Price Variation: The New Hampshire Experience." *Issue Brief* (Center for Studying Health System Change) 128 (November):1–4. http://www.hschange.com:/CONTENT/1095/1095.pdf.

Tuohy, Carolyn J. 1999. *Accidental Logics: The Dynamics of Change in the Health Care Arena in the United States, Britain, and Canada.* New York: Oxford University Press.

Tversky, Amos, and Daniel Kahneman. 1973. "Availability: A Heuristic for Judging Frequency and Probability." *Cognitive Psychology* 5 (2):207–232.

Tversky, Amos, and Daniel Kahneman. 1982. "Judgment under Uncertainty: Heuristics and Biases." In *Judgment under Uncertainty: Heuristics and Biases,* edited by Daniel Kahneman, Paul Slovic, and Amos Tversky. New York: Cambridge University Press.

United States General Accountability Office. 2009. *Fees Could Better Reflect Efficiencies Achieved When Services Are Provided Together.* Washington, DC: United States General Accountability Office.

United States Government Accountability Office. 2015. *Medicare Physician Payment Better Data and Greater Transparency Could Improve Accuracy.* Washington, DC: Government Accountability Office.

US Congress Office of Technology Assessment. 1986. *Payment for Physician Services—Strategies for Medicare.* Washington, DC: US Congress Office of Technology Assessment.

US House of Representatives. 1989. Hearing before the Subcommittee on Health of the Committee on Ways and Means. 2nd Session, May 24, 1988.

US Senate Committee on Finance. 2012. *Roundtable on Medicare Physician Payments* [Transcript]. Hearing before the Committee on Finance, United States Senate. 112th Congress, 2nd Session, May 10, 2012. Washington, DC: Government Printing Office.

US Senate Committee on Finance. 2013. High Prices, Low Transparency: The Bitter Pill of Health Care Costs. Hearing before the Committee on Finance. 113th Congress, 1st Session, June 18, 2013.

US Senate Permanent Subcommittee on Investigations of the Committee on Governmental Affairs. 1979. *The California Relative Value Studies: An Overview and the California Physicians Service, the Corporation, and Its Relationship with the California Medical Association.* Washington, DC: Government Printing Office.

US Senate Special Committee on Aging. 1988. *Committee Print: Medicare Physician Payment: Issues and Options.* Washington, DC: Government Printing Office.

Viebeck, Elise. 2014. "Wyden Open to 'Doc Fix' with War Savings." *The Hill*, March 19, 2014. Accessed September 10, 2014. http://thehill.com/policy /healthcare/201235-wyden-interested-in-war-spending-as-sgr-pay-for.

Vladeck, Bruce C., and Thomas Rice. 2009. "Market Failure and the Failure of Discourse: Facing Up to the Power of Sellers." *Health Affairs* 28 (5):1305–1315.

Wasley, Terree P. 1993. "Health Care in the Twentieth Century: A History of Government Interference and Protection." *Business Economics* 28 (2):11–16.

Weaver, R. Kent, and Bert A. Rockman, eds. 1993. *Do Institutions Matter?* Washington, DC: Brookings Institution.

Weisz, George. 1995. *The Medical Mandarins: The French Academy of Medicine in the Nineteenth and Early Twentieth Centuries.* Oxford, UK: Oxford University Press.

Wennberg, John, and Alan Gittelsohn. 1973. "Small Area Variations in Health Care Delivery." *Science* 182 (4117):1102–1108.

Williams, R C. 1939. "The Medical Care Program for Farm Security Administration Borrowers." *Law and Contemporary Problems* 6 (4):583–594.

Williams, R. C. 1940. "Development of Medical Care Plans for Low Income Farm Families—Three Years' Experience." *American Journal of Public Health and the Nation's Health* 30 (7):725–735.

Wilson, James Q., ed. 1980. *The Politics of Regulation.* New York: Basic Books.

Wynn, Barbara O., Lane F. Burgette, Andrew W. Mulcahy, Edward N. Okeke, Ian Brantley, Neema Iyer, Teague Ruder, and Ateev Mehrotra. 2015. *Development of a Model for the Validation of Work Relative Value Units for the Medicare Physician Fee Schedule.* Santa Monica, CA: RAND Corporation.

Yackee, James Webb, and Susan Webb Yackee. 2008. "A Bias towards Business? Assessing Interest Group Influence on the US Bureaucracy." *Journal of Politics* 68 (1):128–139.

Yackee, Susan Webb. 2014. "Reconsidering Agency Capture during Regulatory Policymaking." In *Preventing Regulatory Capture: Special Interest Influence and How to Limit It,* edited by Daniel Carpenter and David Moss. New York: Cambridge University Press.

Zuckerman, Stephen, Katie Merrell, Robert A. Berenson, Nicole Cafarella Lallemand, and Jonathan Sunshine. 2015. "Realign Physician Payment Incentives in Medicare to Achieve Payment Equity among Specialties, Expand the Supply of Primary Care Physicians, and Improve the Value of Care for Beneficiaries: Final Report." Washington, DC: Urban Institute; Silver Spring, MD: Social & Scientific Systems. Accessed June 14 2016. http://www.urban.org/author/stephen-zuckerman/publications.

Zwolak, Robert M., and Hugh H. Trout III. 1997. "Vascular Surgery and the Resource-Based Relative Value Scale Five-Year Review." *Journal of Vascular Surgery* 25 (6):1077–1086. © 1997 by The Society for Vascular Surgery and International Society for Cardiovascular Surgery, North American Chapter. Reproduced with permission from Elsevier.

Acknowledgments

Writing is a singular activity, but a book's completion depends on the efforts of many. A disclaimer: I should stress that the acknowledgment of any participation in any part of the research process of these individuals and organizations should not imply their endorsement of the book's findings, and all and any errors or omissions are mine alone.

This book would not have been written without the encouragement and assistance of people I am so fortunate to work with, or to have worked with, at Columbia University's Mailman School of Public Health. When I was hired at Columbia, I was guided by an indispensable faculty trio who relentlessly propelled the book forward: Larry Brown, Sherry Glied, and Michael Sparer. They not only wanted me to write it, but helped get it there by generously giving feedback on chapters and continual guidance throughout. They are true gems. I especially thank Larry for his extensive comments on multiple drafts. Thom Blaylock enthusiastically worked on the project at the start and read material at the end. I thank Dean Linda Fried, who was supportive of my work, and the communications team, Peter Taback and Timothy Paul. Other colleagues at Columbia also supported the book process: Sara Abiola, Tal Gross, Nan Liu, Matt Neidell, Lusine Poghoysan, Jack Rowe, Adam Sacarny, Bhaven Sampat, and Claire Wang. Practicum program staff helped me recruit students over several years: Emily Austin, Susan Cohen, Carey McHugh, Debra Osinsky, Rachel Sabb, Rebecca Sale, and Beth Silvestrini. Two students deserve special mention: Sara Mullery, who provided essential support as I completed the manuscript, and Arielle Langer, who ably contributed data collection, coding, and analysis of a superior standard. I am also so grateful for the help I received from Eugenia Cho, David Cloud, Erica Eliason, Samantha Gilman, Larry Joo, Ting-Jung Pan,

Andrea Popovech, Margaret Raskob, Nabeel Quereshi, Nidhie Singh, Amanda Sussex, and Martina Szabo, who helped with this and related projects. Thanks to all of our superb department staff, especially Dahlia Rivera—who helped me with Larry's edits—Dori Lorsch, and Cecilio Mendez, who kept things in order.

The cooperation of the American Medical Association and the Specialty Society Relative Value Update Committee and its staff in the Physician Payment Systems Section was indispensable, and I am extremely grateful for their help during this project. The AMA and the chair of the committee kindly accommodated me at meetings.

Of course, due to research regulations on human subjects, the interviewees shall remain anonymous, but I am grateful to those who took the time to speak with me and shared their knowledge of the RBRVS, the update process, and physician payment policy issues. In addition, I appreciate other individuals who shared material with me, such as their meeting notes.

The research for this book was supported by a Robert Wood Johnson Foundation Investigator Award in Health Policy Research. The foundation's generous support was critical, along with the intellectual and supportive community it fostered, built by David Mechanic, Alan Cohen, Lynn Rogut, Jed Horowitt, and others. I thank David Colby, Lori Melichar, and National Advisory Committee members, including Larry Casalino, Jim Morone, Jill Quadagno, Jeannette Rogowski, and especially Mark Peterson and Mark Schlesinger.

This book really began many years before I started writing it. I thank the National Institutes of Health Agency for Healthcare Research and Quality postdoctoral training program, housed at RAND-UCLA, because it was there that I learned about physician payment from Tom Rice; both he and Ron Andersen were great mentors. At the RAND Corporation, Melinda Buntin and José Escarce developed my interest in physician payment and the committee, and Dana Goldman especially encouraged my work on payment and budgetary issues. Finally I want to thank Eric Chen, who was initially a research intern and later a collaborator on a related paper we published, as well as Jack Needleman and Michelle Ko.

At Harvard University Press, I thank Mike Aronson, who brought the book project to the Press and, through the initial review process, read chapters and guided the book at formative stages. When he retired, Janice Audet enthusiastically took over with patience, kindness, helpful feedback, and great advice. Janice commissioned high-quality peer reviews, and two who waived anonymity were Judy Feder and Dan Carpenter, along with one reviewer who remained anonymous. Their astuteness and care significantly added to the manuscript. Thanks to all the production team, including Lauren Esdaile, for work on the manuscript and the marketing team for their attention to detail. I am also very grateful for the essential and meticulous contribution of copy editor Gillian Dickens and Brian Ostrander at Westchester Publishing Services.

I deeply appreciate the wise counsel of David Smallman at the Smallman + Snyder Law Group.

John Goodson and Chris Koller were constant in their encouragement of my project, and read and contributed great insights and suggestions to the chapters. Health politics and policy colleagues and fellow Investigator Award alums offered sage advice at various times, including Colleen Grogan, Michael Gusmano, Susan Moffitt, Tom Oliver, Eric Patashnik, Harold Pollack, Bert Rockman, Deborah Stone, Frank Thompson, David Weimer, and Joe White. Many others, of course, clarified aspects of the RBRVS and helped by patiently providing answers to factual questions, background relating to the history or intricacies of the physician payment area, and the practice of medicine today. Scott Manaker spent a lot of time on the phone with me addressing technical questions about the RBRVS. Thanks also for related technical and economic perspectives from Kevin Hayes and Ariel Winter at the Medicare Payment Advisory Commission and Stephen Zuckerman at the Urban Institute. Others provided helpful information on medicine and physician payment policy, including Norman Edelman, Oliver Fein, Mark Friedberg, Brian Klepper, Margaret Kruk, Shelah G. Leader, Victor Rodwin, Julie Schoenman, and Zirui Song. Some practicing physicians who did not want to be named gave me frank assessments regarding the reimbursement of specific services in their specialties. Lauren LeRoy and Paul Ginsburg helped address some gaps in the discussion on the Physician Payment Review Commission, as did Ted Marmor on the history of the system. Rick Mayes and Bob Berenson kindly shared some of their interview material from their book on Medicare, and Bob kindly read one of the chapters.

I especially want to thank Andy Sabl, who encouraged me and patiently waited throughout a long gestation. I want to thank all my friends near and far, including Ngawaiata Arkanstall, Jim and Mary Barr, Ashley Cox, Angelique Fris, Michael Gluck, Heather Hart, Alisa Hirschfeld, Michael Hooker, Elizabeth McLeay, Maria Miller, Eddie Miller and Jess Hoffman, Hodi Poorsoltan, Susan Sheu, and Buddy Warren. For all their support and love, I am grateful to my family, Helen and Neville Glasgow and the Laugesens and Yskas: Murray and Jude, Ruth, Mark, Rosa, Ayleen, Daniel, and Redmer.

I am so very grateful for all the love of my son, Benji, who showed great forbearance through a long process.

Everyone—both named and unnamed—please accept my heartfelt thanks.

Index